A

· · ·

BOOK

The Philip E. Lilienthal imprint
honors special books
in commemoration of a man whose work
at University of California Press from 1954 to 1979
was marked by dedication to young authors
and to high standards in the field of Asian Studies.
Friends, family, authors, and foundations have together
endowed the Lilienthal Fund, which enables UC Press
to publish under this imprint selected books
in a way that reflects the taste and judgment
of a great and beloved editor.

The publisher and the University of California Press Foundation
gratefully acknowledge the generous support of the
Philip E. Lilienthal Imprint in Asian Studies,
established by a major gift from Sally Lilienthal.

TWO SYSTEMS, TWO COUNTRIES

TWO SYSTEMS,

TWO COUNTRIES

A NATIONALIST GUIDE TO HONG KONG

Kevin Carrico

UNIVERSITY OF CALIFORNIA PRESS

University of California Press
Oakland, California

© 2022 by Kevin Carrico

Library of Congress Cataloging-in-Publication Data

Names: Carrico, Kevin, author.
Title: Two systems, two countries : a nationalist guide to Hong Kong /
    Kevin Carrico.
Description: Oakland, California : University of California Press, [2022] |
    Includes bibliographical references and index.
Identifiers: LCCN 2021041586 (print) | LCCN 2021041587 (ebook) |
    ISBN 9780520386747 (hardback) | ISBN 9780520386754 (paperback) |
    ISBN 9780520386761 (ebook)
Subjects: LCSH: Nationalism—China—Hong Kong—21st century. | Hong
    Kong (China—Politics and government—1997–
Classification: LCC DS796.H757 C368 2022 (print) | LCC DS796.H757 (ebook)
    | DDC 320.54095125—dc23
LC record available at https://lccn.loc.gov/2021041586
LC ebook record available at https://lccn.loc.gov/2021041587

Manufactured in the United States of America

28 27 26 25 24 23 22
10 9 8 7 6 5 4 3 2 1

CONTENTS

ACKNOWLEDGMENTS

It is not often that one finds an acknowledgments section for a book wherein many people would perhaps be most thankful to not be thanked. For this reason, I will thank very few people by name here.

The political situation in Hong Kong today makes it inadvisable for me to thank anyone there by name. Even if I could do so, however, I still could never express sufficient gratitude for the thoughtfulness, patience, and camaraderie that everyone has shown me throughout my research. This book is dedicated to everyone who has envisioned a better future for Hong Kong, whatever shape that vision might take, and I can only hope that some of you will see your insights reflected in the chapters that follow.

Funding agencies will still be happy to be acknowledged, of course. Early work on this project was funded by a new staff grant at Macquarie University. Subsequent research was funded by a research grant (RG-010-P-17) from the Chiang Ching-kuo Foundation for International Scholarly Exchange, as well as by a Discovery Early Career Researcher Award (DE190101210) from the Australian Research Council.

A few sections of chapter 3 are based on reflections previously published in *Hong Kong Studies* (2, no. 1 [2019]) under the title "Seeing (Exactly) Like a State: Knowledge/Power in the Beijing-Hong Kong Relationship." I thank *Hong Kong Studies* for the opportunity to contribute to this exciting new journal and appreciate their permission to reproduce a few revised and updated sections in this book.

I would like to thank my colleagues in the Chinese Studies program and the School of Languages, Literatures, Cultures, and Linguistics at Monash University, who have been immensely understanding as I have spent large blocks of time away from Melbourne in Hong Kong and endlessly supportive as I have written this book over the past two years. I would like to think that the late Bruce Jacobs, with whom I discussed an early outline of this book over dinner a few years ago, would have appreciated the argument that I have developed here.

From my original submission through review, revision, editing, and now publication, my experience with University of California Press has been fantastic, and I thank everyone for their patience and support throughout this process. I genuinely appreciate all of the hard work that everyone at the press puts into making authors' visions come to life.

I would also like to thank colleagues at *Apple Daily*. I was proud to have an opportunity to share my thoughts with the paper's readership in 2020 and 2021, and these weekly writing exercises helped me think through some of the issues discussed in this book. The extralegal closure of *Apple Daily* in June 2021 and the arbitrary detention of its editors and executives are a genuine disgrace for a once great city.

I also cannot forget to thank my friends at the highly respected newspaper *Wen Wei Po* for their unwavering attention to and eager promotion of my research all these years.

Finally, I would like to thank my family, both in Australia and in the United States, from my grandparents and parents to my aunts, uncles, sisters, and nephews and nieces. I first learned about a place called Hong Kong from my grandparents, who visited decades ago. Although they did not live to see the publication of this book, I would like to think that they would have enjoyed it. My parents have been endlessly supportive and have always encouraged me to follow my passions, even when those passions have led to my being followed by PRC state media. I would like to thank my best friend Leaf for her love and support through this challenging project and look forward to many more years together. My son Teddy may no longer remember much about Hong Kong beyond some toy stores and the monkeys at Hong Kong Park, but I look forward to the day when we can all visit again.

Melbourne, November 2021

Introduction

The Newest Nationalism

If there is one point on which everyone involved in the discussion of Hong Kong's political future could agree, it would be that Hong Kong independence is impossible. This once taboo idea has become increasingly part of mainstream political discussions in the city since 2011, yet remains just as implausible as ever. The Chinese Communist Party (CCP), which rules over the People's Republic of China (PRC), of which Hong Kong has been a part since 1997, would never allow the city to be independent. Furthermore, the fact that Hong Kong has no army of its own and relies on China even for its food and water means that the idea is simply unfeasible.

Hong Kong independence is however more than just unfeasible: the idea, in fact, presents a genuine self-destructive threat to the city's freedoms. China has ruled over Hong Kong since 1997 under the principle of One Country, Two Systems, wherein the Special Administrative Region enjoys a high degree of autonomy and numerous rights and freedoms that are not permitted anywhere else in China: freedom of speech, freedom of the press, and freedom of assembly. Yet the Chinese Communist Party is particularly sensitive and unforgiving toward transgressions against national unity: the Party bases its legitimacy in a narrative of national reunification following a century of humiliation by foreign powers, which began with Great Britain's colonization of Hong Kong in 1842 and officially ended in triumph with the city's handover to Chinese sovereignty in 1997. Using Hong Kong's treasured freedoms to promote separation from China, a practical impossibility, achieves nothing but provoking Beijing and providing the central government with the perfect pretext to further tighten its grip on the city.

What if, however, all these assumptions are actually wrong? What if Hong Kong independence is not just a crazy and impossible idea, but rather a product of genuine reflection on political developments in Hong Kong over the past two decades? What if the group of theorists and activists known as the "Hong Kong independence movement" represent not a singular and inevitably failed ideal, but rather a diverse array of political perspectives contributing to a vibrant and open-ended discussion of the city's future beyond the failed orthodoxies of the past? And what if, furthermore, these theorists and activists in fact understand the central government far better than the central government understands them?

This book is intended as a provocation, asking readers to take seriously the all-too-often casually dismissed idea of Hong Kong independence. Yet like the idea that it explains and analyzes, this book is also far more than a provocation. I first became interested in Hong Kong independence because the emergence of this idea since 2011 provides a rare opportunity for a theorist of ethnic and national identities to observe the formation of such identity in real time. The initial question driving my research was this: Why has the concept of a Hong Kong nation, largely unarticulated just a little over a decade ago, emerged at this moment in history? Pursuing this question for nearly a decade, including conducting fieldwork with enthusiasts of independence since 2016, I have taken the time to engage seriously with concepts and theories that I had also once dismissed as completely impractical. In doing so, I realized that Hong Kong nationalism is not only a case study that could be used to develop a new academic theory of ethnicity or nationalism, but also in and of itself a collection of radically innovative theories of Hong Kong's history, identity, relationship with China, and potential future paths.[1] Thus, while analyzing Hong Kong nationalism to better understand the formative processes of nationalist identity, this book also provides an introduction to the main schools of Hong Kong nationalism, giving readers an opportunity to see the world through the eyes of independence activists and recognize their intellectual contributions to the study of Hong Kong and China.

This book is then a provocation that should not really be all that provocative: I propose that we engage seriously with the ideas of a diverse range of intellectuals and activists who have contributed to a nuanced, theoretically engaged, decade-long debate in a politically complex society. It is all too easy to dismiss Hong Kong independence as an impossibility. It is at once more intellectually challenging and rewarding to seek to understand why ever more people are increasingly enthusiastic about this impossibility: a political reality that demands a complete reassessment of our understanding of Hong Kong's political reality.

FROM ONE COUNTRY, TWO SYSTEMS
TO TWO SYSTEMS, TWO COUNTRIES

On July 1, 1997, after a century and a half of British rule, the colony of Hong Kong was transferred to the People's Republic of China, marking the establishment of the Hong Kong Special Administrative Region. Speaking at the ceremony celebrating the handover on June 30, CCP Chairman Jiang Zemin declared, "On this solemn occasion, I wish to extend my cordial greetings and best wishes to the six million or more Hong Kong compatriots who have now returned to the embrace of the motherland."[2]

Twenty years later, on June 30, 2017, a very different event was held on the campus of Hong Kong Baptist University, where hundreds had gathered to mourn Hong Kong's handover to Chinese rule two decades earlier. Against a backdrop that read "Freedom from Chinese colonizers," Andy Chan of the newly established Hong Kong National Party led the crowd in shouting chants of "we are not Chinese," "we are Hong Kong-ers," and "Hong Kong independence."

Twenty years earlier, no one could have imagined this scene. Hong Kong had been handed over to the People's Republic of China in 1997 under the rubric of One Country, Two Systems first agreed upon by Great Britain and China in the 1980s. Prior to 1997, there were doubts about the notable lack of consultation with the Hong Kong people in reaching this agreement, just as there was rightful anxiety about the city's fate under Chinese rule due to the hard dictatorial turn in PRC politics after 1989.[3] Was Hong Kong being handed over from one colonial master to another? Could Beijing be trusted to abide by the promises it had made regarding Hong Kong's freedoms in the Joint Declaration and the Basic Law?[4] Yet despite these concerns, after 1997 the One Country, Two Systems model appeared relatively successful in protecting Hong Kong's unique political, legal, civil, and press liberties, making the city a simultaneously distinct yet also integral part of China. The apparent initial success of One Country, Two Systems in restraining Beijing and maintaining a genuine degree of autonomy in Hong Kong made a decade of pessimistic predictions about the "fall of Hong Kong" appear hyperbolic and alarmist.

With the passage of time, however, as tensions rose between Hong Kong's relatively open political, legal, media, and social systems and the increasingly restrictive political culture of the People's Republic of China, the most pessimistic of predictions began to seem overly optimistic. In 2002, unprecedented protests brought half a million people onto the streets to voice their opposition to proposed national security legislation that threatened the city's freedom of speech, freedom of press, freedom of association, and rule of law.[5] In 2011 and 2012, another round of student-led protests targeted a patriotic education module that promoted an ideologically restrictive vision of Chineseness for Hong Kong students.[6] And in 2014, after decades of endless delays to the universal suffrage legally guaranteed in the city's Basic Law, unprecedented Occupy Central protests brought central sections of the city to a standstill for seventy-nine days.[7]

Within this context of continually escalating political and cultural tensions, in 2011 Lingnan University academic Chin Wan published a highly idiosyncratic book, *On Hong Kong as a City-State*.[8] In Chin's telling, Hong Kong had heretofore been imagined as either a colony of Great Britain or a Special Administrative Region of the People's Republic of China, but these labels failed to fully capture the reality of the city's historical experience and cultural present. Chin proposed instead that Hong Kong was in fact a city-state, a proposal that may seem quite underwhelming at first glance, and certainly an unlikely candidate for radically changing the face of Hong Kong politics. Yet for Chin, reimagining Hong Kong as a city-state places the city's heritage in the European city-state tradition, envisioning a unique culture for the Hong Kong people distinct from China. Insofar as this distinctiveness enables redirecting the discussion of Hong Kong's future away from inevitable integration with China to a focus on Hong Kong itself as a distinct polity, Chin's intervention realized a genuine paradigm shift in political thinking in the city: imagining a future for Hong Kong beyond the increasingly obviously failed ideal of One Country, Two Systems.

In the ten short yet eventful years since the publication of Chin's book, the world's newest nationalism has left an indelible mark on Hong Kong politics and culture, producing a proliferation of perspectives, publications, protest movements, political parties, and punitive purges. In the city's universities, undergraduate students have compiled special journal issues drawing on the latest·developments in postcolonial theory and scholarship on international law to argue for the existence of a Hong Kong ethnicity with the legal right to self-determination.[9] In local media, a network of news sites and daily online talk shows promoting independence has emerged to fundamentally change how people think and talk about daily realities in the city. In the political field, the Hong Kong National Party has explicitly promoted the goal of establishing an independent Republic of Hong Kong, advocating anti-colonial resistance by any means necessary. A rapidly growing scholarly and popular corpus on Hong Kong independence that traces the city's unique history and envisions its distinct future has expanded across bookstore shelves. There has even been a relatively fringe movement advocating for Hong Kong's return to the United Kingdom on the basis of international law. Across their diverse political visions, Hong Kong nationalists have come together in a common awakening to the failure of One Country, Two Systems and the corresponding need to develop a vision of Two Systems, Two Countries.

These developments raise two sets of pressing questions, which this book examines. First, thinking specifically about Hong Kong and its political and cultural dilemma under Chinese rule, I ask: How can we explain the dramatic transformation of Hong Kong identity and politics since 1997, and in particular since 2011? Why has the once taboo idea of Hong Kong nationalism emerged at this moment in history? What does the once absent concept of a Hong Kong nation mean to Hong Kong nationalists, and how have their various proposals for the city's future attained broader popular resonance? How, in turn, has the Chinese central government responded to these developments? And finally, what are the implications of this unfolding discussion for Hong Kong's political future and its relationship with China?

Second, thinking through broader anthropological concerns of the formation of a novel ethnic-national identity, I ask: How is this new mode of identification (the Hong Kong nation) imagined and enacted by activists? What can this process, occurring in real time for direct observation, reveal about the fundamental processes of national identity construction? And what can we learn about the Hong Kong-China relationship from the thinkers directly involved in the process of its reimagining?

This book seeks answers to these questions. It is based in a decade of research, having followed and even at times contributed to the conversation on Hong Kong nationalism from the first articulation of Hong Kong as a city-state in 2011 to the attempted silencing of this conversation in 2020 with the

National Security Law. In the span of this brief yet very eventful decade, a series of completely unexpected developments pitting newly emergent knowledge against old power has forever changed politics, culture, and activism in this city of seven million people.

At the same time, one after another, the lives of everyone involved in the conversation on Hong Kong independence have also been forever changed, including my own.

A NOTE ON METHOD AND SURVEILLANCE

I first noticed her as I casually glanced around the subway car. We were above ground now, the sun shining radiantly through the MTR (Mass Transit Railway) car's windows on a warm December morning, on our way to Tung Chung on northern Lantau island. Only one of us realized at the time that we were in fact traveling together.

As I looked around the subway car, our eyes met, and she immediately looked down at her phone. A few minutes later, as I glanced around the car again, our eyes met one more time. This was curious. She clearly seemed to be looking at me and only at me, but I could not figure out why: to this day, in fact, I still do not know if she intended for me to notice or not.

Sporting an "I love Hawaii" T-shirt that fit across my rotund figure a bit too tightly, matched with an aging pair of Crocs, I could be certain that her glances were not spurred by romantic interest. I noticed that she was wearing an Oxford University sweatshirt. I had presented a paper on Hong Kong's National Education Center at an Oxford conference seven years earlier. Maybe we had met there? Maybe she was somehow familiar with my research on Hong Kong and happened to recognize me? Yet this struck me as quite unlikely. Believe me, readers, I am not vain, and these are not the kinds of thoughts that I usually think. But then again, I do not usually have someone very obviously staring at me for no reason. Having nothing better to do for the moment, I mulled over each possibility, none seeming terribly likely. Our eyes meeting must just have been a coincidence.

As I arrived at my destination, Tung Chung, my goal for the day was simple: to obtain a sense of the general mood of the area, which had become a site of tensions between locals and Chinese tour groups since the opening of the nearby Hong Kong-Zhuhai-Macao Bridge a few weeks earlier.[10] I would perhaps strike up a few casual conversations along the way, but I had no meetings or interviews scheduled. It would most likely be an uneventful day, always an appealing prospect before a busy week.

As I walked through the Citygate Mall, its corridors crowded with hundreds of Chinese shoppers, opening their suitcases to pack them full of new purchases to smuggle across the border, I could see how this sudden surge of new visitors could be annoying for local residents ... but then as I turned around for a moment to glance behind me, I suddenly noticed that young lady in the Oxford sweatshirt there again. That's really strange, I thought.

About half an hour later, I paid a visit to a bathroom on the basement level of the mall. Exiting the men's room, I noticed that this same young lady was in the foyer area outside of the bathroom. It suddenly became very clear that it was no longer possible to explain these encounters as pure coincidences. Again, all types of explanations raced through my mind, none seeming particularly plausible. Hopping on the escalator to proceed to ground level, I immediately noticed that she followed along. As I disembarked, I stopped, turned around, and held up my iPhone to take a picture. Once she spotted me holding up my phone, however, she turned around 180 degrees, riding the escalator toward me backward. I was so puzzled by this that in the end I completely failed to take a picture. When she reached the top of the escalator, she very conspicuously continued to look away from me as she hurried forward through the mall's crowds.

From that moment, the remaining hour that I spent in Tung Chung was without a doubt the most perplexing of my life. I walked toward the other end of the mall to exit onto the public square outside, only to find that she had followed me there. When I raised my phone to take a picture, she again walked away. I saw two policemen standing outside and thought of speaking with them about the situation, but I honestly had no idea who was following me or how exactly to explain to the police this puzzling experience that I myself was still attempting to process. There was no way to put this situation into coherent words. As I walked out toward the Ngong Ping 360 cable cars to the north of the mall, I noticed that she was again following me. When I walked back toward her to ask what she was doing, she was suddenly led away by an older woman.

I climbed the stairs leading to the Ngong Ping 360 cable cars and could see my two tails standing near a bus stop below awaiting my return. At this point, it was clear that I was not going to get any work done that day; my mind was overrun by the question of who was following me and why they were doing so. Abandoning my plans, I walked back to the MTR and sat in the station through a few train departures, checking to see if anyone was waiting along with me. Once I was as confident as I could be that I was no longer being followed, I boarded a train to return to my Kowloon hotel.

During a series of meetings, interviews, and casual walks through the city over the following week, I occasionally had a vague sense that someone was following me but was never completely certain. As the days passed, in fact, it gradually began to seem crazy to think that anyone had actually been following me. Friends seemed to agree, most appearing perplexed at my narrative of the weekend encounter. Admittedly, I found the creeping possibility that I had not been followed no less perplexing. Had I just been paranoid that day in Tung Chung?

Arriving back in Sydney ten days later after an overnight flight, I planned to take a nap at home before going to pick up my son in the afternoon. Glancing at my phone, I noticed that I had a message from a friend that read simply: "You're famous." The image attached to the message was a screenshot of the cover of the propaganda rag *Wen Wei Po*, owned and managed by the Liaison Office, the representative office of the government of the People's Republic of China in Hong Kong. A series of clandestinely shot pictures of my time in Hong Kong featured under the headline "Australian scholar spreads Hong Kong independence." The subtitle read, "Kevin Carrico has visited Hong Kong many times, is friends with Andy Chan of the Hong Kong National Party, and Wayne Chan of Students' Independence Union came to his presentation." The article included a detailed discussion of my activities during my visit, including the curious factoid that on Tuesday, December 11, 2018, I went back to my hotel to change clothes in between two afternoon meetings. If anyone is still curious, I made this choice because I was sweaty. Amid all of the challenges facing Hong Kong in 2018, the central government had chosen to prioritize dispatching a team to follow my every move and change of apparel.

One function of such surveillance, of course, is collecting information on the meetings and behavior of its targets. In my case, however, I doubt that any remotely valuable information was obtained. I have made no secret of the focus of my research or of my acquaintance with many Hong Kong independence advocates. Nothing that we discussed in any of these meetings, some of which I now know were in fact surveilled, was top secret. Another far more insidious function of surveillance, however, is to affect the thinking of its targets, leaving one pondering questions that can never be answered. Once the

Wen Wei Po cover story confirmed without a doubt that I had been followed, further questions emerged. What was the actual goal of this surveillance? Did the people following me intend to be clandestine and simply fail horribly? Or did they in fact want me to notice that they were following me? If so, why? Why was I obviously followed on some days, but not followed on others? Or was I in fact followed every day, without realizing?

This surveillance obviously changed how I experienced Hong Kong. It has also changed how I have written the final version of this book about Hong Kong. Readers who proceed through the book will be reassured immediately that I am not engaging in self-censorship. This is, after all, a book about the most sensitive topic in Hong Kong politics today: independence. My concern is not for myself. I have long ago abandoned any hope of returning to China and have reached largely the same conclusion about returning to Hong Kong since the implementation of the National Security Law. My concern is instead for the people with whom I worked during my research. As an anthropologist, I have based my research on lengthy conversations with advocates of Hong Kong nationalism over years of engagement. Yet as a result of the surveillance applied to my research since at least July 2017 (if not earlier), combined with the impact of the National Security Law forced on Hong Kong at the end of June 2020, I have had no choice but to adjust how I tell this story.

In the current political and legal climate, there exists a real risk that even anonymous recounting of private conversations in book form could be used by the authorities to persecute people whose lives are already difficult enough, with the National Security Law allowing the authorities to jail critics for life for speech crimes. Considering the intentionally arbitrary nature of this law and its enforcement, there is no way of knowing which of my meetings were being surveilled and which comments, when put on the public record by an "anti-China force" like myself, could be matched up with a particular meeting and thereby used as evidence in political persecution. To eliminate the risk that this book could be used to persecute others while at the same time never shying away from the critical insights derived from these conversations, I have revised this text such that my original recounting of ostensibly private but potentially surveilled conversations has been replaced by the analysis of publicly available written texts or statements that make similar points. To cite one example, my discussion of the potential use of force in fighting for independence, a topic of numerous conversations over the years, has been replaced by analysis of a publicly available article on this topic from the Hong Kong

National Party journal *Comitium* that communicates many of the same ideas that I took away from these conversations.

For the same reason, this book includes no photographs from my time in Hong Kong. I have had a truly fulfilling fieldwork experience over the past few years in this city about which I care deeply, and it is precisely as a result of this deep care that I must also be careful about how I share my experiences publicly.

The National Security Law forced on Hong Kong in June 2020 makes the stakes of independence advocacy higher than they have ever been. At the same time, however, this law also makes sharing the story of Hong Kong's ongoing struggle even more urgent than it already was. I have thus chosen to tell the story of Hong Kong's independence discussion in a way that is at once brutally honest and ethically responsible. My friends in Hong Kong can be reassured that this text cannot be mined by the authorities for evidence to engage in politicized persecution: all data recounted here are in the public record in other publications. At the same time, these friends in Hong Kong and beyond can also be reassured that I am avoiding self-censorship, speaking honestly without concern for the increasingly voracious anaconda in the chandelier, and drawing fully upon insights from our conversations over the years.

Finally, the fact that I have had to think about these matters at all and have been left with no choice but to take these fairly drastic steps in the final stages of manuscript preparation is a testament to the foresight of the people and ideas discussed in this book. As Hong Kong independence activists have told me for many years, and as I myself have gradually come to realize, there was never any chance of maintaining Hong Kong's freedoms under One Country, Two Systems. Everything that they predicted has come true.

LAYOUT OF THE BOOK

The three chapters of this book are organized thematically, examining (1) the origins of Hong Kong nationalist thought, (2) the main factions in the Hong Kong nationalist conversation, and (3) the central government's response to these developments.

In the first chapter, "Hong Kong Ethnogenesis," I begin my analyses from the question of why, since the transfer of Hong Kong to Chinese sovereignty in 1997, ever fewer residents of the city identify as Chinese, with ever more embracing visions of a Hong Kong nation. My analysis proceeds through four distinct theoretical exercises, trying on each one to see how it fits these phenomena, finally tracing Hong Kong's ethnogenesis to the intersection of political affect and logical critique. The reimagining of Hong Kong as a nation distinct from China is undoubtedly a response to Beijing's increasingly interventionist approach to Hong Kong matters, meeting the central government's provocations with a counterprovocation of independence that gleefully crosses all of Beijing's red lines. At the same time, however, Hong Kong nationalism is more than a counterprovocation: it presents a sustained political critique of One Country, Two Systems, seeking enlightenment from the once-soothing mythologies of Hong Kong's future under Chinese rule. The Hong Kong nation is thus not only an imagined community but also an imaginative community, seeking new and inventive paths out of the city's increasingly dire political situation.

The second chapter, "Two Systems, Two Countries: New Directions in Political Thought in Hong Kong since 2011," examines these paths. This chapter is based on years of dialogue with independence activists and close readings of their foundational writings, developing the first comprehensive English-language introduction to the four main schools of nationalist thought: city-state theory, self-determinationism, Hong Kong independence, and returnism. Chin Wan's paradigm-shifting intervention in *On Hong Kong as a City-State* (2011), calling for the recognition of Hong Kong as a city-state with a distinct culture, launched a wide-ranging public discussion of politics and identity in Hong Kong that has over the past decade expanded far beyond his original vision. Self-determinationism, for example, is based in the application of international law to Hong Kong's political situation, envisioning adherence to the law as both a distinguishing feature of the Hong Kong people and a solution to their political dilemma via a referendum on self-determination. Hong Kong independence, by contrast, sees no point in compromise with a power that refuses to yield to the law, promoting instead the development of an anti-colonial community forged in resistance to Chinese rule by any means necessary. Finally, advocates of returnism paradoxically propose decolonization via recolonization, arguing that Hong Kong's sovereignty needs to be legally returned to the United Kingdom on account of China's repeated violations of the Sino-British Joint Declaration. This chapter reflects the full diversity of opinions and proposals exchanged under the label of Hong Kong nationalism, reinterpreting this nationalism not as a single movement but rather as an ongoing and open-ended conversation based on a common awakening to the failure of One Country, Two Systems.

In the third and final chapter, "Seeing (Exactly) Like a State: Knowledge/ Power in the Hong Kong-China Relationship," I analyze Beijing's response to these intellectual and political developments. I first immerse myself in the official Chinese academic corpus on Hong Kong nationalism, drawing upon and developing Edward Said's knowledge/power framework from *Orientalism* by applying it to a novel colonial relationship: Beijing's rule over Hong Kong. Analyzing four core tropes in official Chinese scholarship, namely the spoiled child, the hysteric, the outlaw, and the virus, I trace an imaginary structure of state power that sees Hong Kong as invariably deficient and irrational, need- ing support from China in order to return to normalcy and health. The central state's analyses of Hong Kong's revolt against central control always already find a solution in further central control, such that Beijing seeks solutions in precisely the types of policies that produced current tensions. Beijing's exer- cise of power against the knowledge produced in Hong Kong's decade-long debate on nationalism is thus further intensifying tensions and making the city's political future increasingly uncertain. At the same time, however, Bei- jing's policies are also providing the clearest evidence yet in support of Hong Kong nationalists' arguments. Knowledge and power are thus not one and the same, but rather exist on distinct sides of this colonial binary, feeding off one another in perpetually escalating conflict, with no clear resolution.

In the conclusion, I reflect on recent events in this conflict, from the 2019 anti-extradition protests to Beijing's unprecedented 2020 decision to force a centrally drafted National Security Law on the city. These developments reveal the lasting impact that the Hong Kong nationalist discussion has had on politics and identity in the city, as well as demonstrating the value of Hong Kong nationalists' analyses for understanding Hong Kong-China relations, even as Beijing attempts to erase these now inerasable ideas.

CHAPTER I

Hong Kong Ethnogenesis

On June 30, 2017, hundreds traveled from across Hong Kong to a remote corner of Baptist University in Kowloon Tong to mark the twentieth anniversary of Hong Kong's handover to the People's Republic of China. In stark contrast to the festivities of twenty years prior as well as the elaborate ceremonies that would take place just twelve hours later alongside Victoria Harbor, this gathering did not celebrate but rather mourned Hong Kong's 1997 handover.

This event encapsulated the degree of change in Hong Kong over the preceding twenty years. Andy Chan of the Hong Kong National Party, who had organized the event in collaboration with the student unions of various Hong Kong universities, succinctly summarized this shift as follows: "We disagree with the thinking of the past, and with the approaches of the past. We do not want to build a democratic China. We do not feel that we are Chinese. We feel that we are Hong Kong-ers. We don't want to remain confined within this One Country Two Systems trap." The ideas expressed here, reorienting matters of politics and identity away from China toward an explicit focus on Hong Kong, are so novel that they would have been unthinkable just a few short years earlier. At the time of Hong Kong's handover to Chinese rule in 1997, 31.6 percent of young people aged eighteen to twenty-nine identified as "Chinese in the broad sense" (meaning having a sense of Chinese identity while not necessarily identifying with the People's Republic of China). By 2017, that number had jarringly dropped to just 3.1 percent.[1] Polling has also indicated growing support for the idea of independence: one 2016 poll found that 40 percent of respondents aged fifteen to twenty-four supported the only recently articulated idea of Hong Kong independence.[2] Paradoxically, identification as even broadly Chinese has plummeted precisely as Hong Kong has been integrated into China, while the once taboo idea of Hong Kong independence has found growing resonance among an ever larger group of residents.

The twentieth anniversary of Hong Kong's handover to China was supposed to be cause for celebration. Chairman Xi Jinping had rented out the entire Renaissance Hotel adjacent to Victoria Harbor and was to present a triumphant speech the next morning. An ever smaller minority, however, took Xi's boastful declarations of the success of One Country, Two Systems even remotely seriously. At Baptist University, Chan continued: "We need to tell the world that July 1st is nothing to celebrate. Rather, this is a day to be mourned. 20 years ago, the United Kingdom handed us over to a ruthless dictatorship. And from that moment, our fall began." As if to prove Chan's argument, the Hong Kong government had gone to great lengths to prevent this gathering from happening at all. Originally to be held at the clock tower at Tsim Sha Tsui, directly across the harbor from Xi's hotel and the Wan Chai Exhibition Center where official celebrations would be held the next day, the clock tower area had been conveniently cordoned off for unspecified "repairs." Threatened with arrest while setting up at an alternate location in Tsim Sha Tsui East, the event finally found a home in a remote corner of Baptist University, far removed from the symbolic center of the city. In a suitably paradoxical situation that reflects the conflicted nature of this idea in practice, One Country, Two Systems was to be defended from its critics by denying them the very freedoms of speech and assembly that One Country Two Systems had promised.

I sat among other speakers from the university student unions as Chan concluded his remarks by leading the crowd in chants. In both Cantonese and English, the crowd shouted, "Hong Kong independence," "we are not Chinese," and "no Chinese colonization." As my gaze wandered to the stage's maroon backdrop, which read "freedom from Chinese colonizers," I thought to myself how we had all arrived here. Just ten years earlier, not to mention two decades earlier, no one would have believed that in 2017 a political party would be holding a rally to mourn the handover and advocate independence from China. The One Country, Two Systems model that, in providing a supposed solution to the "Hong Kong question," was also supposed to provide a path forward for the "Taiwan question," had ironically opened a reverse path of political imagining: rather than the people of Taiwan seeing hope in One Country, Two Systems as Beijing had hoped, ever more people in Hong Kong living under One Country Two Systems had instead come to find hope in Taiwan's model of a free nation independent from China.

How exactly did this happen? Why have ever more people's visions of themselves and their city's future coalesced at this historical moment around the idea of a Hong Kong nation distinct from China? What can we learn about the formation of ethnonational identity by observing this process in real time? This chapter examines four theoretical frameworks for interpreting the emergence of the idea of a Hong Kong nation, tracing the formation of this identity in the interaction between political affect and logical critique of the founding myths of the Hong Kong Special Administrative Region.

TAKE ONE: THE PSYCHOPATHOLOGY OF IDENTITY

The first book-length English-language study of Hong Kong independence to reach library shelves was Zhu Jie and Zhang Xiaoshan's *Critique of Hong Kong Nativism*, published by Springer in 2019.[3] Zhu and Zhang are members of the Chinese Association of Hong Kong-Macao Studies, an official academic organization under the Hong Kong and Macao Affairs Office of China's State Council, about which I have more to say in chapter 3. For now it will suffice to say that, according to its own official mission statement, the association's main objective is to "plan and coordinate research on the theory and practice of One Country Two Systems" across its three main research clusters: politics and law, economics, and society and administration.[4] Zhu and Zhang are legal scholars who have focused their research on the emergence of the idea of a Hong Kong ethnicity and the corresponding vision of a Hong Kong nation. Their research focus is thus largely the same as my own: Why has Hong Kong nationalism emerged at this particular moment in history? And what are its implications for Hong Kong-China relations?

Zhu and Zhang's take on these matters, however, is quite different from mine: in short, they characterize Hong Kong nationalism as at once pathological, growing out of a perverse relationship with the city's motherland, and fundamentally impossible, taking Hong Kong down an irreversible path of self-destruction.

Zhu and Zhang analyze the development of Hong Kong nationalism from a historical perspective, dividing Hong Kong's history into three stages: (1) a period of blurred borders and mutual exchange from 1842 to 1949, (2) a period of closed borders and growing distinction from 1949 to the late 1970s, and (3) a period of inverted hierarchy and emergent pathology from the 1980s to the present. Belying the heavily Sinocentric assumptions of their framework, each stage of Hong Kong's history is defined solely by the city's relationship with China, disregarding all other factors, with a particular emphasis on whether the relationship adheres to the authors' underlying assumption of a natural pan-Chinese unity.[5]

For the first stage, from the establishment of the colony of Hong Kong in 1842 to the communist takeover of China in 1949, Zhu and Zhang portray the border between Hong Kong and China as largely open, facilitating a constant flow of people and goods.[6] Such fluidity and openness, they argue, was manifested not only in cross-border movements but also in identity: even long-term residents of Hong Kong at the time, according to Zhu and Zhang, viewed the city less as a permanent home than as a temporary shelter from the series of tumultuous events that reshaped politics and society in China in the nineteenth and twentieth centuries.[7] This argument coheres on one level with the general scholarly consensus on the flexibility of identity in Hong Kong's first century as a colony, but this consensus is very obviously being deployed by Zhu and Zhang on another level to ignore non-national modes of identification, such as local hometown identities, thereby projecting rigid pan-Chinese nationalist assumptions back across time.

In the second stage, from 1949 to the end of the Maoist era in the late 1970s, the Hong Kong-China border hardened considerably, with both the British colonial administration and the Maoist regime enforcing border controls from 1950 onward.[8] Zhu and Zhang's singular focus on the border as a line between the two territories alludes to the considerably more complex identity processes produced by this border. The development of distinct visions of culture, society, and identity on either side of such a border is a natural process of community formation, but insofar as it deviates from Zhu and Zhang's racial teleology of unitary Chineseness, these developments are labeled as anomalous. The hierarchy emerging between the two societies in this period is in their view even more disconcerting. The emergence of a distinctive Hong Kong identity coincided with the rise of Hong Kong as a major regional economic center from the 1950s through the 1970s, a period in which China itself remained trapped in the self-defeating, yet also as a result perpetually self-reproducing, cycle of political mobilization toward an imaginary Maoist utopia. Confidence in the city's economic and social developments led to a certain pride in Hong Kong as a site of "rapid development, high efficiency, incorrupt administration, and political freedom," which contrasted with the perpetual turmoil and poverty to the north of the border.[9] According to Zhu and Zhang, the people of Hong Kong came to see themselves in this period as not only distinct from China but also distinctly better than China, a belief that Zhu and Zhang call "Hong Kong chauvinism."[10]

In Zhu and Zhang's third historical stage, from the late 1970s to the present, this unnatural chauvinism has been subverted by the rise of China. In 1997, Hong Kong was handed over to China, making the city "China's Hong Kong." And since this handover, China's rapid economic growth has challenged Hong Kong's status as a regional economic center.[11] The historical inferior now not only has higher GDP growth rates but is also the city's sovereign ruler. Zhu and Zhang argue that as the hierarchies of the past are overturned and Hong Kong's perceived superiority fades away, the people of the city have grown increasingly determined to repress these realities: "Mentally and psychologically, many Hong Kong residents are stuck in the middle 1980s, and they have not been prepared for all the changes that happened after 1997."[12] This is where Zhu and Zhang trace the origins of the idea of Hong Kong independence: as a pathological response to China's unstoppable rise. Seeking to maintain their imagined superiority relative to China yet feeling that superiority rapidly slipping away, Hong Kong residents have in Zhu and Zhang's analysis turned to Hong Kong nationalism, which the authors interpret as little more than an angry cry of despair emanating from a city that time has left behind.[13] The chauvinism of past eras has, in the relative marginalization of the present, mutated into pathological self-affirmation, obsessively repeated in a failed attempt to cover over its own deep insecurities amid the inexorable historical trend of China's rise.[14]

Having laid the city down on the analyst's couch to reveal its psychopathologies, the authors proceed to introduce their analysands to the reality principle: Hong Kong independence, they tell us, is not only pathological but also impossible. The arguments that Zhu and Zhang deploy in this regard are neither particularly novel nor interesting, so I cover them only briefly. First, Hong Kong's livelihood and entire economy are reliant upon China, whether for basic supplies like food and water or for economic growth.[15] Second, China will never allow Hong Kong to be independent, particularly on account of the torturous modern history of national division and humiliation that the CCP heralds itself as overcoming.[16] Finally, Hong Kong independence is illegal because it violates Article 1 of the Basic Law, which states, "The Hong Kong Special Administrative Region is an inalienable part of China."[17] Zhu and Zhang are not aiming for subtlety here: Hong Kong independence, they tell us, is not only pathological but also illegal, impractical, and at the end of the day fundamentally impossible. This idea's fundamental impossibility, they argue, means that it contains within itself an inevitable drift toward violence, attempting to overcome its own insurmountable failures by ever more forceful means: "In order to keep their influences and realize their separatist dreams, separatists in many countries are spreading panic and fears by street violence, arson, assassination, abduction, massive slaughter and bombing. In China, 'Xinjiang independence' and 'Tibet independence' were not accepted by the society, so they became extremism and terrorism."[18] A similar path, they tell us, is inevitable in Hong Kong.

There can be no compromise with such trends, Zhu and Zhang warn. Earlier compromises by the central authorities, such as the decision to withdraw Article 23 legislation in 2003 or the national education program in 2012, gave the unruly natives of the south the wrong impression of the central state's determination: "Unfortunately, this kind of compromises [sic] are seen as the sign of 'weakness,' so that many democrats believe that as long as they 'play hard' and mobilize the masses, Beijing would give in at the final moment."[19] They continue: "The folk [sic] also have the mindset of 'the solution to a big problem is a big fuss, the solution to a little problem is a little fuss; all in all, no fuss, no solution."[20] Continued indulgence of such pathological impracticality, driving politics in Hong Kong toward the impossible, is fundamentally unsustainable. The central authorities thus need to "explain to the [sic] Hong Kong society the impossibility of 'Hong Kong independence' in a way that is acceptable to Hong Kong residents," "press charges against those separatists who infringed the law," and address economic and livelihood issues so that the people of the city will not be so perpetually hopeless and angry.[21]

To think that Hong Kong is just one more explanation, one more arrest, or one more massive infrastructure project away from finally acquiescing to Beijing's will is to fundamentally misunderstand everything. Yet as official academics working in the Chinese Association of Hong Kong-Macao Studies, Zhu and Zhang's job was never to develop independent analyses explaining the dynamics of contemporary politics that have led to the emergence of a feeling of ethnic and national difference in Hong Kong. Their job is to attack new and potentially liberating developments in Hong Kong politics, as well as to rationalize Beijing's predetermined solution of further tightening its grip as the best and indeed only option. Accordingly, the authors tellingly never bother to provide readers with any details about their research process. There is no explanation of their methods, no literature review, no mention of interviews, nor even any reference to any time spent conducting research in Hong Kong: the pathological and impossible nature of the idea of Hong Kong independence is not even worthy of being taken so seriously. Rather, simply by right of their positions as official Hong Kong-ologists, they know Hong Kong better than the city's residents ever could, and their responsibility is to communicate the truth that they always already had. The irony of developing a critique of what Zhu and Zhang call the "ideology" of Hong Kong nationalism from within the infinitely more restrictive confines of official state ideology does not seem to give the authors even the slightest pause. In fact, it gives them a false sense of confidence and certainty.

Rather than providing a convincing analysis of the emergence of Hong Kong nationalism, Zhu and Zhang's book provides a far more revealing case study of the type of misunderstandings and misrepresentations that shape Beijing's policy toward Hong Kong and thus Hong Kong-China relations, a topic to which I return in chapter 3. For the moment, it will suffice to note that the reliably condescending tone of Zhu and Zhang's arguments and the control-focused policy implications of their conclusions in fact provide a far more convincing explanation of the origins of and driving forces behind Hong Kong nationalism than their own theories.

TAKE TWO: NONCOMPLIANCE CYCLE

Zhu and Zhang claimed to provide a historical analysis of the emergence of Hong Kong nationalism, but their periodization grouped all events from the 1980s to the present under a single era, characterized solely by China's rise, which they claim has literally driven the Hong Kong people insane with envy. Upon closer examination, however, the idea of independence did not enter mainstream political discussions in Hong Kong in the 1980s, but rather only in the 2010s. Zhu and Zhang's analysis, for all of its shortcomings, thus shows its greatest weakness in its fundamentally ahistorical historical framework. What, then, has actually happened in Hong Kong since 1997? What specific factors have led to the emergence and popularization of the idea of Hong Kong independence at this particular moment in history? And why are Zhu and Zhang so eager to elide the discussion of recent history, summarizing the past four decades through the singular metanarrative of China's rise? My goal in fieldwork in Hong Kong has always been to develop a framework for understanding the rise of ethnic feeling and independence sentiment in the city, seeing the recent rise of such sentiment as a unique intellectual opportunity to observe and thereby understand ethnic and national thought in the process of formation. Engaging in dialogue with supporters of Hong Kong independence to think through the events of the two decades since Hong Kong's handover to China, my thoughts were often drawn back to a seemingly unlikely reference: a 1969 book chapter by G. William Skinner and Edwin Winckler, "Compliance Succession in Rural Communist China: A Cyclical Theory."[22]

Skinner and Winckler analyze state-society relations in rural areas of Maoist China, a social and political environment far removed from contemporary Hong Kong. Yet through their detailed analysis of state policy shifts in the first two decades under Mao (1949–1969), Skinner and Winckler propose a concept that resonated with my impressions of events in Hong Kong: a compliance cycle.

In this cycle, radical state-driven mobilization for the purpose of Maoist ideological projects, attempting to force reality to comply with unreal political doctrines, produced disastrous outcomes that eventually pushed society and the leadership to demobilize in reluctant compliance with reality. By contrast, what I was witnessing in post-1997 Hong Kong was the evolution of a noncompliance cycle, wherein state attempts to force reality in Hong Kong to comply with its doctrines of Chineseness produced a sense of difference and resistance. Rather than making adjustments in response to this reality, the difference and resistance produced therein have fueled ever greater paranoia and desire for control from the central state, which in turn has fueled ever greater difference and resistance. The result is a non-compliance cycle wherein the Chinese state and Hong Kong civil society continue to provoke one another in a self-reproducing cycle of escalating mutual provocation that pulls the two sides ever further apart. In the following sections, I explain the main components of Skinner and Winckler's theory and my revision thereof, before demonstrating how this noncompliance cycle can explain developments elided in Zhu and Zhang's analysis.

Compliance and Noncompliance Cycles

In a dense twenty-page essay published in 1969, G. William Skinner and Edwin Winckler analyze a cyclical pattern in state policy and thus in relations between the Chinese Communist Party and rural residents (whom the authors call "the peasantry") through the first two decades of the Maoist era, which they call a compliance cycle.[23] This macrolevel cycle is composed of three distinct yet mutually interrelated subcycles: a goal cycle, a power cycle, and an involvement cycle. The goal cycle, referring to official goals ordered from the top of the political hierarchy, consists of three potential policy priorities: economic goals, ideological goals (i.e. "redness"), and order (what would now be called "stability").[24] The power cycle, referring to the shifting modes of exercising power to mobilize the populace toward official goals, also consists of three main types: normative (i.e., relying on moral pressures), remunerative (i.e., relying on rewards), and coercive (i.e., relying on explicit pressures from and enforcement by the state).[25] Finally, the involvement cycle, tracing rural residents' attitudes and responses toward these varying modes of mobilization for policy goals, consists of six largely self-explanatory cyclical steps tracing a trajectory from unfamiliarity to involvement to eventual disappointment: indifference, partial commitment, commitment, ambivalence, partial alienation, alienation, and a return to indifference.[26]

These three mutually affected and affecting micro-cycles (goals, power, and involvement), when superimposed upon one another, come together to form Skinner and Winckler's macrolevel compliance cycle, through which they explain shifts in policy and political participation in the first two decades of Maoist China. The six steps in this compliance cycle are normalcy, mobilization, high tide, deterioration, retrenchment, and demobilization.[27] If readers' eyes are beginning to glaze over from this overly compact retelling of a complex theoretical framework, allow me to briefly summarize how the authors apply this framework to reality:

1. There are periods of moderation, with policy focused primarily on economic goals using remunerative mobilization, which produce normalcy and stability.[28]

2. The positive outcomes of these periods of moderation and stability produce overconfidence among decidedly immoderate state leaders, creating a hotbed for the type of "radical" ideological fantasies that proved so reliably destructive throughout the Maoist era.[29]

3. State leaders push for more radical measures and mobilization of "the masses," prioritizing ideological goals and deploying normative (i.e., non-remunerative) power to mobilize rural residents in the service of these ideological fantasies (e.g., the Great Leap Forward following the considerably more moderate initial transition to "socialism").[30]

4. The impractical nature of these radical measures, however, leads to a disastrous clash with reality that is at first repressed, with normative power driving cadres to falsely report "miracles" (remunerative in terms of sociopolitical capital) regardless of realities.[31]

5. As the impractical nature of policy grows increasingly apparent, unable to bridge the distinction between Maoist fantasy and reality, society gradually deteriorates into crisis such that residents' attitudes shift from state-driven commitment to reality-based ambivalence and eventually alienation.[32]

6. Finally, policy makers respond first with retrenchment and then eventually demobilization, returning to the more moderate policies from which the cycle began, which return a degree of order to society.[33]

The core insight of Skinner and Winckler's analysis lies in their notion of compliance as a keyword for understanding state-society relations in the Maoist era. On the one hand, they examine the manifold ways in which the Party-state mobilized rural residents to comply with policy goals, and thereby attempted to also make reality comply with Maoist ideological fantasies. On the other hand, Skinner and Winckler also show how Mao's self-declared, ever-victorious dictatorship of the proletariat inevitably had to yield to and comply with the unforgiving dictatorship of reality. This single keyword of compliance thus provides a revealing entry point for understanding the relationship between the state, society, and reality in Maoist China.

Redesigning this framework to interpret state-society relations over the past two decades in Hong Kong's history, the most suitable keyword would by contrast be *noncompliance*. On the one hand, this concept highlights the ways in which the Chinese Communist Party has failed to abide by its promises of a high degree of autonomy for Hong Kong. On the other hand, this concept also captures how civil society in Hong Kong has refused to comply with the central state's increasingly noncompliant model of rule. These two refusals, each feeding off of the other, have produced a noncompliance cycle of mutually escalating and thus self-reproducing provocations over the past two decades of Chinese rule over Hong Kong.

Unpacking this noncompliance cycle in Hong Kong, there are three distinct yet interacting cycles parallel to Skinner and Winckler's framework: a goal cycle, a power cycle, and a response cycle.

The goal cycle refers to the PRC state's goals in its handling of Hong Kong affairs, operating primarily along the binary of autonomy and centralization, or difference and assimilation. There have indeed been periods, such as the first five years after Hong Kong's 1997 handover, in which the central leadership seemed comparatively more committed to complying with the autonomy and corresponding rights promised to Hong Kong, and thereby in the maintenance of Hong Kong's difference. By contrast, there have been far lengthier periods, particularly from 2014 onward, in which Beijing has been considerably more focused on centralization and assimilation, thereby refusing to comply with the high degree of autonomy promised to the city.

Operating within these two primary policy directions, Beijing's power cycle, referring to its shifting modes of exercising power over Hong Kong toward these policy goals, consists of three main types: benevolent, punitive, and identificatory. The benevolent and punitive modes of power are relatively self-explanatory: the former largely coincides with moments of autonomy in the goal cycle, while the latter coincides with moments of control-oriented centralization.[34] The third mode of identificatory power refers to the official invocation of a shared identity of Chineseness, appealing to an idea of commonality so as to deemphasize difference. This mode of power thus combines both benevolent and punitive elements: for those who agree with the oft-repeated mantra "we are all Chinese" (*dajia dou shi Zhongguoren*), there is comfort to be found in this will to identity, producing a disciplining micro-power; yet for those who disagree with this idea, the assertion that both PRC and Hong Kong citizens are Chinese is not a statement of solidarity, but rather a declaration of ownership and a corresponding punitive warning to recognize oneself in and submit to a particular normalizing ideological vision of Chineseness dictated from Beijing.

Emerging in interaction with these goal and power cycles is a response cycle from the Hong Kong public, which can also be mapped along the two poles of sameness and difference, or compliance and noncompliance: the cultivation of identificatory power equating the central state itself with "Chineseness" has produced a false equation between sameness and compliance. Although the distribution of power between the two sides is grossly mismatched, Hong Kong civil society's noncompliance with the central state's drive for escalating control only further escalates its desire for control, which in turn drives further refusal and noncompliance from civil society. The result is a mutually escalating noncompliance cycle, pulling the central state and Hong Kong society ever further apart.[35]

Compared to a singular narrative of "China's rise" as presented in Zhu and Zhang's analysis, the interactions traced in this noncompliance cycle, as shown in the following sections, provide a considerably more illuminating framework for understanding Hong Kong's post-1997 history.

The Opening Salvos: SARS and Security

Writing in 2000, James Hsiung described Hong Kong's fate after its handover to China as a super paradox: "We can safely say, over two years later [i.e., after 1997], that life in Hong Kong after reversion is paradoxically quite normal, contrary to the doomsday prophecies of many 'people of little faith.'"[36] Hsiung was in a sense correct: there were indeed a few largely peaceful years after 1997 in which the difference between Hong Kong and Chinese societies was generally acknowledged and respected by Beijing under the rubric of One Country, Two Systems. Yet his optimism was in retrospect extremely premature. For example, in his discussion of the success of One Country, Two Systems, Hsiung proceeds to recommend the framework as a possible solution for disputes surrounding autonomy and sovereignty in Quebec, Catalonia, Puerto Rico, Kurdistan, Kashmir, and of course Taiwan, a recommendation that has not aged well.[37] It was indeed true that Hong Kong's handover had proceeded relatively smoothly for the first few years after 1997, and that none of the most pessimistic predictions for Hong Kong's fate came true. At the same time, however, it was also true that there was no institutional guarantee for such success, and as a result no guarantee that the most pessimistic predictions for Hong Kong's fate would not come true at a later point, as they indeed have. Rather, the initial success of One Country, Two Systems was derived solely from self-restraint on the part of the leaders of the People's Republic of China: a resource that has historically been in notably short supply, particularly regarding matters of autonomy.

In his closing reflections in his edited volume *Hong Kong the Super Paradox: Life after Return to China*, Hsiung states:

Critics have made hay of Article 23 of the Basic Law, which requires that the HKSAR "enact laws on its own to prohibit any act of treason, secession, sedition, subversion against the Central People's Government." . . . Despite the jitters this Basic Law provision had given to many bona fide democracy advocates before 1997, the fact remains that at the time of this writing, two years after the handover, the SAR government is in no hurry to introduce such bills in the Legco. Nor is Beijing known to be in such a hurry.[38]

Less than two years after Hsiung's book was published, however, the government hurriedly began work on national security legislation under Article 23. Due to the lack of any pressing threats in this regard, prioritizing national security legislation at this particular moment was a curious policy decision, made even more curious by the fact that a minimalist reading of the Basic Law indicates that no further legislation was in fact necessary to meet the requirements of Article 23.[39]

Considering these facts, the overreach of the proposed legislation and its conflicts with legally guaranteed rights were beyond comprehension. The government consultation document's definition of treason could be used to prosecute people exercising their legally protected right to peaceful protest; the draft law's definition of offenses under "secession" could criminalize legally protected free speech on such sensitive issues as PRC rule (or lack thereof) over Tibet, Xinjiang, or Taiwan; the definitions of "subversion" as well as "state secrets" were overly broad, opening the door for the type of politicized manipulation of these charges commonly seen in China; and finally, the legislation called for the banning of political organizations deemed illegal in the PRC, without noting that the PRC lacks even the semblance of a rule-of-law-based system for declaring organizations illegal.[40] The draft national legislation was, in sum, centralizing in a punitive mode, a move that was particularly shocking after a few initial years of relatively benevolent (although clearly not institutionally guaranteed) autonomy. National security legislation under Article 23 of the Basic Law was the first step in the rapidly unfolding noncompliance cycle whose effects we see today.

The Hong Kong government spared no effort in rushing this deeply flawed legislation through a hurried consultation process toward passage.[41] It might even have succeeded were it not for one of the great ironies of history: the draft national security bill was presented to the Legislative Council on February 25, 2003, just three days after Dr. Liu Jianlun, who had treated patients suffering from an unknown respiratory disorder in Guangzhou, checked out of the

Metropark Hotel Kowloon and into the Prince of Wales Hospital in Sha Tin with a high-grade fever and shortness of breath. Within a month of Dr. Liu's arrival, over sixty new cases of severe acute respiratory syndrome (SARS) were emerging each day in Hong Kong. This first crossing of paths between national security legislation and an epidemic, both products of the Chinese Communist Party's culture of secrecy, not only derailed this legislation but also forever changed the path of Hong Kong's history under Chinese rule.[42]

Plagues are often read as metaphorical reflections of problems plaguing a society, and the origins of the 2003 SARS outbreak proved particularly amenable to such a reading.[43] The transfer of power to a new generation of leaders in Beijing in late 2002, which was supposed to be cause for celebration, meant that the Chinese state was obsessed with ensuring that no bad news would be allowed in this period.[44] There is, of course, no way to stop unfortunate things from happening, but the approach to these unfortunate events, such as the emergence of a novel and fatal respiratory illness, was simply to hide these developments and suppress all discussion. Secrecy is not however an effective anecdote for a highly infectious virus, in fact providing the ideal environment for its proliferation. Like the novel coronavirus eighteen years later, SARS proliferated within China's state-enforced silence and cover-ups to the point that it spread to Hong Kong via Dr. Liu.[45] The Hong Kong media's revelations about SARS, alerting the world to the dangers of this outbreak, highlighted the relative strengths of the city's system, precisely the systemic advantages that the proposed national security legislation threatened to destroy: the language on state secrets therein, after all, could have made illegal precisely the type of revelatory and life-saving reporting that the Hong Kong media produced on SARS.

Just as the spread of SARS in 2003 revealed public and even at times private realms across Hong Kong as potential spaces of fatal infection, so the threat of the revocation of the city's liberties made these life-sustaining yet often taken-for-granted freedoms an object of reflection and finally action.[46] Hoping to halt the seemingly inevitable passage of the national security legislation, which was proceeding to a second reading in July, the Civil Human Rights Front called for a protest against the bill on July 1, 2003, the sixth anniversary of Hong Kong's handover. Organizers' most optimistic projections estimated attendance of perhaps two hundred thousand. On the day of the protests, no less than half a million people filled the streets, producing the "largest indigenous social movement in Hong Kong history" and leaving the

SAR government in shock.[47] The public's refusal to comply with Beijing's non-compliance, their reassertion of autonomy over centralization, had never been clearer, and the prematurely declared success of One Country, Two Systems had never looked more uncertain.

Beijing's "New" Hong Kong Policy: Political, Economic, and Cultural Centralization

The proposed national security legislation was shelved after the July 1 protests and withdrawn before the end of 2003. Punitive centralization had generated massive pushback from Hong Kong civil society: the government was not complying with its promised protections of Hong Kong's freedoms, and the people refused to comply with such invasive policies. The resignation of Secretary for Security Regina Ip, who had played a prominent role in overseeing and promoting the legislation, as well as the eventual removal of Chief Executive Tung Chee-wah, could all be read as benevolent compromises. Yet it was also precisely at this moment that Beijing began implementing what has become known as its new Hong Kong policy, employing benevolent, punitive, and identificatory modes of power in the fields of economics, politics, and culture in an attempt to force Hong Kong's reality to comply with the central state's vision.[48]

Benevolent centralization was implemented in the economic field, as seen in the Closer Economic Partnership Agreement, a free trade agreement between the People's Republic of China and Hong Kong signed in late June 2003. This agreement provided a framework for the promotion of trade between the two parties. Its most consequential measure, however, was the Individual Travelers' Scheme, which gradually made individual travel to Hong Kong available to residents of forty-nine cities across China.[49] This single step literally opened the Hong Kong tourism market to hundreds of millions of new visitors. The resulting new growth model revitalized the tourism and retail industries in the aftermath of SARS, but also in this process structurally transformed Hong Kong's economy to be more reliant on the PRC than ever before, as well as intensifying the overcrowding of an already overcrowded city and producing escalating cultural conflicts between Hong Kong residents and Chinese visitors.[50] As a result, even such benevolent centralization sparked a counterwave of noncompliance in the 2012 protests against Chinese tourists and the 2015 Gwongfuhk protests against parallel traders, who smuggle goods from tariff-free Hong Kong into China to sell at a profit.

Punitive centralization was implemented in the political field, preventing the city from achieving genuine self-governance.[51] The Article 23 controversy and the downfall of Tung Chee-wah had bolstered discussion of political reform, based on the eminently reasonable assumption that a more representative government accountable to the people of Hong Kong could avoid similar policy failures.[52] Yet by April 2004, the Standing Committee of the National People's Congress had reinterpreted the Basic Law to assert its absolute control over the political reform process: Hong Kong would have no say in the pace or extent of reforms.[53] Within a month of that interpretation, in a pattern that has been repeated countless times since, Beijing used the power that it had just generously granted to itself to rule out reform toward universal suffrage in the 2007 chief executive and 2008 Legislative Council elections.[54] In 2007, when Chief Executive Donald Tsang alluded to developing a timetable for political reform for the next round of elections in 2012 under pressure from pan-democrats, Beijing again stepped in to remind the city that, regardless of eminently reasonable interpretations of the Basic Law that suggest otherwise, only the central government could decide the pace for expanding suffrage.[55] Unsurprisingly, Beijing yet again used this power to determine that there was no need for expanded suffrage in 2012.[56] The timeline for substantial political reforms toward universal suffrage was thereby pushed back to 2017.

The proposal for direct election of the chief executive in 2017 was only finalized in 2014, seventeen years after the handover. Based on Deng Xiaoping's vague and extralegal musings that the Chief Executive of Hong Kong must "love the motherland," the "Decision of the Standing Committee of the National People's Congress on Issues Relating to the Selection of the Chief Executive of the Hong Kong Special Administrative Region by Universal Suffrage and on the Method of Forming the Legislative Council of the Hong Kong Special Administrative Region in the Year 2016" required any candidates for the position to be nominated and approved by the Beijing-controlled Nominating Committee.[57] Despite the 2014 Decision's obvious failure to abide by the promise of universal suffrage, it is worth noting in the analytical context of this noncompliance cycle that the proposal likely could have been accepted by both the Legislative Council and broader society if it had been put forward a decade earlier. However, as the wait for the final goal of universal suffrage had heightened expectations, or as the provocations of growing central interference and perpetual delays in democratization led to growing demands for substantive reforms from Hong Kong civil society, the 2014 proposal, demonstrating Beijing's perpetual obsession with control and its lack of understanding of Hong Kong society, was roundly rejected when it finally arrived. Illustrating the implications of this escalating noncompliance cycle, decades of delays in realizing promised universal suffrage, ostensibly securing Beijing's control over political developments in Hong Kong, had precisely the opposite effect, sparking the Occupy Central protests of 2014, a major turning point in state-society relations.

Identificatory centralization was implemented in the field of education. In the immediate aftermath of the 2003 protests that led to the withdrawal of national security legislation, the SAR government convened the National Education Working Group to initiate an educational program for Hong Kong students with the self-referential goal of "enhancing identification with national identity."[58] The program's main components included developing "patriotic" curricula and textbooks; promoting field trips to a National Education Center in Tai Po managed by the unabashedly pro-Beijing Hong Kong Federation of Education Workers; and the development of "educational exchange" trips for Hong Kong students to China, packed full of patriotic propaganda.[59] The program bore a revealing resemblance to the patriotic education curriculum implemented in schools across China in the 1990s after the nationwide protests and state massacre of protesters in 1989. Patriotic education's emphasis on pre-1949 national humiliation at the hands of foreign powers externalized the violence that the Chinese Communist Party had just enacted against its own citizens, successfully recasting the state as the people's savior rather than oppressor. The national education program far less successfully recast a once-shared pan-Chineseness not as a broad cultural umbrella with diverse manifestations but rather as a demand for centralizing ideological unity: I spent a considerable amount of time at the National Education Center in Tai Po in early 2009, and the Party-state messaging there was just about as subtle as a *Global Times* article. Such eagerness for ideological control again failed to have its intended effect: the central state's noncompliance in matters of culture, education, and identification again produced noncompliance from Hong Kong civil society, sparking the 2012 protests against national education, the activism of which forever transformed Hong Kong politics.[60]

There was then nothing new about Beijing's "new" Hong Kong policy. It was in reality little more than an ultimately failed attempt to copy the Party's post-Tiananmen stability formula of economic rewards, political repression, and patriotic education in a fundamentally different social context: Hong Kong.

Such policy duplication not only demonstrates a substantial lack of imagination on the part of the central government, but also in its effects shows Beijing's fundamental inability to understand Hong Kong society and deal with a political situation in which any semblance of an independent civil society still exists. The fields of politics, economics, and culture that were the focus of Beijing's post-2004 centralization have in turn become battlegrounds in this escalating noncompliance cycle, producing an increasingly noncompliant civil society that targeted national education and its patriotic ideology in 2012, the central government's political reform proposal and the central state's control over that process in Occupy Central in 2014, and the challenges of economic integration with China in 2015's Gwongfuk protests. The transformation of these attempted spheres of influence and integration into sites of confrontation and rebellion, demonstrating the failure of central policy, has not however led the central government to adjust its policies, but rather to simply reproduce its hard-line approach, further deepening resistance.

The more that the CCP attempts to forcefully integrate Hong Kong into China, the greater the distance between the central government and civil society grows. The more that Beijing tells the people of Hong Kong that they are Chinese, along with all of the political and ideological baggage that accompanies this official construction, the more people come to feel that they are not in fact Chinese. And the more people feel that they are not Chinese, the more Beijing feels the need to tell them that they are. Four decades into the era of "reform and opening," in a special administrative region ostensibly designed to serve as a model example of Beijing's willingness to abide by its international guarantees of two distinct systems and genuine autonomy, one ironically finds a state that is even less responsive to public opinion and more confined by ideological orthodoxy than the Maoist regime analyzed by Skinner and Winckler five decades earlier. It is precisely within this noncompliant context of a mutually escalating cycle of provocations and counterprovocations, passed over by Zhu and Zhang, that the idea of Hong Kong independence has emerged. This proposal is without a doubt the greatest provocation of all, the most defiant form of noncompliance challenging Beijing's sacred conception of national sovereignty. As the two parties to this increasingly tense relationship test each other's red lines, Hong Kong independence activists gleefully leap over the central government's reddest of red lines, in a move that, like Article 23 legislation, has forever changed the dynamics of the Hong Kong-China relationship.

This all makes sense and would seem to provide a contextualized and coherent explanation of the origins of Hong Kong independence advocacy. Yet on closer reflection, is this really all that the idea of Hong Kong independence is? Is it simply a confrontational way to let off some steam among activists disillusioned with China's rule? Is it just a provocation, intended to test and challenge Beijing's control and its political taboos? If we are to believe this interpretation, then even after thinking through political developments in Hong Kong since 1997, the time span that Zhu and Zhang's analysis evaded, our conclusions nevertheless ironically circle back to their claim that Hong Kong politics is about nothing more than "making a fuss." Yet even if we refuse to embrace such a casually dismissive logic, following the logic of the noncompliance cycle, one can reach the comforting conclusion that the best way for the central government to push back against the idea of Hong Kong independence would be to step back from this cycle of provocation and grant Hong Kong universal suffrage and genuine autonomy. The sole issue with such an eminently reasonable proposal is simply that it could never happen. It is in fact far more unlikely than the idea of Hong Kong independence, which is reliably dismissed as an impossibility. There is thus, I propose, far more to Hong Kong nationalism than simply provocation: it is an awakening to the repressed reality of the impossibility of autonomy, democracy, and freedom under Beijing's rule.

As One Country, Two Systems is propelled through its own internal contradictions toward the erasure of its basic distinction, moving from two systems toward one, the proposal to rescue the promised ideal of two systems via two countries indeed leaps over all of Beijing's red lines. This proposal is, however, far more than a provocation: it is a fundamentally logical reorientation of political aspirations. The concept of Hong Kong independence has thus produced far more than Beijing's ire; it has given rise to a rapidly expanding body of journal articles, political commentaries, book-length monographs, online television networks, and even political parties promoting new visions for the Hong Kong-China relationship. The following section moves beyond the analytical macro-framework of a noncompliance cycle to engage directly with the words and visions of Hong Kong independence enthusiasts. If we set aside our theoretical frameworks attempting to interpret and explain the rise of Hong Kong nationalism within the Hong Kong-China relationship, we can begin to see these thinkers developing their own sophisticated theoretical frameworks for radically reinterpreting this relationship. Hong Kong nationalism, then, is neither the sign of an underlying pathology nor simply a blunt provocation in a noncompliance cycle: it is a novel and unyielding critique of the city's path under Beijing's rule, ushering in a political awakening from the mythologies of One Country, Two Systems.

TAKE THREE: TOWARD A CRITIQUE
OF HONG KONG UNDER CHINESE RULE

Hong Kong was transferred from the United Kingdom to the People's Republic of China in 1997 under the framework of One Country, Two Systems. Under "one country," Hong Kong became a part of the People's Republic of China; under "two systems," Hong Kong was guaranteed genuine autonomy as a Special Administrative Region.[61] This autonomy protected the city's rights and legally guaranteed its eventual progression toward universal suffrage. Hong Kong's political progress could even provide a model for greater political openness in the People's Republic, which would in turn further safeguard the city's freedoms. Regardless of China's political progress or lack thereof, however, the legal guarantee for the city's continued autonomy and political development was to be found in the Basic Law, which explicitly limited Beijing's role in Hong Kong affairs to matters of diplomacy and defense. Further support for maintaining Hong Kong's autonomy would be provided by the city's open and vibrant political culture, in particular by the pan-democratic camp, which has served as the city's dynamic and indeed popular opposition, reliably winning the overwhelming majority of the popular vote. Beyond politics, Hong Kong's economy would benefit from its continued integration with the rapidly expanding Chinese economy. And despite all of the differences between Hong Kong and China, Hong Kong is first and foremost a Chinese city, meaning that the city had left behind the disgrace of colonization and now enjoyed a high degree of autonomy.

At first glance, each of the preceding assertions seems completely reasonable. Yet in the two decades after the 2003 Article 23 controversy, emerging realities repeatedly undermined these hopeful assumptions. Hong Kong nationalism is, I propose, a critical awakening from these once comforting mythologies: it breaks out of the confines of past ideologies to promote open discussion of the situation in which the Hong Kong people find themselves today, deconstructing overly optimistic metanarratives of China's political development, Hong Kong's own legal and political defenses, the economic benefits of integration, and pan-Chinese identity and decolonization. The emergence of the idea of

Hong Kong independence is, in sum, Hong Kong's political enlightenment, casting aside the burdensome mythologies of the past to imagine a new path forward.

A Realpolitik Intervention?

Despite the commonplace dismissal of Hong Kong independence as fundamentally unrealistic, the initial reflections that brought this idea into mainstream political discussion explicitly claim to have been based in realpolitik calculations. This "realpolitik" analysis, proposed by former Lingnan University professor of Chinese Chin Wan in his 2011 book *On Hong Kong as a City-State*, begins from an unflinching demolition of overly optimistic assumptions about democratization and the city's relationship with China, derived from what he calls the "theory of democratic return (*mahnjyu wuihgwai leuhn*)."[62]

Chin begins his book by explaining his interpretation of the distinction between idealpolitik and realpolitik, proposing that the former is based in ideals, while the latter is based in interests.[63] Hong Kong politics, Chin tells us, have been trapped in a self-defeating mode of idealpolitik that sacrifices the city's real political interests to fantastic hopes about China. In Chin's telling, the first wave of discussion on a "democratic China" emerged after the 1984 announcement of the Sino-British Joint Declaration, which dictated that the city was to be handed over to China in 1997.[64] The first version of this theory was the "theory of democratic return" (*mahnjyu wuihgwai leuhn*), which posits that the development of a democratic system in Hong Kong prior to 1997 would protect the city's distinct political culture after the handover, while also serving as a model to facilitate greater political openness in the People's Republic.[65] Should Beijing choose to follow Hong Kong's lead on political liberalization, the city's export of democracy to China would in turn provide an ideal environment for protecting Hong Kong's rights and freedoms.[66] The optimism of this theory reflects the spirit of the times; in the early years of the PRC reform era in the 1980s, anything was possible, and economic opening was teleologically assumed to lead naturally to political opening.

Chin builds his critique of this proposal on a close reading of the two central terms in the theory of democratic return: "return" (*wuihgwai*) and "democracy" (*mahnjyu*). First, Chin points out, the term "return" draws upon the emotionally charged language of official Chinese nationalism, which portrays Hong Kong's colonial years as an era of "humiliation" and its 1997 "return" as a moment of glory achieved by the CCP.[67] Yet how can the colonial era be considered one of solely humiliation if hundreds of thousands of refugees sacrificed everything to escape Maoist China to resettle in Hong Kong? And how can one be "returned" to a nation that one has never known? Such ideologically loaded language represses the full complexity of Hong Kong's experience of British colonization, as well as obscuring through the language of pan-Chinese racial nationalism the subsequent experience of PRC control. Chin thus recommends replacing the term "return" with the far less emotionally laden phrase "transfer of sovereignty" (*jyukyuhn gaauyihk*) in discussions of the events of 1997.[68] Second, Chin incisively notes the temporal disconnect apparent between Hong Kong's "return" and the realization of "democracy." Whereas the "return" always had a clear timetable, to be completed on July 1, 1997, the timetable for "democracy" has remained consistently indeterminate, perpetually located in an undefined future: democratization is perpetually promised but also endlessly deferred to an unspecified and increasingly distant moment.[69] There was hope that real democratization in Hong Kong could help to promote real political change in China, but at the end of the day precisely the opposite occurred: neither China nor Hong Kong achieved democracy.

The temporal tension between return and democratization was most apparent after the 1989 Tiananmen massacre, which left Hong Kong facing its immanent "return" to a regime that had just gunned down citizens in the streets of the nation's capital. According to Chin, on account of the loss of hope for democratization in China after the events of 1989, the original "theory of democratic return" transformed into its second iteration: a "theory of democratic resistance to the communists (*mahnjyu kong'guhng leuhn*)."[70] Hong Kong could no longer be a model for China's nonexistent democratization, but at the very least substantive democratization in the city before 1997 could protect against the Chinese Communist Party's destruction of Hong Kong's way of life after 1997.[71] This was again an overly hopeful theory: Beijing's dissolution of the 1995 Legislative Council, followed by its perpetual stalling on democratization, displayed the futility of such optimism.

One can certainly debate whether the ideas that Chin labels idealpolitik are truly unrealistic, and whether the ideas that he labels realpolitik (discussed in more detail in the next chapter) are really all that realistic. Regardless, Chin's pointed critique of the endlessly hopeful yet also hopeless struggle for democracy in China gave resonant voice to a growing sense of exasperation within Hong Kong society with the city's self-declared motherland. Democratization in China is a worthy goal: indeed, a goal with which few would disagree in principle. Yet with the passage of time and the perpetual hardening of Beijing's politics, this worthy goal has only ever grown increasingly distant: rather than economic reforms making democratization inevitable, economic growth in an era of self-declared opening has in fact reinforced the Party-state system and its closed politics to a point that other dictatorships have been unable to achieve. Watching this anachronistic Leninist juggernaut charging undeterred into the future, Chin emerges from the shadows of hopes past to tell the people of Hong Kong that they have neither the resources, the ability, nor the responsibility to democratize China.[72] Their sole responsibility, he says, is to look after themselves and their city, so as to preserve their way of life. Chin's 2011 intervention, calling for abandoning the type of wishful thinking that dominated discussions of Chinese politics throughout the 2000s, is reminiscent of James Mann's controversial but also increasingly obviously prescient call for the United States to drop its "China fantasy" of inevitable liberalization in Beijing, published just a few years earlier.[73]

Yet as is characteristic of Chin's general style, which I discuss in more detail in chapter 2, he takes the logic of his argument one very unexpected step further: he suggests that the elusive ideal of a democratized China may not actually be in Hong Kong's interests. The Chinese Communist Party, Chin argues, benefits from the One Country, Two Systems arrangement, which enables the Party to use Hong Kong as a trading and technology transfer outpost unaffected by sanctions and other restrictions on international trade, as seen for example in the US Hong Kong Policy Act's recognition of the city as a treaty port separate from the People's Republic of China.[74] As a result, Chin argues, the Chinese Communist Party has an interest in maintaining at least a veneer of autonomy in Hong Kong so as to maintain the city's "special" trading relationship with the outside world.[75] By contrast, Chin asks, would a democratic China necessarily make the same cost-benefit calculations? A new and more democratic government emerging after the collapse of the Chinese Communist Party, he speculates, might not continue to grant Hong Kong its autonomous status. In a best-case scenario, Hong Kong would need to renegotiate the terms of the relationship with a new ruling party that would be suddenly accountable to reliably nationalistic public opinion in China.[76] In a worst-case scenario, a democratic China might completely dismantle Hong Kong's government, demand that the city open its borders, and even force Hong Kong to begin paying taxes to the central government.[77] If a directly elected, fully representative legislature was established in China to replace the rubber-stamp National People's Congress, Hong Kong as just one city within a massive nation-state would have extremely limited representation, leaving the city vulnerable to unpredictable political developments.[78] The endpoint that so many had been seeking for so long, a democratic China, could ironically be the fastest route to Hong Kong's feared endpoint of becoming "just another Chinese city."

The first chapter of Chin's book is provocatively titled "Give Up on a Democratic China, Preserve the Hong Kong City-State."[79] The Hong Kong nationalist conversation that these reflections initiated is first and foremost an awakening from the myth that democratization in China, or in Hong Kong under Chinese rule, is inevitable, or even for that matter possible. Since its 2011 publication, ever more people have taken Chin's advice, actively redirecting the focus of political activism from China to Hong Kong itself and its local concerns, with dramatic implications for the city's political culture.

Study the Basic Law!

The Basic Law, the mini-constitution of the Hong Kong Special Administrative Region, outlines Hong Kong's legally guaranteed autonomy and freedoms very clearly: equality before the law; the right to stand for office and the right to vote; and freedom of speech, press, association, assembly, religion, and conscience, all while guaranteeing progress toward direct elections with universal suffrage.

From a legal perspective, one could read the Basic Law as granting particular rights and freedoms to the Hong Kong people. Yet from a practical political perspective, the maintenance of these rights and freedoms that Hong Kong already had can only be guaranteed after 1997 by constraining the central government from revoking them. Articles 13 and 14 of the Basic Law are particularly important in this regard: they explicitly limit Beijing's role in the city to diplomacy and defense.[80] The Basic Law thus not only grants freedoms to Hong Kong, but also preempts Beijing's all too predictable interventions in these freedoms.

Yet if the Basic Law is to protect Hong Kong's freedoms by proscribing interventions by the central government, the law also contains within itself a fatal flaw. Article 158 states, "Power of interpretation of this Law shall be vested in the Standing Committee of the National People's Congress."[81] Article 159 further states, "Power of amendment of this Law shall be vested in the National People's Congress."[82] The final right of interpretation of and amendment to the Basic Law is thereby curiously granted precisely to the party that is supposed to be constrained by the law: the Chinese Communist Party. Whereas James Hsiung characterized the initial success of One Country, Two Systems as a "super-paradox," in reality the most perplexing of paradoxes is to be found in the Basic Law: a law that should place restraints on an overbearing state power with a long-standing record of crushing the autonomy of "autonomous" regions grants to that same power the final authority to interpret and amend this law that ostensibly guarantees Hong Kong's autonomy. Beijing's powers in Hong Kong thereby include not only diplomacy and defense as stated in the Basic Law, but also the interpretation of the Basic Law that is supposed to limit Beijing's powers in Hong Kong, thereby making its powers limitless.

Beijing has predictably used its powers of interpretation to continually expand its powers beyond the constraints of the Basic Law, all while claiming to be operating within the Basic Law, which clearly (but also clearly insufficiently) restricts its powers. The first interpretation of the Basic Law was requested by the Hong Kong government in 1999. In January of that year, the Court of Final Appeal ruled in *Ng Ka Ling v. Director of Immigration* that permanent residents as defined in the Basic Law, including any children of residents born outside of Hong Kong, had the right to enter and settle in Hong Kong freely without delay.[83] This was one of those uncomfortable situations in which a reasonable reading of the law produced a politically unpopular ruling, suddenly opening the city to a potential influx of 1.67 million new residents from China.[84] As Hong Kong nationalist historian Eric Tsui observes in his history of the city's experience both beyond and under Chinese rule, "in this decision, rule of law and the preservation of Hong Kong's local identity came into open conflict."[85] By May 1999, Chief Executive Tung Chee-wah and his Executive Council had asked the National People's Congress Standing Committee (NPCSC) to provide an interpretation of Article 24 of the Basic Law, which defines permanent residence in the city. The NPCSC concluded that any legal permanent residents of Hong Kong who had been born in China needed to receive permission from the Chinese authorities before moving to Hong Kong. The central government issues 150 one-way permits per day for this purpose, meaning that the 1.67 million people granted the right to relocate to Hong Kong according to the Final Court of Appeals ruling would need to wait in line for their one-way permits to be issued. A city already suffering from extreme population density heaved a sigh of relief.

Yet in the long run, this relief was misplaced: the NPCSC's interpretation of the Basic Law targeted not only the Court of Final Appeals' inconvenient decision but also the judicial autonomy displayed therein.[86] As Tsui notes, asking the Chinese Communist Party to override local court rulings in an interpretation of the Basic Law that had nothing to do with Beijing's stated purview of diplomacy and defense not only damaged the sovereignty of the city's legal system but also set a dangerous precedent for further interventions.[87] There is no one to whom one can appeal against such interventions, as the NPCSC's interpretations are final regardless of whether they actually make any legal sense (which they usually do not).

In its subsequent interventions, the central government has used its powers of interpretation to expand its control over matters far beyond its legally affirmed jurisdiction in diplomacy and defense: declaring control over the electoral reform process, the transition between chief executives, matters of diplomatic immunity, and, as discussed in more detail in chapter 3, determining who is eligible (or not) to hold office in Hong Kong.[88] In the continual unfolding of these interpretations from Beijing that unsurprisingly only ever give Beijing ever more power, there no longer remain any functional checks nor balances on the CCP's powers in Hong Kong: there remains only a blank check, under the guise of law, for the central state to make whatever choice it pleases under the guise of legal interpretations, even going so far as explicitly violating rights guaranteed in the Basic Law under the pretext of "defending the Basic Law."

There was a time when I was genuinely puzzled by the central government's repeated calls over the years for the Hong Kong people to study the Basic Law. Soon after two interpretations of the Basic Law in the mid-2000s, there was a series of calls from senior PRC leaders, state media, and local Beijing-linked elites for the people of Hong Kong to study and "understand the Basic Law" (*liuhgaai geibun faat*).[89] While visiting the National Education Centre in Tai Po in 2009, I was given a copy of the Basic Law, and teachers repeatedly emphasized their eagerness for everyone to "study" the Basic Law.[90] I wondered why the authorities would so fervently encourage the Hong Kong people to study the law that grants them autonomy and freedoms. I have gradually come to realize, however, that there is far more to the call to study the Basic Law: the notion of understanding here is a very particular type of understanding. First, the call to study and understand constructs a hierarchy between those who understand and those who do not, just as there exists a hierarchy between those who interpret the law and those who are left to study and obey it. Like a teacher assigning homework to students, those calling for others to study the law, namely the Chinese state and its representatives, are presumed to have a complete grasp of the law, while those who are summoned, the Hong Kong people, are in need of further study. The call to study the Basic Law is thus reminiscent of Althusser's description of interpellation, with those hailed in this process not only being rendered as subjects of the Party's latest interpretation but furthermore as inadequate subjects in need of completion from the higher power engaging in the calling: Hong Kong citizens are hailed here as "hey, you who do not understand the Basic Law!"[91] Through this hierarchical framing, any understanding of the law that diverges from Beijing's interpretation is thereby rendered as inherently lacking in understanding, requiring further study. The law is no longer a topic of public debate or deliberation and can no longer constrain official power; it is to be studied and understood in a particular way dictated by the state.

Second, insofar as the law is read strictly within this hierarchy, and in particular against the backdrop of Beijing's increasingly interventionist approach to Hong Kong affairs far beyond its legally defined purview in the Basic Law, the Party-state's call for people to "study" and "understand" the Basic Law is reminiscent of the pseudo-liberating commands "you are free," "do what you will," and "you are right to rebel" analyzed by André Glucksmann in *The Master Thinkers*.[92] In Glucksmann's analysis, the Maoist slogan "you are right to revolt" (*zaofan you li*) encapsulates the contradictions inherent within the nominally radically egalitarian Maoist revolution, insofar as the call to revolt is a hierarchical command from higher powers, precisely those against whom one could revolt: "If I obey you, I am disobeying you, but if I disobey you, I am obeying you."[93] The only truly authentic test of one's freedom to rebel in this context would be to rebel against Maoism, a possibility that is of course strictly forbidden. One is thus in the act of rebelling "replacing one kind of discipline with another," submitting in rebellion or rebelling in a submissive mode.[94]

Similarly, in the demand to study and understand the Basic Law, whereas actual study of the law tells the people of Hong Kong that "you are free" and "you are autonomous," the freedom and autonomy dictated in this understanding preclude the possibility of questioning whether one is in fact free and autonomous in practice. This is a matter on which Beijing alone is free to reach a final interpretation. You are not free to question whether the central government understands and abides by the Basic Law, nor to ponder whether the city's rule of law system has been maintained under the Basic Law. These are also matters that Beijing alone is left to decide. As Beijing has increasingly granted itself the unrestrained freedom to interpret any and all matters far beyond its legally justified jurisdiction toward the goal of limiting Hong Kong citizens' freedoms, the Basic Law is no longer an effective means of constraining Beijing or of protecting residents' rights, if it ever actually was at any point. Rather, the Basic Law has become, like the Maoist invocation to rebel, "a device for governing," ideologically weaponizing respect for the rule of law to gradually eclipse Hong Kong's rule of law institutions by means of a law that can mean whatever Beijing wants it to mean.[95] Hong Kong nationalism is an awakening to this extralegal function of the law and the corresponding need to operate beyond its oppressive limits.

Hong Kong Has No Opposition

Even after abandoning hope for democratization in China and recognizing the fundamental inability of the Basic Law to restrain the central government, one can still nevertheless find hope for Hong Kong in its pan-democratic opposition. The pan-democrats have, election after election, won the overwhelming majority of votes and have (at least until 2020) thereby maintained enough of a bloc in the Legislative Council to prevent Beijing's allies in the legislature from implementing their agenda unopposed. Beyond its legislative efforts, the pan-democratic camp has also been essential to political activism in the city, organizing the July 1 protests in support of universal suffrage, the largest annual protest on Chinese soil. The pan-democrats, in sum, have managed to keep Hong Kong's political opposition alive in an unfair electoral system and a civil society under growing pressure. One could say that their efforts have saved Hong Kong from complete (dis)integration into China.

Not so fast, says Lewis Loud, a commentator who has been on the front lines of the evolving Hong Kong independence discussion. Loud's 2018 essay "Elections as an Imperial Examination" begins with the unsettling assertion that despite appearances to the contrary, Hong Kong has never had a real opposition, nor even any real civil society movements.[96] Loud of course acknowledges that the pan-democratic camp exists and recognizes that it has been very active. Yet Loud analyzes the pan-democrats not as contributing to the democratic ideal of civil society based in solidarity among citizens of equal stature, but rather as contributing to the reinforcement of a rigidly stratified political hierarchy that despite its appearance of opposition in fact only serves to reinforce and reproduce the current political system. At the top of this hierarchy are people with political power and access to the Legislative Council, he tells us, while at the bottom lies everyone else. In a deeply cynical yet also deeply resonant reading of Hong Kong political culture, Loud argues that it is in fact the democratic opposition that has blocked the emergence of genuine oppositional activism in Hong Kong.

Loud begins by questioning whether the ritualized annual events of the opposition movement have any genuine oppositional potential.[97] Consider, for example, the July 1 march: year after year, decade after decade, hundreds of thousands of people have come onto the streets on the anniversary of Hong Kong's 1997 handover to China, using this symbolically resonant date to call on the central government to grant the city genuine universal suffrage. Considering that such a protest could never go forward anywhere else in China, the annual march appears at first glance to be a testament to the vitality of Hong Kong's freedoms. Yet such a perspective, in setting the bar so low as to simply celebrate the ability to still hold protests, points to the generally Sinocentric approach of so much activism in Hong Kong. Loud digs deeper to pose a different set of questions: What do these annual marches in fact achieve? Have these marches, with their demand for universal suffrage, had any actual effect on China's Hong Kong policy after decades of such annual gatherings? Or have they only provided a platform to air discontent while Beijing continues to tighten its control over the city? These previously unasked questions are at once revealing and deeply discomfiting. Although the July 1 protest has been central to the opposition movement since 2003, Beijing's Hong Kong policy over this period has indeed only become ever more heavy-handed and intrusive.

The intrinsic value of political activism of course cannot be judged solely on its direct outcomes, a fact of which any enthusiast of Hong Kong independence is undoubtedly keenly aware. Yet at the same time, activism cannot be completely and permanently detached from such considerations. As political backsliding accelerates in the People's Republic and Beijing's Hong Kong policy becomes increasingly hard-line and recalcitrant, Loud poses a necessary question: Is there anything that can be done beyond marching every year on July 1? After decades of these peaceful protests without any change for the better, are we to simply continue like this endlessly, hoping that there will be change at some point?

Reassessing the meaning of these annual events, Loud cynically argues that their real purpose is little more than fundraising for pan-democrats' electoral campaigns: in a most provocative statement, he declares that "all civil society activities in Hong Kong are nothing but an extension of elections."[98] Anyone who has ever attended a July 1 protest in Hong Kong will undoubtedly remember with fondness the flood of emotions, the feelings of solidarity, and the insistent hope for change. Yet participants will also undoubtedly remember the sight of politicians shouting slogans and asking for donations all along the march's route. In Loud's interpretation, pan-democratic politicians at the top of the political hierarchy have year after year mobilized the people of Hong Kong in a literal pyramid scheme disguised by lofty ideals to contribute to their own never-ending reelection campaigns: "The people at the bottom of the pyramid want change, but they went to the wrong place for it. All of these activities are nothing more than showcases and election rallies for the people at the top of the pyramid."[99]

Yet even if the only practical outcome of these annual gatherings has been fundraising for the pan-democratic camp, is there not still value to be found in helping to ensure a healthy bloc of pan-democrats in the Legislative Council? Giving voice to what Malte Phillip Kaeding has called nationalists' "two-front campaign" against both pro-establishment and pan-democratic politicians in the city, Loud's answer is a resounding "no."[100] "So, the more that these types of protests are held, the more stable the pan-democrats' seats in Legco are ... the more stable their base votes and thus their political careers. But Hong Kong's situation has not improved as a result. Rather, things have only become worse."[101] In attempting to understand the continued deterioration of Hong Kong's political situation amid the growth of political activism and the expansion of pan-democratic power, Loud turns to the imperial examination, the cornerstone of the Chinese empire's system for appointing officials from the Song dynasty onward.[102] The imperial examination tested aspiring officials' knowledge of obscure details of the classics, but the possibility of becoming an official provided by this exam drew in aspirants from across society. Some spent the majority of their adult lives in preparation, believing that the examination provided a fair system for determining who was in fact qualified to serve.

Loud, unsurprisingly, provides a far more cynical reading of the system's appeal and social impact: "Generating false hope among so many for an extremely small number of openings, the imperial examination was able to seduce anyone with any skills or talent into dedicating all of their energy to exam preparation."[103] The examination system thereby drew the greatest talents of countless eras into a lifelong project of test preparation and thus a lifetime dedicated to working inside the system. Those who failed to pass and obtain officialdom had wasted their lives on an impossibility, missing the opportunity to apply their intellects to more practical political activities that might effect genuine social change. Those who succeeded and became officials, by contrast, had also wasted their lives, allowing their intellects to be domesticated by state ideologies and thereby being transformed in their success into shareholders in the imperial system: "The imperial court's bottom line immediately became their bottom line."[104]

Hong Kong's electoral system, Loud argues, produces precisely the same outcomes. Like the imperial exam, conventional democratic politics in Hong Kong draws in millions of enthusiastic people and convinces them that the only way to effect change and realize a better future is by applying their intellects and activism in the service of the current system.[105] Those who have managed to place themselves at the top of the pyramid, whether by examination in the past or by election in the present, naturally become dedicated to the system's reproduction, ensuring that amid all of this activism nothing in fact changes. Loud thus argues, quite provocatively, that the pan-democratic opposition in which so many have placed their hopes for decades is nothing more than another part of the colonial system that has disenfranchised the Hong Kong people. Putting a new spin on the concept of the administrative absorption of politics proposed by King, Loud proposes instead the electoral absorption of political opposition: "The people in power use their Legislative Council seats to remotely control any and all potential opposition movements. We always thought that the half of Legislative Council seats that are directly elected are the rare democratic elements in this entire system. But the truth of the matter is that Legislative Council elections are in fact the biggest United Front activities in Hong Kong. Their logic is the same as the imperial examination system, which managed to seduce all capable and talented people to dedicate all their energies to exam preparation for millennia."[106] Then, just as "all civil society activities in Hong Kong are an extension of elections," so "all elections and all civil society activities surrounding them are, at the end of the day, nothing more than an extension of the regime."[107]

Loud's analysis of the conundrum of simultaneously limitless yet also limiting political activism is dark yet also illuminating in its unrestrained scorn for long taken-for-granted assumptions: conventional activism of the type that works within Hong Kong's system is not promoting genuine democratization but rather keeping the city trapped inside a failed system, ironically endlessly reproducing nonrepresentative colonial rule via endless political activism. Hong Kong nationalism, seeking the city's independence from Chinese rule, represents a genuine awakening from this self-reproducing system that has co-opted opposition in its service, finally recognizing that genuine opposition and thus genuine change can only be found in a total break with this system. This is why, Loud tells us, the central government has been so eager to suppress the emergent discussion of Hong Kong independence: it represents the city's first genuine opposition.

The Economic Embrace of the Motherland

Setting aside political and legal concerns, economic integration with China should be uncontentious. After all, there could be far worse fates than having an increasingly close relationship with a rapidly expanding economy on a truly unprecedented scale. The cornerstone of post-1997 economic integration is the Closer Economic Partnership Agreement (hereinafter referred to as CEPA), a free trade agreement between the People's Republic of China and Hong Kong. Reminding us yet again that 2003 was a year of far greater significance than 1997, CEPA was signed on June 29, 2003, in the aftermath of the SARS disaster and just two days before half a million people took to the streets to protest against proposed national security legislation.

According to its preamble, the goals of the agreement are "to promote the joint economic prosperity and development of the Mainland and the Hong Kong Special Administrative Region (hereinafter referred to as the "two sides"), [and] to facilitate the further development of economic links between the two sides and other countries and regions."[108] Toward these goals, CEPA promotes trade between China and Hong Kong via three primary avenues: the gradual cancellation of import tariffs on goods of Hong Kong origin into China; the opening of the Chinese market to Hong Kong service providers in particular sectors; and encouraging the expansion of "bilateral exchanges of goods, capital, and people."[109] In the aftermath of the negative economic impact of SARS, CEPA was an attempt at the benevolent exercise of integrative power.

Almost immediately upon the signing of CEPA, pro-Beijing commentators characterized the agreement as a "big gift from the central government."[110] There is, one must note, a significant difference between an act of charity and an economic partnership agreement between two parties with their own respective comparative advantages. As any student of anthropology knows, gifts do not move about without an underlying reason; they carry with them "a spirit," namely the spirit of the giver.[111] No gift, furthermore, is purely disinterested: a gift fundamentally changes relations between the two parties involved, carrying within itself the obligation to accept the gift, the obligation to accept the bond established therein, and the obligation within this bond to reciprocate.[112] Despite (or perhaps precisely because of) the charitable appearance of the gift, the bond established in such an exchange is never truly equal, insofar as gifts and the obligations to receive and reciprocate are inextricably intertwined with power and its imaginaries.[113] The relationship constructed in this particular gift exchange imagined a massive emerging market offering charity to a smaller and increasingly marginal market. And in a case of doing things with words, the unfolding of CEPA in the years that followed made this construction a reality.

The relationship was, from the start, deeply unequal, and was made only more so by the effects of the agreement. Siu Kit, in his history of Hong Kong nationalist thinking, even draws upon the affectively loaded language of the century of humiliation to portray CEPA as an "unequal treaty (*bat pihngdang tiuhfun/bu pingdeng tiaokuan*)."[114] Despite the promises of mutual opening and recognition, the opaque and arbitrary nature of the People's Republic's legal and business environment made the market access promised to Hong Kong companies under CEPA little more than an illusion. Siu argues that whereas CEPA brought benefits for Hong Kong shipping and logistics companies expanding into the China market, it has had minimal impact on China market access for the type of high-value-added industries that are the cornerstones of the city's economy: accounting, securities, insurance, finance, and film.[115] Yet CEPA has indeed had a massive impact on China's role in the Hong Kong market. In his nationalist history of Hong Kong, Eric Tsui argues that CEPA has had a deeply distorting effect on the city's economic development, promoting excessive reliance on finance, the service industry, and tourism, all with a near exclusive focus on the China market.[116] Rapid growth in these China-focused fields produced, as it has the world over, a lack of interest in economic diversification and further innovation, thereby forming a self-perpetuating trap of ever greater reliance on the China market. In Tsui's analysis, the central government's "big gift" functioned effectively as a means of economic colonization.[117]

The CEPA measure that had by far the greatest impact on Hong Kong's economy and society was among the least discussed in 2003: the Individual Visit Scheme, which permitted residents of designated Chinese cities to visit Hong Kong without a tour group, as had been previously required. By 2007, the scheme had expanded to cover residents of forty-nine cities across China, from Shenyang in the north to Nanning in the south, and from Shanghai in the east to Chengdu in the west, opening the Hong Kong tourist market to literally hundreds of millions of potential new visitors. In 2003, with a population of just 6.74 million people, the already crowded city of Hong Kong had hosted a total of 15.5 million visitors, 8 million coming from China. Yet following the implementation of the Individual Visit Scheme, Hong Kong's tourism numbers grew exponentially over the decade that followed. The city hosted 21.81 million visitors in 2004, 28.17 million visitors in 2007, 42 million visitors in 2011, and a total of 60.8 million visitors in 2014, with 77.7 percent of visitors that year coming from China.[118]

Bruce Lam, in his history of Hong Kong's democratic movement, acknowledges that this unprecedented expansion brought unparalleled growth to Hong Kong's tourism industry from 2003 onward. Tourism revenues more than quadrupled between 2002 and 2014, at which point tourists from China were bringing $359.04 billion in annual inbound tourism expenditures.[119] Yet Lam argues that these developments not only distorted the development of Hong Kong's economy, like many other aspects of CEPA, but also brought unprecedented pressures on society. Tourism revenues were concentrated primarily in the hands of hotels, chain stores, and real estate magnates.[120] Expanding sales made landlords confident enough to demand higher rents from store tenants. Smaller stores left behind by the rush of business found themselves unable to stay open amid rising costs, which also made gaining a foothold in the market a near impossibility for start-ups.[121] The vibrancy and diversity of the Hong Kong market was gradually squeezed out by external factors, producing an increasingly monotonous market focused on luxury brands, jewelry, cosmetics, and pharmaceutical items.[122] Retailers no longer catered to the needs of residents, but rather to tourists, a development that had a deeply alienating effect on locals.[123] Streets were also increasingly overflowing with people, occupied by visiting shoppers filling their suitcases with items to take back across the border. In a skewed distribution of benefits and costs, while only a few benefited directly from tourism revenues, anyone who rode the MTR or walked through a shopping mall was forced to face the negative side effects of this tourist boom.

Following an economistic approach to its logical endpoint, subsuming everything to the logic of profits could produce extremely disconcerting results. Consider, for example, China's milk powder scandal. In September 2008, soon after the conclusion of the Beijing Olympics, news broke that numerous dairy companies had been adding melamine to watered-down milk: its presence mimicked protein in quality tests' nitrogen readings, enabling watered-down milk to pass inspections. Companies were then able to profit from selling this adulterated milk at the same unit price as unadulterated milk. Yet melamine-tainted milk can cause serious illness in infants who consume it, leading to kidney stones, kidney failure, and even death. At least three hundred thousand infants in China were exposed to such intentionally poisoned milk. Over fifty thousand became ill to the point that they required hospitalization. At least six died.[124] In my discussions with enthusiasts of Hong Kong independence, the milk powder scandal was often cited as a turning point for people's thinking about the city's relationship with China. There was of course shock at the puzzling cruelty of such behavior. Yet one interlocutor told me that he felt a deeper sense of shock at the logic behind this cruelty: he saw it as a crystallization of the type of purely economic logic, embracing profits above all else, that had been unfolding in the expansion of China-Hong Kong relations. When profit appears to provide the answer to everything, it also becomes the source of all problems.

The milk powder scandal at once inverted and reproduced CEPA's economic hierarchy. From one perspective, this hierarchy was inverted as Hong Kong became a source of hope for countless Chinese parents, supplying imported milk powders that they could trust to feed their children. Whereas state nationalist narratives have long portrayed Hong Kong as reliant on China for its most basic needs, such as water, food, and even economic growth itself, the Hong Kong market after the 2008 milk powder scandal in fact stepped in to provide for one of China's most basic needs, reminding us that the Hong Kong-China relationship is far more complex than official narratives acknowledge (a point to which I return in chapter 3). Hong Kong's status as a well-regulated economy and rule-of-law society that could guarantee "better quality, safer, [and] more trustworthy" goods turned this crisis into an opportunity for the city.[125]

From another perspective, however, this crisis only reproduced and further reinforced the Chinese economy's hierarchical domination of Hong Kong. Driven by the Individual Visit Scheme and the multiple entry permits made available to Shenzhen residents, smugglers known as "parallel traders" began buying up milk powder supplies in Hong Kong and smuggling them across the border to China, avoiding import tariffs while selling the powder at double profits or higher. Stores in the northern New Territory towns of Sha Tin, Sheung Shui, Tai Po, Yuen Long, and Tuen Mun began stocking seemingly infinite supplies of milk powder for a market with seemingly endless demand. The fading market diversity already present in the effects of CEPA became only ever more apparent as these towns' economies were completely rebuilt around the smuggling market. Milk powder was both everywhere and nowhere: nearly every store sold it, but sudden shortages could also leave local parents unable to procure the supplies they needed.[126] Paradoxically, this crisis highlighting the strengths of the Hong Kong system in fact only drew the city ever further into China; Hong Kong's strategic advantage became the source of further integration with and reliance on the China market.

Familiar spaces became unrecognizable in this process. Stores that once served locals now served parallels traders, as train stations and sidewalks were occupied by groups of eager shoppers with a notably different sense of etiquette and personal space.[127] Demonstrating the often baffling trends in this parallel trading market, I learned during a visit to Sheung Shui in early 2017 that cross-border trade had in recent months shifted attention to boxed wine, which was supposedly a hot item at the time in China. Walking down one stretch of road, I observed a series of stores, one after another, all selling boxed wine and milk powder. "Are you supposed to mix the two," I joked. The friend accompanying me held up his hands, shook his head, and sighed in exasperation, "It just makes no sense." He described to me the shops and restaurants of his childhood, telling me about a restaurant here, a general goods store there, and a bookstore there, all replaced by an endlessly expanding milk and boxed wine warehouse.

There was a mimetic relationship between smugglers, once presented as compatriots but now experienced as strangers, and the local streets that they occupied, once familiar but now increasingly unrecognizable and alien. Wandering through these crowded streets, observing the endlessly expanding frenzy of activity that was also all fundamentally the same, I could not help but come away with the distinct impression that Hong Kong was at once not China yet was also in a sense becoming China. I could also see that this becoming China, presented as a return home in matters of identification and an endless gift in matters of economics, was in fact deeply and irreparably alienating.

One Country, Two Systems/Two Systems, Two Countries
and the Politics of Impossibility

The most lasting and resilient myth that Hong Kong nationalism explicates is the idea that Hong Kong is naturally part of China.

This belief is based not in any historical or cultural understanding, but rather in blunt racial thinking. According to this logic, the majority of residents of Hong Kong originally came from the geographic space now known as "China," and as a result they have "Chinese blood;" therefore, they always have been and always will be Chinese, and as a result, Hong Kong always has been and always will be a part of China. These assumptions, based in dated yet still emotionally resonant ideas of blood and belonging, erase the city's ethnic diversity, oversimplify the city's complex historical relationship with China, and obscure the sociocultural distinctions emerging from unique historical experiences over the past two centuries.

The racialized vision of pan-Chineseness pushed by Beijing represses a more nuanced constructivist vision of identity, which would recognize the vastly divergent historical experiences of the people of Hong Kong and China from 1841 to the present and the ways in which these experiences have produced fundamentally distinct societies and cultures. The false belief in racial commonality feeds an assumption that Hong Kong's 1997 handover was only natural and that the resulting increased contact between peoples and cultures would produce enhanced "understanding" and thus belonging. This has been true in one sense: unprecedented degrees of contact have produced unprecedented degrees of familiarity and understanding in Hong Kong with regard to the politics and culture of the People's Republic of China. Yet in this knowing, many Hong Kong residents have not found themselves reunited with long-lost brothers and sisters but rather have come to feel a growing sense of difference and distance from their newly proximal relatives.

An anonymous local artist working under the pseudonym Local Studio gave voice to these feelings in a series of illustrations titled *Hong Kong Is Not China*, self-published as a booklet in 2015.[128] Each page of the booklet compares political, cultural, economic, or social phenomena in China and Hong Kong, repeatedly emphasizing the contrast between the two. Historically, the booklet shows that Hong Kong was established in 1841, while the People's Republic of China was established in 1949.[129] Politically, the booklet highlights that Hong Kong has separation of powers between the executive,

legislative, and judicial branches, while China's political system is characterized by a centralized model.[130] Culturally, the booklet highlights the distinctions between linguistic cultures in Hong Kong and China, as well as access to
free media and an open internet in Hong Kong.[131] Economically, the booklet
highlights that Hong Kong uses the Hong Kong dollar rather than RMB, and
that it is home to a stock market that is considerably more strongly regulated
than China's.[132]

The Local Studio booklet unambiguously portrays Hong Kong's political,
social, economic, and cultural systems as not only distinct from but also superior to China's. Some of the contrasts can be admittedly crude and off-putting.
For example, the artist makes mocking references to the use of squat toilets in
China and claims that the Chinese people "love to be enslaved and manipulated
by the Chinese Communist Party."[133] Yet if one can set aside such hyperbolic
and at times offensive statements, one finds a significant kernel of truth in the
booklet's portrayal of two unique peoples, produced by the distinct historical
experiences of the past two centuries, the reality of which has been obscured by
the racialized conceptualization of a singular Chinese nation. The declaration
that "Hong Kong is not China" is not the product of chauvinism and prejudice as Beijing would have us believe, but rather the open acknowledgment
of fundamental irresolvable differences that had been heretofore repressed by
anachronistic pan-Chinese racial nationalism; it is a product not of misunderstandings, prejudice, and caricatures (the "Hong Kong chauvinism" criticized
by Zhu and Zhang), but rather of interaction, knowing, and reflection.

The revelation of this irresolvable difference explicates the comforting
mythologies of decolonization under One Country, Two Systems. The British
colonization of Hong Kong indeed came from a remote land, as compared to
Beijing's post-1997 rule over Hong Kong. Yet the institutions and values that
were built over the course of the colonial experience from 1841 to 1997 came
to be recognized and experienced by many residents as local. Beijing's post-
1997 rule over Hong Kong, by contrast, comes from an adjacent territory, with
assumptions of racial commonality. Yet the political culture that the central
government and its allies in the local government have fostered in Hong Kong
since 1997 feels by contrast different and unnatural. Politically, the perpetual
delays in promised reforms toward universal suffrage and the suppression of
political participation have created widespread disappointment and frustration.
Legally, the redeployment of the Basic Law for the purposes not of restricting
the central government but rather further empowering it to intervene in Hong

Kong affairs has undermined the city's rule of law traditions. Culturally, the pressures on independent publishers and the promotion of a patriotic education framework have been blatant infringements of the territory's established freedom of speech and conscience. The racial mythology of underlying sameness has been deployed to repress undeniable and irresolvable difference.

In his reading of Lyotard's writings on the Algerian War, Mohammed Ramdani has traced initial outlines of the concept of the differend that Lyotard would only articulate decades later: the basis of the Algerian conflict, he argues, lies in a fundamental affect-driven difference that needs to be expressed but is also beyond any resolution.[134] In his eponymous book, Lyotard defines the wrong of the differend as "a damage accompanied by the loss of the means to prove the damage," insofar as this wrong is inexpressible in prevailing idioms: take for example return, reunification, or decolonization.[135] Building on this idea, Ramdani cites Algerian historian Mohammed Harbi, who notes that "between the two worlds, that of the colonizer and the colonized, there is not only an incompatibility in terms of language: the two are not even describing the same object."[136] The task of thinking through such differends is then not to provide a singular, certain path toward a solution, but rather to transcend the hegemonic language of the oppressors to develop new languages and visions to better understand the conditions, and more specifically the wrongs, that have produced this difference.[137] If one is able to set aside our conventional imagining of colonization as something that Western nations do to underdeveloped nations on the other side of the world and instead reimagine colonization as simply the insupportable domination of one people by another, one can then easily see the colonial nature of Chinese rule over Hong Kong and the irresolvable difference therein. This colonization first occupies people's identities through the encompassing racial unity of Chineseness in "one country," before in turn masquerading colonial rule as autonomy under "two systems," repeating this mantra ad nauseam to the point that there is indeed no space within this illusory autonomy to express the genuinely colonial nature of the relationship. There is then genuine power to be found in recognizing and expressing this fundamental intractable difference in the declaration "Hong Kong is not China," a novel concept that this booklet expresses and establishes in its blunt and insistent repetition.

In his 2014 article "Should Hong Kong Have the Right to Self-Determination" (discussed in more detail in chapter 2), published in *Undergrad*, the journal of the Hong Kong University Undergraduate Student Union,

Jack Lee presents another vision of this difference through a comparison of the Chinese colonization of Tibet and Hong Kong.[138] In one section, Lee highlights the eerie similarities between the Seventeen-Point Agreement for the Peaceful Liberation of Tibet, the Orwellian-named treaty signed in 1951 between the Chinese and Tibetan governments promising genuine autonomy, and the Basic Law that promises Hong Kong a high degree of autonomy under One Country, Two Systems. For example, the Basic Law's authorization for Hong Kong to enjoy a high degree of autonomy, as well as exercising executive, legislative, and independent judicial power (Article 2), is reminiscent of the guarantees of national regional autonomy and the proscription of Chinese interference in Tibet's political system (points 3 and 4 in the Seventeen-Point Agreement). The promises to respect Hong Kong's way of life, protecting freedom of speech, freedom of the press, freedom of assembly, freedom of conscience, and freedom of religion (Articles 27–34), are reminiscent of the promises to protect Tibet's religious beliefs, customs, and habits (point 7 in the Seventeen-Point Agreement). And just as China was supposed to only be responsible for Tibet's foreign affairs and defense (points 14 and 15 in the Seventeen-Point Agreement), so Hong Kong was promised the same (Articles 13 and 14). Lee thus raises the troubling question: Will the fate of Hong Kong's autonomy be the same as Tibet's?[139]

Having researched self-immolation in Tibet, I distinctly remember feeling discomfited by Lee's comparison when his article was first published in 2014. After all, at that time Hong Kong was holding a public debate on a proposal for political reform, which was followed by the large-scale peaceful occupation of large sections of the city by protesters for months on end. In the same year, residents of Tibet lived under an all-encompassing security state that left them no option to express their opposition to central government policies through any means other than self-immolation.[140] Yet in retrospect Lee's jarring comparison in fact presented a far more clear-eyed and indeed prescient vision of the future of Hong Kong-China relations than any mainstream academic work has been able to do: Hong Kong nationalists know the power that they are facing all too well. It is always so easy to dismiss such comparisons, pointing out that the situation in Hong Kong is nowhere near as dire as that in Tibet. Yet in doing so we lose sight of the fact that these two nations are governed by the same power in similarly colonizing ways. In 2020, as the National Security Law provided a pretext for mass arrests for speech crimes and political activists fled the city to take refuge in exile, what seemed unimaginable a few short years before suddenly became an inescapable reality. Whether we are talking about an Autonomous Region or a Special Administrative Region, the end point is always the same. Few saw this coming, and even fewer dared to openly raise this prospect, but could Hong Kong's promised autonomy under Beijing's control ever have possibly ended any other way?

Hong Kong nationalism is thus this city's political enlightenment, giving voice to the irresolvable differences repressed by narratives of racial unity and national regeneration. The declaration that "Hong Kong is not China" is not just an angry response to the central state's provocations but rather an intellectual confrontation with and critique of said provocations. It unflinchingly casts away the false solace of the mythologies of the past, awakening from the ideological deployment of Chineseness, the Basic Law, promises of autonomy and political reform, patriotism, decolonization, and economic growth, revealing these political-cultural representations as ideological supports for Beijing's creeping domination over all aspects of life and thereby revealing One Country, Two Systems itself as a closed system inevitably proceeding toward One Country, One System.

As One Country, Two Systems inexorably approaches its own erasure in One Country, One System, those who are invested in two systems logically come to see the only path to their preservation in Two Systems, Two Countries. The counterproposal of independence may seem unreal, but in its impossibility it reveals the impossibility of the system that it critiques. As Bruce Lam notes in the first volume of his two-volume history of Hong Kong's resistance movement, "Only when our government is truly endorsed, controlled, and monitored by the Hong Kong people will it really understand the Hong Kong people's needs and serve their interests."[141] The seeming impossibility of Hong Kong not being China, of Hong Kong people in fact truly ruling Hong Kong as promised by Deng Xiaoping, is not then an indictment of the idea of independence itself but rather an indictment of the fundamentally impossible situation in which the city finds itself two decades after its handover. Trapped between an inescapable reality constructed around fictions and an impossible fiction that provides the only real path to promised rights and freedoms, there is real power to be found in finally articulating this irresolvable difference in the at once jarring but also revelatory declaration, "We are not Chinese."

TAKE FOUR: ON THE ETHNICIZATION
OF THE HONG KONG POLICE FORCE

The second section of this chapter analyzed the evolution of Hong Kong ethnic and nationalist thinking as one step in an escalating process of mutual provocation between the central government and Hong Kong civil society, a process that I called a noncompliance cycle. By leaping over the reddest of red lines, the idea that Hong Kong always has been and always will be a part of China, Hong Kong nationalists recapture agency from an increasingly interventionist central government. As the third section of this chapter showed, however, simply because Beijing views Hong Kong nationalism as a major provocation does not mean that it is nothing more than a provocation. There is in fact far more to ethnonationalist thought as both a product and producer of political enlightenment with regard to Hong Kong's fate under Chinese rule. Hong Kong nationalism explicates a series of comforting myths that people have been told, or have told themselves, about the fate of Hong Kong under Chinese rule: that democratization in China is inevitable, that the Basic Law could maintain the city's unique system, that the opposition camp could guard democratic values, that economic integration with China would be mutually beneficial, and that colonization had come to an end. The vision of a distinct Hong Kong ethnicity deserving of its own nation thus emerges in the interaction between escalating affective confrontations with the central state and sober-minded analysis of these confrontations, awakening to the impossibility of maintaining Hong Kong's way of life under Chinese rule. In the concluding section of this chapter, I reapply this model of affect and analysis to a distinct yet also related example: the emergence of ethnic thinking regarding the Hong Kong Police Force during the 2019 protests.

I was in Admiralty when protesters gathered outside the Legislative Council on June 12, 2019, to block a second reading of the proposed extradition bill that would allow anyone in the city to be extradited to China. I watched, slightly bewildered, as protesters occupied the central thoroughfare of Harcourt Road just a little after eight o'clock in the morning. I was still standing among the crowd on Harcourt Road later that afternoon when the police used an unprecedented degree of force to clear protesters who had by that point occupied roads throughout Admiralty, extending outward toward Central. I of course not only watched but also ran as police shot one round of tear gas after another, chasing protesters, observers, and bystanders with batons raised, and even firing bean bag rounds and rubber bullets indiscriminately at unarmed civilians.

Meeting with a friend the next day, each of us intermittently breaking into coughing fits from the tear gas, we reflected on June 12's unique mix of optimism and despair, completely unaware of all that was ahead in the coming months. During a lull in our conversation, he posed an unexpected question: "Do you think all of those police yesterday, the police who chased after us and fired tear gas at us, were actually Hong Kong police? Or had they come across the border from China?" I was initially taken aback. Even with the accelerating erosion of One Country, Two Systems, sending in PRC police posing as local Hong Kong police to put down protests would have been an extremely provocative move in 2019. The possibility had thus not crossed my mind, and even when this possibility was placed before me for consideration, it still struck me as highly unlikely.

Nevertheless, as I thought about it, I could understand why someone would feel this way. To imagine the police that day as outsiders simply made more sense than to think of them as locals. Because the city of Hong Kong has a lengthy tradition of public protest, and because the right of assembly is legally protected in the Basic Law, people were not accustomed to the police force treating protestors like they did on June 12. Even at a recent low point in police-civilian relations, the 2014 Occupy protests, the already fairly aggressive and politicized police force nevertheless still showed infinite constraint compared to its behavior in 2019. Yuk-man Cheung has noted, drawing upon polling done by Chinese University of Hong Kong's Center for Communication and Public Opinion Survey, that strong distrust of the Hong Kong Police Force rose from 6.5 percent to 51.5 percent between June and October 2019, reflecting a dramatic shift in public opinion.[142] Something had clearly changed: How could one make sense of these changes? The simplest and thus most appealing explanation possible was to imagine that the police who had chased and beaten protesters the day before were actually not Hong Kong police, not people who had grown up in the same city and vowed to protect this community and its laws, but rather people raised within a different system, with different sociocultural structures and a decidedly different way of dealing with protests. One could say that the idea that Hong Kong police had been replaced with Chinese police was simply a case of essentializing othering via a conspiracy theory: as I have analyzed in my previous book on Han Clothing, in their positing of absolute binaries that provide complete explanations of events, conspiracy theories provide the last refuge of singular, clearly differentiated, and fully comprehensible identities in today's world.[143] Yet at the same time, I could never quite shake the feeling that these reflections in Hong Kong were far more than that. They were a genuine attempt to apply ethnic boundary thinking to make sense of experiences that otherwise could not be comprehended.

I followed rumors of Chinese armed police hiding among the Hong Kong Police Force as they spread throughout the summer of 2019. The weakness of these theories, in retrospect, lies in their continued optimistic faith that there was any actual difference between the two systems of policing: the subsequent willingness of the Hong Kong Police Force to transform into the regime's private militia shows that people were in fact giving far too much credence to the continued distinction between "two systems" in regard to matters of policing, public protest, and rule of law.

The baselessness of such optimism was made apparent on August 31, 2019, when members of the Hong Kong Police Force launched a violent attack on civilians inside Prince Edward MTR Station. Video from inside the station that evening shows police randomly beating and pepper spraying cowering MTR passengers. Soon thereafter, the police began making mass arrests, expelling media from the station and, in clear violation of the law, refusing to allow paramedics to enter the station to treat the injured.[144]

I returned to Hong Kong three days later to find a city enraged by the police brutality on display. In my discussions after this attack, I noted that the rumors of PRC infiltration of the Hong Kong Police Force had largely disappeared. There was no longer much suspicion of an other infiltrating a group that was perceived to be one's own. Rather, members of the Hong Kong Police Force were now seen explicitly through the lens of ethnic difference as an other in and of themselves: a group distinct from and opposed to the city's civilians, serving an external power. Upon the awakening to this difference, this boundary was reenacted and thereby reinforced one night after another in early September 2019 outside of the Mongkok Police Station directly above Prince Edward MTR Station. Almost every night brought a tense standoff between two rival groups who detested one another. Protesters would bring traffic on Prince Edward Road to a halt, pointing laser beams at the police while shouting such slogans as "the Hong Kong Police Force knows the law but ignores the law" (*Heunggong gingchaat jifaat faanfaat*), "corrupt police" (*haakging*), and "may your whole family die" (*sei chyun ga/hahm gaa ling*).

Tensions would finally build to a point that the police would open fire, shooting rubber bullets or bean bag rounds, and eventually come charging out of the station, firing tear gas and chasing us with their batons raised, unleashing their anger on anyone they managed to catch, continuing their vengeful blows long after their detainees had been subdued. This was repeated night after night, each side seemingly relishing the opportunity to further reinforce the previously unrecognized and unarticulated boundary between the self and the other through these clashes.

The recognition of difference and corresponding evolution of ethnic thought with regard to the Hong Kong Police Force that I observed over the summer of 2019 are a microprocess following paths similar to the broader identity processes analyzed in this chapter. As Hong Kong passed through a simultaneously hopeful but also exhausting summer of protests, a cycle of mutual provocation and escalation emerged in the relationship between police and civilians: excessive use of force by the police led protesters to take more aggressive steps in pushing back and defending their right to protest, which in turn led the police to use more aggressive force in dealing with protesters. Yet the risk in viewing this as simply a cycle of continually escalating, affect-driven mutual provocation is that such a view flattens this experience and ignores the genuine knowledge production unfolding in the observation, construction, and subsequent enactment of two mutually exclusive and opposed groups. This distinction was made painfully clear on August 31, 2019, when the violence unleashed in Prince Edward MTR Station led protesters to see the police force as no longer simply infiltrated by an ethnic other but indeed an other in and of itself. This pseudo-ethnic othering was a recognition of a difference irresolvable within the current sociopolitical system, as well as a critique within this recognition of the system that had transformed the force from defenders of the rule of law to defenders of a lawless and alien dictatorship.

There are, I must admit, few times in my life that I have felt more uncomfortable than during a march on September 8, 2019, as protesters shouted an endless stream of the crudest insults at police standing on the edge of the procession; "while corrupt police are out doing overtime, their wives are at home doing two other guys" (*haakging OT, gingsou 3P*). Yet one of those few times that I did feel even more uncomfortable was just a few hours later in Mongkok as I watched a crowd of at least five police officers surround and beat a fleeing protester senseless for no clear reason, refusing to halt their blows long after the young man lay motionless on the ground.

The unfolding of this differend, this previously unexpressed yet also intractable difference, was a microversion of the macroprocess of relations between China and Hong Kong civil society since 1997. The microinteractions of mutual provocation that occurred in the summer of 2019 transforming the police force into an outside group are just a smaller subset of a much larger historical process since 1997. These processes are characterized not only by affect and provocation, but also by observation, analysis, and emerging recognition of a self-styled protecter as an external colonizing power. There is power in casting aside false ideologies of racial unity, critically analyzing the origins and development of difference, and in turn expressing this once repressed differend through the declaration that "Hong Kong is not China." Precisely because colonization is understood as the exercise of power by an other, it is through the recognition of power as an other that its colonizing nature is understood and can in turn be resisted.

Two Systems, Two Countries

New Directions in Political Thought in Hong Kong since 2011

What is Hong Kong nationalism? What are the main perspectives and proposals for a Hong Kong nation articulated by advocates of this idea? This chapter provides the first comprehensive English-language introduction to the main schools of thought in Hong Kong nationalism: (1) city-state theory, (2) self-determination, (3) independence, and (4) returnism. These schools of thought share a common awakening to the fact that One Country, Two Systems is a failure. Yet beyond this shared political enlightenment, theorists of the four schools draw upon vastly different philosophical and political perspectives, proposing in turn vastly different visions for Hong Kong's future. Hong Kong nationalism is thus less a singular movement than an open-ended, taboo-free, participatory, and hopeful conversation about the city's future.

This chapter presents an intellectual history of Hong Kong nationalism, with a focus on the development of ideas rather than on particular figures or events. Some figures are indeed so essential to the development of these thought trends that discussion of their contributions and personalities is necessary. Yet I have found in the process of writing this chapter that a focus on individual contributors and their inevitably big personalities can easily leave one mired in the unnecessarily complex and often highly contentious relations between these personalities, which yield little of intellectual value beyond the insight that political activists do not always hold one another in high regard. Similarly, certain seminal events, such as the 2014 Occupy protests or the 2016 Fishball Revolution, are discussed in this chapter only insofar as they are inextricably linked to the intellectual developments analyzed herein. I have accordingly focused not on providing a full history of events related to Hong Kong nationalism during the 2010s, but rather on interpreting and tracing the theoretical debates emerging from and contributing to these events, such as the question of the possibility of democratization under Chinese rule raised by the Occupy protests or the ethics of the use of force raised by the Fishball protests.[1]

In this overview of the development of Hong Kong nationalist thought, I particularly want to highlight the genuine diversity of the ongoing debate around this concept. At the same time, while recognizing the relative improbability of any of the proposals for Hong Kong's separation from China, this chapter highlights the usefulness of this discussion for producing novel critiques of Chinese rule over Hong Kong, as well as of pan-Chinese nationalism more broadly.

FROM CITY-STATE THEORY TO ETERNAL BASIC LAW

Everyone has an opinion about Chin Wan. Chin is a former government official and former professor of Chinese studies at Hong Kong's Lingnan University who in the course of the 2010s transformed into a political prophet reimagining Hong Kong-China relations.[2] Predictably, Chin and his contributions are viewed with disdain by establishment pro-China figures, who claim that he peddles a Sinophone Sinophobia. Yet even among today's more outspoken advocates of outright independence from China, simply mentioning Chin's name inevitably produces an eyeroll and a laugh. When they are pressed further, however, I have yet to meet anyone among this group of independence activists who denies Chin's central role in radically reorienting the discussion about Hong Kong's relationship with China. He did so by becoming an uninhibited medium giving voice to sociopolitical tensions in Hong Kong under Chinese rule, as well as by proposing new concepts to envision a future beyond these tensions. His 2011 book, *On Hong Kong as a City-State*, spoke extremely frankly about the failings of One Country, Two Systems and proposed a vision of Hong Kong as a city-state distinct from the rest of China.[3] In doing so, Chin singlehandedly prompted a paradigm shift in the city's political culture: voicing urgent yet previously unarticulated concerns within society while at the same time developing a new thought system that has forever changed how people in Hong Kong see and talk about the city's future.

As a thinker, Chin is decidedly disdainful of convention, confrontational, and eager to tackle even the most sensitive of taboo topics; these characteristics have enabled him to rise in a Nietzschean manner above the stale and leveling orthodoxies of Hong Kong politics, dealing a fatal blow to standard political discourse in the city. These same transgressive characteristics that made Chin influential in the first half of the 2010s, however, have also led to his declining popularity in the second half of the 2010s. If we follow the previous metaphor, one can easily imagine just how simultaneously fascinating and frustrating it would have been to follow Nietzsche in real time on social media. Chin's unconventional and confrontational nature, which drove him to write books that forever changed Hong Kong politics, has with the passage of time also made him a polarizing and even unpopular figure in the ongoing debate on Hong Kong's future, a debate that his work initiated.

The Hong Kong City-State

Chin's revolutionary thought exercises begin from his relatively mundane proposal in his 2011 book that Hong Kong is a city-state.[4] At first glance, few declarations could be less interesting. Hong Kong is, after all, a city that has its own borders, currency, policies, and its own ostensibly autonomous government. Yet in the process of unfolding this idea of a Hong Kong city-state through his ever-expanding series of city-state books, Chin proceeds to give this concept and Hong Kong itself a novel sense of meaning. Recasting the Hong Kong Special Administrative Region of the People's Republic of China as a Hong Kong city-state is thus far more than a simple matter of academic wordplay.

What is a city-state? In Chin's reading, it is a lot of things. He tells us that the city-state is a Western tradition that can be traced back to ancient Greece, where the foundations of classical politics in Plato's *Republic* and Aristotle's *Politics* were imagined through the city-state (polis).[5] He tells us that city-states are small, autonomous entities with a city at their core; they serve as gathering points, generally on the periphery of a greater power, for talented individuals, capital, goods, cultural customs, and scholars from many lands to come together.[6] Sometimes, he tells us, a city-state is independent, but most often it is linked to another sovereign entity that provides resources and defense.[7] Politically, Chin tells us, the city-state is the birthplace of democracy; rather than envisioning people as serving the state, the city-state exists for the people.[8] Even more fundamentally, Chin cites Aristotle to argue that the main purpose of the city-state is realizing "the good life."[9]

Aristotle ... ancient Greece ... the polis. This all feels quite far removed from the matter at hand: Hong Kong and its relationship with China. Yet that is precisely the point: the city-state tradition as articulated by Chin completely rewrites the history of Hong Kong and its relationship with China. Chin explicitly argues that envisioning Hong Kong as simply a colony (under British rule) or a Special Administrative Region (under Chinese rule) presents a woefully incomplete picture of the city's cultural realities, as well as its possibilities.

To envision Hong Kong under British rule as simply a colony characterized by the standard colonial fare of injustice and oppression is to overlook the complexity of the city's history. In Chin's portrayal, the 1842 founding of the Hong Kong city-state was less a moment of colonization and shame, as invariably portrayed in official Chinese historiographies, than the establishment of a novel political and cultural tradition in East Asia.[10] Residents, after all, were not simply colonized but in many cases actively chose to move to this city-state from China to pursue "the good life" available in this polis. Politically, Chin argues, although dispatched from London the governor was given near total autonomy in handling local matters, thereby developing a tradition of independent political and economic policies focused on local interests that enabled the city to prosper.[11] Accordingly, Hong Kong provided a safe haven from the cultural destruction, political upheaval, and humanitarian disasters that characterized China's long nineteenth and twentieth centuries.[12]

To envision Hong Kong as a Special Administrative Region, the official name for the city after 1997, is in Chin's reading an even more impoverished description. The characteristics that ostensibly make Hong Kong "special," such as rule of law, freedom of association, and freedom of the press, are not in fact "special" in the contemporary world; they are simply "normal" universal values.[13] Hong Kong's commonsense freedoms could only be interpreted as in any way "special," Chin tells us, as a result of the abnormal political, sociocultural, and legal situation in the People's Republic of China today.[14] Insofar as neither colony nor special administrative region are able to reflect Hong Kong's historical and contemporary realities, Chin proposes in their place the concept of the city-state, which he characterizes as an "objective" term to describe the city's reality.[15]

The distinct city-state experience in turn produces a distinct Hong Kong culture. Based on historical immigration patterns to the city, Chin proposes a tripartite vision of the much-discussed (and all too often horribly clichéd)

Hong Kong character, combining aspects of culture from Qing China, the Republic of China, and Victorian-era England.[16] From the Qing, the people of Hong Kong have inherited what Chin sees as a certain conservatism and serenity.[17] From the Republic of China, the people of Hong Kong have inherited that era's spirit of courage and exploration.[18] And from Victorian England, the people of Hong Kong have inherited a spirit of liberalism, skepticism, and reason.[19] I am personally highly skeptical of any discussion of national character, and it is of course extremely easy to criticize this caricature of a "Hong Kong character" built on different spirits from different epochs. Yet this instinctive academic reaction, which I could have easily typed out in a few short minutes and been done with this paragraph, misses the deeper point of Chin's analyses and their resonance. Chin is here appropriating a mythology of national characters as collected sediments of various historical eras, bringing history back into identity construction, to deconstruct the central state's mythology of a timeless pan-Chinese racial unity that ignores Hong Kong's distinctive historical experience.

Can this distinctiveness survive Beijing's increasingly restrictive rule? Chin's answer is not only that it can, but that it must. According to standard narratives, the Chinese Communist Party gifted the idea of One Country, Two Systems to the people of Hong Kong for fifty years and can theoretically withdraw this arrangement whenever it pleases. As the years pass, and as the city no longer plays the central role that it used to play in economic matters in the region, Hong Kong is perpetually imagined to be on the verge of eclipse by such cities as Shenzhen or Shanghai. Hong Kong's future is in China: Hong Kong needs China. Chin again demonstrates his unique ability to turn conventional thinking upside down by reversing this narrative to argue that, in fact, China needs Hong Kong. First, One Country, Two Systems is in Chin's reading neither a major theoretical innovation by Deng Xiaoping nor a gift to the Hong Kong people from the Chinese Communist Party. Rather, One Country, Two Systems is simply a relatively face-saving way for the Chinese Communist Party to acknowledge the strength and superiority of Hong Kong's system under British rule. Insofar as the Party had nothing of political value to offer the city, and insofar as it benefited economically from the city's system, Beijing had no choice but to maintain this system after the handover: One Country, Two Systems.[20] Second, despite the incessant hype about Shanghai or Shenzhen overtaking Hong Kong, such hype remains at the end of the day nothing but hype: Chin says Shanghai's city-state legacy was completely destroyed by the CCP in the 1950s, thoroughly assimilating the city into Party culture, and Shenzhen has never been anything more than an appendage to Hong Kong's city-state legacy.[21] Neither is fit, in his reading, to play the essential financial and technological role that Hong Kong plays in China's development.[22] Chin's inversion of hierarchies here is a paradigm-shifting argument that has had a truly revolutionary impact on Hong Kong political culture and the city's relationship with China: rather than seeing Hong Kong as destined to be absorbed by China, Chin argues that the CCP in fact needs Hong Kong, and that as a result Hong Kong has real power and agency in this relationship.[23]

While China needs Hong Kong, Chin argues, the Chinese Communist Party is resistant to acknowledging this fact, meaning that its policies are split, wavering erratically between a pragmatic structural functionalism meant to maintain Hong Kong's place in China's future and irrational "controlocracy" driven to destroy the city's uniqueness.[24] At one level, the CCP recognizes that Hong Kong plays an irreplaceable role in China's development and relations with the world and thus strives for a measured, realpolitik approach. At another level, however, Chin analyzes CCP leaders and their nationalist supporters as emotionally distressed by the fact that Hong Kong's great legacy, the legacy that the CCP must maintain, was created by Great Britain and the people of Hong Kong rather than the Party, China's self-declared omnipotent creator.[25] Official discourse attempts to repress this founding lack by claiming that the people of Hong Kong exist in debt to China. According to these narratives, Hong Kong plundered China's best and brightest at difficult times in the country's history, the city relies on China for the basics of its existence today, and the support of the PRC government is all that keeps the city's economy running.[26] Yet these ideological constructions are only temporary fixes. Chin argues that the Party, left to its own erratic devices, will be unable to maintain a rational policy toward Hong Kong and will eventually destroy the very qualities that make Hong Kong worth possessing.[27] Reading these words from a decade earlier in the year 2021, they seem uniquely prophetic.

To prevent this coming destruction, Chin proposed his city-state vision.[28] How was this vision to be realized? What does it actually mean, practically speaking, to recognize Hong Kong as a city-state, or to build it into a city-state? Chin provides few concrete details in this first book. Perhaps anticipating the paradigm-shifting nature of this idea, Chin's main proposal therein is to simply acknowledge Hong Kong's history as a city-state; such recognition would then, ideally, lead to what he calls a "city-state movement" with a focus on local political interests, and this city-state movement would then make use of Hong Kong's strategic advantages in its relationship with China to clearly articulate, based in the rule of law, the clear delegation of powers between Hong Kong and the CCP.[29] The idea of the city-state, in and of itself, is to be a game changer.

Chin's well-documented self-confidence was in this case correct: in any discussion of the books that have had the greatest impact on Hong Kong politics since 2011, *On Hong Kong as a City-State* should be at the top of the list. When Chin published his first book in the city-state series, localist sentiment was just beginning to take shape as an influential school of thought in Hong Kong politics, and *On Hong Kong as a City-State* provided its first systematic theoretical articulation, initiating a more sophisticated discussion of the city's future. Ironically, considering the paths that this conversation has subsequently taken, Chin is particularly careful in *On Hong Kong as a City-State* to emphasize that he is decidedly not advocating Hong Kong independence. As he states near the end of his book: "The right to autonomy granted by the Basic Law is in fact considerably more expansive than anything formally recognized under British rule. The issue is that China is attempting to impede this autonomy, and the Hong Kong people are not being proactive enough in fighting for it. Genuine autonomy for Hong Kong is simply a realization of 'One Country Two Systems,' and is certainly not Hong Kong independence."[30] Although city-state advocacy is not the same as independence advocacy, the transformation of the political discursive field that Chin's intervention produced opened the door to independence advocacy. Yet long before such proposals for outright independence entered mainstream Hong Kong politics, Chin had already taken his thinking in new and genuinely unexpected directions.

Long Live Feudalism!

Chin's first book in the city-state series realized a paradigm shift in how people think and talk about Hong Kong's relationship with China, and has, whether people like to acknowledge it or not, left a lasting legacy on Hong Kong politics. The second book in the series went a step further by attempting a further paradigm shift within this paradigm shift, revealing the simultaneously exciting and imperfect dynamism of Chin's reliably tumultuous thinking.

Chin's second book is *On Hong Kong as a Bastion of Loyalism*. And just as *City-State* tells us that Hong Kong is a city-state, so *Loyalism* tells us that the

Hong Kong people are the true loyalists of a great lost past. Whereas Chin highlighted the distinction between Hong Kong and China in his first book through his promotion of the city-state concept, he does the same in his second book through a spirited defense of Chinese culture and feudalism. Yes, you read that sentence correctly. To summarize Chin's fascinatingly paradoxical argument in the most concise manner possible, he says that in order to fulfill their historical role as the true loyalists of pure Chinese tradition, the Hong Kong people need to abandon the concept of "cultural China" so as to promote Chinese culture, epitomized in the modern Hong Kong city-state, which revitalizes the feudal system of the Western Zhou (1047–772 BCE) distinct from China. Hopefully the exegesis that follows will make this argument somewhat clearer.

"Cultural China" (*mahnfa Junggwok/wenhua Zhongguo*) is a concept frequently deployed in discussions of identity in Hong Kong. This concept has popular resonance, insofar as it allows people to identify as culturally Chinese while at the same time maintaining political distance from the tragedies unleashed on China by the Communist Party since 1949.[31] Yet Chin points out that this idea of "cultural China" (*mahnfa Junggwok*), in its attempt to rescue Chineseness as a cultural ideal from the Chinese Communist regime, still uses the geographical term for China, *Junggwok/Zhongguo*, a term that clearly denotes the space in mainland East Asia that has been controlled by the Chinese Communist Party for the past seven decades.[32] "Cultural China" is thus a false distinction, making a seemingly deterritorializing term in fact decidedly arborescent in its geographic focus.[33] Chin proposes instead a total deterritorialization of the idea of China, abandoning the geographic space of *Junggwok/Zhongguo* altogether by declaring that it has been permanently and irreparably transformed beyond all hope by the Chinese Communist Party's seven decades of rule: "The Chinese Communist Party has kidnapped China" and as a result "the China in your heart is . . . not a real country."[34] Chin proceeds to deploy a decidedly more vulgar metaphor to emphasize this point, comparing anyone who continues to embrace the ideal of cultural China to a cuckold who wants to deceive himself into believing that his lover, engaged in a long-standing and certainly not so clandestine relationship with the Chinese Communist Party, still genuinely loves him.[35]

Yet after criticizing "cultural China" (*mahnfa Junggwok*)," Chin proceeds to promote the idea of "Chinese culture (*wah-hah mahnfa/huaxia wenhua*)."[36] Chin's rendering here replaces the term *Junggwok/Zhongguo*, referring to China as the geographic locus of a particular vision of culture, with the term *wah-hah/huaxia*, a cultural concept which, in Chin's argument, remains unbound by geographical constraints.[37] *Huaxia* is in fact not to be found in China, Chin adds, but rather solely in Hong Kong, which he argues needs to reterritorialize this ideal through "cultural nation-building (*mahnfa gingwok/wenhua jianguo*)" based in traditional "Chinese culture (*wah-hah mahnfa/huaxia wenhua*)" beyond today's China.[38] At first glance, it may seem that we have fallen into the old cliché that Hong Kong, by right of avoiding the Maoist struggle against "old culture," has managed to preserve a purer form of traditional Chinese culture compared to the Mainland. Yet Chin is in fact pursuing a far more provocative and indeed subversive argument than this, reinterpreting the Maoist struggle against the old culture of feudalism as a form of old culture itself. Feudalism, Chin tells us, is not a hindrance from the past preventing the building of a modern republic, as May Fourth discourses claim; rather, it is the foundation of a great lost tradition and the sole pathway to a modern republic. All of the shock value absent from Chin's initial declaration that Hong Kong is a city-state has managed to find its way back into his unexpected declaration in 2013 that "if China wants to become a real Republic, it needs to revitalize feudalism."[39]

Feudalism is of course an affectively loaded yet also often meaningless term deployed in the discussion of Chinese history, supposedly encapsulating everything that was wrong in the "old society" prior to the rise to power of the Chinese Communist Party in 1949.[40] Demonstrating his usual skill with concepts, Chin provides the idea of the feudal with one of its more concrete definitions: "local separation and insubordination to the center by the various provinces and municipalities," based in the literal sense of *fengjian*, meaning "defining borders and establishing states."[41] Chin portrays this feudalism, wherein local politics were handled without intervention by a centralizing emperor figure, as a feature exclusive to the Western Zhou era, constructed in contrast to the unificationist approach subsequently taken by the Qin dynasty: what official histories celebrate as national unification was in fact the birth of an all-controlling centralizing state suppressing an otherwise promising tradition, and what official histories denounce as feudal was in fact a lost Golden Age of vibrant political and intellectual diversity.[42]

Here Chin's reflections bear notable parallels with the arguments put forward by Fei-ling Wang in his study *The China Order*, a critical reading of the centralizing traditions of the Chinese state from the Qin dynasty to the

People's Republic.[43] Also looking back toward the pre-Qin era, in a section memorably titled "The Glory and Peacefulness of the Warring States," Wang argues that the "Warring States era" was, despite its name, considerably less violent than subsequent eras of centralized rule, and was characterized by political pluralism and intellectual vibrancy, as demonstrated by the formation in this tumultuous era of such lasting philosophical traditions as Confucianism, Taoism, Mohism, and of course Legalism.[44] The real Warring State, Wang argues, emerged only with the arrival of the Qin, which in its celebrated drive for centralization and control strangled the political and intellectual dynamism of earlier eras.[45] The remainder of history from the Qin to today has been characterized by the eternal return of the same, repackaged first by the Han dynasty in a sugar-coated Confucian shell. Whenever this burdensome system collapsed under its own centralizing weight, it was reconstructed under a new name by new rulers with the exact same aspirations for centralizing control, producing an endless cycle of state disintegration and recentralization.[46]

For Chin, feudalism was not a lasting scourge on Chinese history that needed to be eliminated in order to realize modernity. Rather, feudalism, meaning the rule of various local lords over fiefdoms largely independent of central power, was a promising yet transient moment in Chinese history, from which the rest of history has fallen unredeemed.[47] The real scourge on this history is the centralizing and controlling state, of which the current regime, despite its ostensibly revolutionary and modern rhetoric, is simply another iteration.[48] The grand cycle of dynastic history that once led eternally back to the founding of a newly pure imperial order fuses here with the unrealized vision of total revolution that dominated China's twentieth century to produce a genuinely radical break portrayed as a traditional return: the abandonment of the centralizing and autocratic China Order via the construction of a voluntary Federation of Chinese States with the Hong Kong city-state at its core, recapturing a long-lost feudal tradition that affirms diversity, decentralization, and dynamism. Chin argues that "if we want China to become China again (*Junggwok/Zhongguo*), to become Chinese (*wah-hah/ huaxia*), we need to return to an arrangement similar to the Western Zhou. This means overcoming the centralizing totalitarianism of the Qin and eliminating the center's irrationally violent rule. This means building a nation through mutual agreements between local regimes. This is a grand new vision to revitalize Chinese (*wah-hah/huaxia*) culture."[49]

Unexpectedly, Chin's path to the Western Zhou is paved with the Basic Law. In his reading, the Sino-British Joint Declaration and the Basic Law mark the first time in post-Qin history that relations between the central government and localities were formalized through a legally binding agreement that restricts the central government's powers.[50] If the Joint Declaration and the Basic Law were in fact fully respected and implemented (a large "if"), such restraint would mark a significant step in the development of rule of law in modern China.[51] Yet it would also be far more than that. The Joint Declaration and Basic Law shatter the seemingly eternal legacy of the intrusive centralizing state to recapture a lost tradition of local self-rule, wherein the son of heaven remains uninterested in everyday local affairs and is primarily responsible for managing peaceful relations between fiefdoms: precisely the fields of diplomacy and defense clearly articulated as the sole purview of the central government in the Basic Law.[52]

Recentering Chinese culture in the Hong Kong city-state and its model of free contractual relations between the center and local states will, in Chin's vision, facilitate the emergence of a voluntary Federation of Chinese (Wah-hah/Huaxia) States including Hong Kong and Taiwan, and gradually expanding to include Macao, China, Mongolia, Tibet, and Xinjiang.[53] Each member of this federation will maintain its own independent administrative, financial, and legal systems, as well as minimal local defenses, while making contributions to centralized defense.[54] Diplomacy will be managed centrally, but the various states in this federation will still be able to enter into international agreements and multilateral institutions as they please; the precise limits of each state's power, Chin argues, will be determined in consultation between the various member states under the guiding principle of mutual benefit.[55] Chin's inclusion of Taiwan in this admittedly unlikely vision has proven controversial, particularly because Taiwan's status as an independent nation-state serves as a growing inspiration for many in Hong Kong who have lost hope in One Country, Two Systems. Yet Chin remains adamant that Taiwan would proactively join his Chinese Federation; insofar as the cornerstone of this federation is Hong Kong, which he claims shares with Taiwan a purer form of traditional culture compared to China, Chin believes that the people of Taiwan would see this federation not as an attempt at annexation but rather as a logical next step in their own peaceful cultural nation-building process.[56] Practically speaking, Chin adds, as an already independent nation, Taiwan's participation will also help to ensure that all states in this federation can enjoy genuine autonomy and full state-level powers.[57] Chin envisions the federation eventually building close relations with other countries that have been influenced by Chinese culture, including Japan, South Korea, Singapore, and Vietnam, forming a newly united Asian bloc on the global stage.[58]

Chin's critique of "cultural China" for the purpose of revitalizing the Western Zhou feudal system is peppered with esoteric quotes from *The Analects*, *The Commentary of Zuo*, and *The Book of Changes*. Soon after the publication of this volume, Chin began appearing in public in Han Clothing (*hanfu*), the recently invented style of traditional clothing that is imagined in China as the ethnic clothing of the Han nationality from time immemorial, passed down from the Yellow Emperor.[59] He called for a revitalization of the Zhou era rites that Confucius and his followers believed were vital to keeping the world in proper order and balance, realizing a Golden Age to which all later eras could only aspire.[60]

From the start, everyone knew that the path to reimagining Hong Kong's relationship with China was going to be long and uncertain. No one, however, could have guessed that it was going to be quite this confusing.

Eternal Basic Law

If we continue to draw out the initial comparison between Chin Wan and Nietzsche as thinkers dedicated to overturning convention, we could say that the first book in Chin's city-state series is comparable to *The Antichrist*, unforgivingly shattering orthodoxies to provide a completely novel perspective on Hong Kong and China. The second book in the city-state series then proceeds to unveil and celebrate a previously ignored tradition, bearing echoes of the Apollonian and Dionysian visions from *The Birth of Tragedy*. Yet by 2015, four years after his first city-state book, Chin was already writing his *Ecce Homo*, reflecting in a very self-assured manner on his own life work. Instead of such chapter titles as "Why I am So Wise" and "Why I Write Such Good Books," Chin's main argument in *On Hong Kong's City-State Sovereignty* (2015) and *On City-State Sovereignty II: The Politics of Hope* (2016), the two final books in his city-state series, basically boiled down to "Why I Need to Be in Hong Kong's Legislative Council."[61]

By this point in Chin's career, the once central role of the city-state was eclipsed by a new concept, "Eternal Basic Law." So anyone who was still following Chin's thinking sighed, grabbed his or her reading glasses, and began trying to figure out exactly what Eternal Basic Law was supposed to mean. Chin traced the source of Hong Kong's many problems to Article 5 of the Basic Law, which states: "The socialist system and policies shall not be practiced in the Hong Kong Special Administrative Region, and the previous capitalist system and way of life shall remain unchanged for 50 years."[62] In the grand sweep of history from the Zhou to the present with which Chin is concerned, fifty years is nothing, and this is precisely the problem. The mid-twenty-first-century deadline of 2047 undoubtedly seemed quite remote in the 1980s when One Country, Two Systems was first proposed, and naturally remained so in 1997 when all attention and anxieties were focused on the transition to PRC sovereignty at that moment. Yet by 2015, 2047 was no longer a distant point in the future; people were beginning thirty-year mortgages that would finally be paid off right before 2047, and the hope of maintaining Hong Kong's distinct system even to that moment was already disappearing due to the Chinese Communist Party's increasingly interventionist policies. By focusing on Article 5, Chin yet again demonstrated his unique ability, apparent since his first city-state book, to give voice to the city's political anxieties and envision innovative new paths forward.

Employing the type of earthy metaphor that he frequently uses to powerful effect in his writing, in a 2017 Facebook post Chin explained his new vision, comparing Hong Kong's situation to a store whose rental contract will expire in a few months. The store manager, representing the Hong Kong people, naturally will not expend much time or effort on building client relations or invest in renovating the space, because after all this space will not be his or hers in just a few months. The owner, representing here the Chinese Communist Party, will also naturally feel increasingly unconstrained by the stipulations of the soon-to-expire contract, asking the current manager for all types of exceptions to the agreement to prepare for retaking this space. Here, Chin claims to have found the root of the Chinese Communist Party's increasingly interventionist approach to Hong Kong affairs, as well as of the Hong Kong people's resigned attitude to this escalating intervention: the uncertain certainty of 2047.

To resolve this dilemma, Chin proposes a simple solution: strike a deal with the Chinese Communist Party to revise Article 5 of the Basic Law, removing the fifty-year expiration date for One Country, Two Systems and thereby inaugurating Eternal Basic Law. This deal would be agreeable to the Chinese Communist Party insofar as it would affirm the PRC's sovereignty over Hong Kong in perpetuity, as well as being agreeable to residents of Hong Kong, to the extent that it would protect their unique system and lifestyle in perpetuity.[63] Tellingly, the first step in Chin's plan for this deal was for him to be elected to the Legislative Council, where he would dedicate all of his energies to promoting Eternal Basic Law. He tells us that his proselytizing on this topic would not be limited to the Legislative Council (and of course the voters and constituencies who elect Legislative Council members), but would also include Hong Kong representatives to the National People's Congress and the broader political establishment in Beijing, which, Chin acknowledges, would need to grant final approval.[64] In a passage that succinctly captures a certain shift in Chin's discourse from developing novel ideas to assigning himself a grandiose historical mission, he declares: "Only a critic like myself who has earned the respect of the Chinese Communist Party can achieve this. Only Chin Wan is able to use his political rhetoric so effectively as to maintain face for the CCP and protect Chinese officials' highly complex but also very fragile feelings."[65] According to Chin's vision, once all parties concerned had been enlightened by the logic of extending the Basic Law in perpetuity, a proposal to this effect would be submitted for a vote in Hong Kong's Legislative Council, to be subsequently confirmed and approved by the National People's Congress in Beijing.[66] This extension of the Basic Law, by eliminating the uncertainty of the 2047 deadline, would reassure the people of Hong Kong about their future, and they would accordingly reinvest their energies in the city: precisely the hopeful change from which Chin's reflections in his first city-state book began.[67] At the same time, by affirming China's sovereignty in perpetuity, Beijing would also benefit from the stability and certainty provided by Eternal Basic Law. Rather than abandoning all hope for China, as Chin had argued in his first book, the key to resolving Hong Kong's dilemma was now to strike a grand deal with China.[68]

The process of revising Article 5 to realize Eternal Basic Law would, however, have far broader implications. In Chin's description, this revision would mark the beginning of a new epoch, insofar as through this process China and Hong Kong would be engaging in free and open negotiation toward an agreement that would be legally binding for both parties: what he calls, drawing upon ideas from his second book in the series, "contractual politics (*daiyeuk jingjih/diyue zhengzhi*)."[69] This would at once constitute a recognition of the previously denied sovereignty of the Hong Kong city-state by China, as well as thereby changing the dynamics of the relationship such that Hong Kong could take the initiative in confronting long-standing challenges therein. After Article 5 of the Basic Law, Chin's next goals were Article 22, which has instituted the one-way permit scheme for immigration from China to Hong Kong, and Article 24, which grants permanent residence to all Chinese citizens born in Hong Kong.[70]

The one-way permit scheme enables 150 Chinese citizens to immigrate to Hong Kong per day, as discussed in chapter 1, and has been a source of public anger in the city for years. A particularly pressing matter in the public discussion of this scheme has been the total lack of local oversight: the PRC government administers the one-way permit scheme completely on its own, and the Hong Kong government lacks the power to even review any of the decisions made, not to mention any potential veto power.[71] On account of the deep-rooted and long-standing issue of corruption under CCP rule, there have been repeated allegations that the distribution of one-way permits is at least partially determined by official connections, with some claims of permits even being auctioned off to the highest bidder.[72]

Article 24 has been even more controversial because its granting of Hong Kong residency to children born in Hong Kong, and then eventually their families, has driven the explosive growth of maternity tourism from China. Hong Kong residency is appealing to citizens of the People's Republic because it includes twelve years of quality public education free of charge, considerably more advanced health-care services, and more complete social services than are available in China, as well as a passport that allows visa-free entry to multiple countries around the world. Accordingly, whereas the number of births in Hong Kong hospitals to Chinese mothers hovered between seven thousand and ten thousand per year in the early 2000s, constituting roughly 15 to 20 percent of live births in the city, as the Individual Visit Scheme expanded to cover ever more cities in China, ever more women came to Hong Kong with the explicit goal of giving birth there.[73] Travel agencies in China even set up maternity tourism packages expressly for this purpose, providing expectant mothers with accommodation near hospitals that had obstetric units as well as transport to the emergency room once labor began.[74] By 2011, the number of Chinese women giving birth in Hong Kong had risen to 43,982, accounting for roughly 46 percent of all births in Hong Kong that year.[75] The city's medical infrastructure was unable to keep pace with such extremely rapid growth, leaving many local mothers unable to find public hospital spaces for childbirth.[76]

Chin's focus on these two articles of the Basic Law as the next step in the renegotiation of Hong Kong-China relations is thus not simply a nasty, xenophobic appeal to people's basest instincts, as some may claim. It is an attempt to envision a solution, no matter how fantastic, to some of the most contentious issues in the Hong Kong-China relationship today.[77] The contractual politics developed in these renegotiations between the center and the periphery provide, in Chin's vision, a virtual panacea for any and all problems. Chin's next goal was to be negotiating for full universal suffrage and a fair and open election for both the Legislative Council and the Chief Executive, followed by a Greater City-State Plan in which Hong Kong leases land from China that the city is then allowed to administer according to its own governance model, beginning from sections of Shenzhen and gradually expanding outward to Dongguan and eventually Huizhou in Guangdong Province.[78] These newest of new territories would provide Hong Kong with greater space, the city's rarest of resources, in order to continue development and even revitalize its industrial base, while at the same time affirming and exposing Guangdong residents to the strengths of Hong Kong's system.[79] Such newfound autonomy, furthermore, would insulate Hong Kong from the economic collapse of China and its inevitable rising conflict with the democracies of the world, developments that Chin Wan had been predicting for years. With plans like this, no one can question Chin's ambition, yet even sympathetic readers may question his practicality.

However unreal the conclusions of Chin's realpolitik reflections may be, the price that he has paid for his thought has been all too real. Chin was removed from his teaching post at Lingnan University in 2015 following warning letters from the university's president advising him to mind his words.[80] His 2016 Legislative Council bid, based on Eternal Basic Law, was eventually unsuccessful, losing in the New Territories East geographical constituency to, among others, the next generation of nationalists represented by Sixtus Baggio Leung of Youngspiration.[81]

The spirit of the city-state and Eternal Basic Law, however, lives on. Cheng Chung-tai of Civic Passion, another academic turned activist, won his 2016 Legislative Council election in New Territories East on a platform of Eternal Basic Law inspired by Chin's vision. In 2017 Cheng published a book together with Jonathan Kan titled *A Preliminary Discussion of Reforms to the Basic Law*, a detailed study of aspects of the Basic Law that could be revised to enhance legal protections for Hong Kong's way of life.[82] These include

> changing the term "capitalist lifestyle" used to describe Hong Kong's way of life in Article 5 to the more specific phrase "Hong Kong's pre-1997 lifestyle";[83]

drafting an anti-interference law to keep CCP money out of the political process and requiring local approval for the establishment of any PRC-run offices;[84]

legally requiring the maintenance of a surplus in healthy economic times while permitting deficit spending only during economic downturns;[85]

granting the Hong Kong Immigration Department veto power over one-way permits from China;[86]

recognizing permanent residents of the city as "citizens" (*gungmahn*) rather than just "residents" (*geuimahn*);[87] and

legally recognizing the official languages of Hong Kong as Cantonese (written in traditional characters) and British English.[88]

Cheng and Kan's book is a genuinely thought-provoking contribution to the discussion of Hong Kong's future. The main blind spot in these proposals, of course, is the need for the Chinese Communist Party to agree to any of them. Chin clearly has no problem assigning himself and his proposals such a grand world historical role, but the reality of the matter is considerably more uncertain: however compelling one's case might be, one cannot strike a grand bargain with a power that does not even acknowledge one's right to negotiate. Cheng Chung-tai, for example, was the last nonestablishment legislator remaining in the Legislative Council after the National Security Law, continuing to promote city-state theory and Eternal Basic Law within an increasingly repressive political environment, when he was finally disqualified by a new vetting body assessing all legislators' patriotism in August 2021. This raises the question: If the PRC government refuses to abide by the Basic Law as it currently stands, with the power of interpretation working completely in its favor, how can one expect it to abide by a renegotiated Basic Law that grants Hong Kong considerably more autonomy and thereby places considerably more restrictions on Beijing? If the PRC government cannot abide by internationally binding agreements like the Sino-British Joint Declaration, as it has demonstrated with increasing frequency since 2014, how can one place hope in this same government's abiding by a renegotiated relationship with Hong Kong within a hypothetical Federation of Chinese States? The end point of Chin's initial realpolitik intervention has shifted from imaginative proposals toward increasingly imaginary proposals crushed by the reality of broken promises and ever-escalating repression. Although Chin's city-state theory may have been left behind by history, the complete and utter destruction of the obstinate orthodoxies of the Hong Kong-China relationship brought about by his reliably unconventional mode of thinking has left a lasting legacy, sparking the productive imaginations of a new generation of activists.

SELF-DETERMINATION: AN UNREQUITED SOCIAL CONTRACT

As Chin underwent his metamorphosis from professor to city-state visionary to advocate for feudalism to proponent of Eternal Basic Law, his initial paradigm-shifting reassessment of Hong Kong-China relations opened the possibility of a taboo-free discussion of the city's political situation and future. Another proposal to emerge in this space is democratic self-determination for the people of Hong Kong as a nationality distinct from the people of China. This proposal first gained traction in a groundbreaking issue of *Undergrad*, the official journal of the Hong Kong Undergraduate Student Union, "Hong Kong Nationality, Self-Determination of Our Future" (*Heunggong mahnjuhk, mihngwahn jihkyut*), which was later republished in book form under the title *Hong Kong Nationalism* (*Heunggong mahnjuhk leuhn*).[89] While undoubtedly inspired by Chin's initial irreverent intervention, the authors went beyond Chin's vision of a Hong Kong city-state based in a lost Chinese tradition to envision instead a Hong Kong nationality distinct from China with the right to self-determination based in international law.

Brian Leung Kai-ping begins his introduction to the "Hong Kong nationality" collection by directly referencing Chin Wan's city-state idea, while at the same time immediately moving beyond it: "The most intensely debated concepts in Hong Kong over the past few years have been 'local consciousness,' 'city-state autonomy,' and 'ethnic identity.' These ideas have enabled us to begin developing new perspectives on our history, identity, and politics by envisioning Hong Kong as an independent and self-ruling entity. The Hong Kong people no longer see Hong Kong as just a borrowed place on borrowed time, but rather as a homeland with genuine and lasting roots."[90] Even just a few years after these words were first published, it is easy to lose sight of how daring they were in 2014, when open advocacy for self-determination was largely unheard of in Hong Kong. In his introduction, Leung acknowledges the still "politically incorrect" nature of Hong Kong nationalist thinking, while at the same time prophetically predicting its growing influence, citing local historian Eric Tsui's insight that once ethnic thinking emerges, such thinking cannot be easily taken back or erased. It forever transforms a people's perception of itself.[91]

The main innovation in Leung's brief introduction is his pushing the self-description of the Hong Kong community beyond the idea of "ethnicity (*juhk-kwan/zuqun*)" within a city-state employed by Chin Wan to the concept of "nationality (*mahnjuhk/minzu*)" which, Leung points out, evokes such ideas as equality among citizens, self-rule, and sovereignty.[92] China researchers familiar with the concept of *minzu* may not associate this term with these ideals, insofar as the country's ethnic politics have been characterized by false promises of "autonomy" providing the foundation for controlocratic micro-management and a language of multiculturalism providing a thin cover for Han-centric colonization. Yet Leung is of course not proposing that the Hong Kong people be recognized as a minority *minzu* by the bureaucrats of Beijing. Rather, Leung draws upon Liah Greenfeld's work on the relationship between nationalism and democracy to reappropriate the concept of nationality toward the goal of democratization in Hong Kong.[93] A bounded community with a clearly defined citizenry is a precondition for a genuine democratic politics, and such a genuine democratic politics in turn guarantees the preservation of this bounded community and its citizenry. As Leung concludes, "Before Hong Kong can make any progress toward democracy, the Hong Kong people's identity is a question that must be answered."[94]

The Undefined Community

Leung unfolds this relationship between nationalism and democracy in the issue's first article, wherein he examines the public reaction to the 2014 Court of Final Appeals ruling in *Kong Yunming v. Director of Welfare*. If only the very coolest of nationalists could be fired up by reading a newspaper, as Jonathan Rée has suggested in a critique of Benedict Anderson's theory of nationalism, who among us will feel the passions of nationalism surging through us while reading a court ruling?[95] The conscious choice of this unexpected starting point, however, renders explicit the logical foundations and implications of the self-determinationist vision.

In *Kong Yunming v. Director of Welfare*, an immigrant from China by the name of Kong Yunming applied for welfare in Hong Kong in 2006. Her application was denied because applicants under the Comprehensive Social Security Assistance Scheme were required at the time to have resided in Hong Kong for at least seven years before receiving assistance. Kong had only arrived four months earlier in 2005 on a one-way permit.[96] She chose to pursue legal action against this restriction, and in 2014 the Court of Final Appeals ruled in her favor, shortening the seven-year Hong Kong residency requirement to just one year. Estimates have suggested that the resulting expansion of welfare eligibility would necessitate an additional 800 million HKD in state expenditures.[97] Opinion polls, as a result, unsurprisingly showed that this ruling was deeply unpopular among the broader Hong Kong public, who would be footing the bill.[98]

Leung acknowledges that one could analyze this ruling through a financial lens, assessing whether the government would be able to handle these new expenditures. One could also analyze the ruling through a legal lens, assessing its soundness under common law.[99] Yet Leung points out that these factors in and of themselves cannot explain people's strong feelings about the ruling. Rather, the case has evoked such a strong response because it relates to basic matters of identity and rights: Who belongs to the Hong Kong community? Who, at the end of the day, is entitled to support from the rest of the community? And who decides?[100]

Leung himself mockingly predicts criticisms of his focus on new arrivals' welfare benefits: Isn't questioning the provision of social welfare benefits to new immigrants nothing more than discrimination against people from China? Might his reflections be the first sign of an incipient fascism in Hong Kong?[101] Might the exclusionary logics of PRC nationalism be reproduced in Hong Kong nationalism? This is the easiest argument to make on this topic in an academic mode. I would certainly know, as I have admittedly pursued similar lines of argument in two of the first articles that I wrote on the topic of Hong Kong nationalism.[102] Such near instinctive criticism, pointing out the seeming contradictions inherent in competing nationalisms, achieves the academic's social function of producing seemingly new information without having to put too much effort into thinking, while in drawing a moral comparison between these two nationalisms for the purposes of self-congratulatory political condescension, an author is reaffirmed as a lecturer in the moralizing sense of someone who literally lectures people on what they are supposed to think and do. It is the easiest possible exercise of academic capital: an article is written, new materials are processed and analyzed in a comforting and safe way, there is a perception of nuance despite the painfully obvious nature of the argument, and at the end of the day no one is likely to strongly disagree with or criticize one's analysis. Yet if we step out of the predictable reproduction of moralizing academic discourse, which often works against its stated goal of thinking, a real issue exists: supporting limits to welfare benefits or questioning the Hong Kong government's complete lack of control over immigration to the city via one-way permits from China is simply not realistically comparable to the type of xenophobic nationalism that Beijing deploys as a legitimizing ideology. So why, then, does it seem so easy to group them together?

Niklas Luhmann has observed that the easiest and thus most common way to classify and thereby appear to understand political matters is according to the progressive/conservative binary.[103] This binary maps easily onto the *Kong* case: welcoming immigration is progressive; openness to granting social welfare to new immigrants is also progressive and thus of course good. By contrast, questioning immigration policy is considered conservative at best, with a corresponding assumption of underlying racism. Questioning new immigrants' eligibility for social welfare assistance is, according to this binary, simply beyond the pale and approaching fascism.[104] Yet as Luhmann has pointed out, this coding within which the affairs of the world seem to fall naturally into place in fact makes matters fall a bit too easily into place, resulting less in actual understanding than in "extreme simplifications" of complex matters.[105]

In actual policy situations beyond these binary simplifications, Luhmann notes, "for the sake of preservation the conservative position may require that many changes are made. And the progressive position depends on preserving things the way they are, at least on preserving those structures and measures through which it wants to create change."[106] Precisely by right of its geographical setting and political fate, Hong Kong's reality requires a certain progressive conservatism or conservative progressivism in order to maintain its continued existence: it is a city with a higher standard of living and considerably stronger social services than the nation that rules over it, which one must note also has a population of at least 1.3 billion versus Hong Kong's seven million. Hong Kong is an already overcrowded city, with its infrastructure, medical services, and social services all existing under immense population pressures, which have only been further exacerbated by the increasingly rapid growth of tourism and immigration from China. Preservation of the city's social services, which should be universally recognized as a progressive endeavor, thus requires a more conservative approach to eligibility.

This is what people found most outrageous about the *Kong* ruling, Leung tells us: the seeming clarification of Kong's welfare eligibility only further blurred the boundaries of an already amorphous community, offering benefits without reciprocal obligations. This initial insult is further compounded by a second insult of this newly open welfare scheme's producing an endless supply of demands on the still legally limited community of taxpayers: a termless contract forcibly signed with only one party actually having any obligations. There is an evocative political metaphor in the figure of the new immigrant to Hong Kong, imposed on the community without consultation with its members, who demands benefits without the slightest consideration for obligations. In a case of political synecdoche, this new arrival comes to embody the unconstrained central government, forcing itself upon Hong Kong without consultation, ignoring public sentiment, and doing as it pleases without reference to its legally binding obligations under the Sino-British Joint Declaration and the Basic Law, all while of course ostensibly operating in accordance with the law, which it conveniently rewrites according to its whims. *Kong Yunming v. Director of Welfare* is thus the perfect introduction to the concept of self-determination, insofar as this case defining matters of identity, rights, and obligations metaphorically reveals the fate of Hong Kong as a community denied a say in determining its own boundaries and future: a nationality at once bound yet also wronged by the law.

A New Social Contract

Rather than the Hong Kong people abiding by yet also being wronged by the law as seen in the *Kong* case, the self-determinationist vision that grew out of this *Undergrad* issue recaptures the law as a means to give the Hong Kong people a say in their own future. In the final article in this collection, "Should the Hong Kong People Have the Right to National Self-Determination?," Jack Lee explicitly argues that by any reasonable definition the Hong Kong people constitute a nationality distinct from the people of China, and that they accordingly have the right under international law to determine the future of their own community.[107]

In his writing, Lee demonstrates a firm grasp of the latest research on the topic of ethnonational identity. Yet in making his argument for the Hong Kong people having the legal right to self-determination, Lee draws upon Joseph Stalin's antiquated four characteristics of a nationality: a common language, territory, economic life, and psychological makeup.[108] In terms of a common language, Lee convincingly cites the use of Cantonese, English, and traditional Chinese characters as distinguishing Hong Kong linguistically from China.[109]

In terms of a common territory, Lee sees Hong Kong's territory extending from the sea directly south of Hong Kong Island toward the border with Shenzhen in the north.[110] In terms of a common economic life, Lee cites the city's free market system, overseen by its common law legal system, as distinct from Beijing's vision of socialism with Chinese characteristics.[111] And in terms of a common psychological makeup, Lee openly acknowledges the difficulty of according any "common psychology" to the people of Hong Kong, yet from 1842 to the present, he notes, the people of the city have indeed had unique historical experiences that have produced a culture clearly distinct from that of the people of China.[112]

The Hong Kong people thus fully satisfy the conditions for recognition as a nationality, leaving just one lingering question: Why would one base the self-construction of one's national identity on an outmoded theory developed by, of all people, Stalin? The Stalinist framework for determining nationality is admittedly alluring in the blunt simplicity and misplaced confidence characteristic of such Marxist formulas: Stalin of course knew nothing about such issues, yet as the master planner and sole arbiter of all truths he nevertheless developed four supposedly objective characteristics through which one can exercise illusory mastery over the nationality question. The framework's simplifying appeal is given a further boost by the Hong Kong people's obvious satisfaction of all four requirements. Yet neither Lee nor newspaper columnist Joseph Lian Yi-zheng, from whom Lee borrowed these criteria, is a devotee of Stalin or of simplistic objectivism, and neither is prone to quoting Stalin in other contexts.[113] Reflecting on this curious use of sources, one might see a deeper level of critique in this rhetorical move, insofar as Lee is here deploying the Stalinist framework not only to construct a nationality, but also to construct this idea in opposition to the ethnonational constructions of a state that ostensibly relies on this very same framework. Certainly the Stalinist framework of nationality is stale and scientistic and difficult to take particularly seriously, yet there is at the same time a deep subversive joy in redeploying this stale framework, ostensibly applied by the Chinese Communist Party, against the Party's own tenuous constructions of Hong Kong as simply "Chinese." The choice of the Stalinist framework not only validates the Hong Kong people's status as a nationality, but also in the same moment invalidates the Party-state's own contradictory narrative of nationality. Lee's analysis is in this sense avowedly deconstructive, using the official language and logic of China's ethnic policy to explode its own ethnic framework.

There is, however, still another layer to this initially curious but symbolically rich turn in Lee's argument. While the Stalinist standards for a nationality provide evidence for a distinction between Hong Kong and China, and thereby invalidate the Party-state's own narrative of nationality, at the same time the Party-state's apparent inability to abide even by its own self-declared standards for recognizing a nationality reaffirms the distinction between Hong Kong and China already established by these standards, highlighting the distinct relationship to the law in the two nations analyzed therein. Utter disregard for the rules, manifested as well in the central state's relationship to the Basic Law analyzed in the previous chapter, is then a difference that makes a difference, reintroducing the distinction initially affirmed through the standards into the distinction that the standards themselves construct.[114] Because the Chinese Communist Party is even unable to abide by the supposedly objective standards through which it determines and thereby masters the existence of a nationality, Hong Kong's rule of law-based culture is reaffirmed as distinct from such arbitrariness.

In this legal difference that makes a difference, we also begin to see how other authors in this influential *Undergrad* collection trace the boundaries of a Hong Kong national community. The final version of these articles, published in book form under the title *Hong Kong Nationalism*, includes a new introduction by Keyvin Wong Chun Kit that explicitly bases Hong Kong nationalism in civic values.[115] In contrast to a racial nationalism based in ideas of blood and soil, Wong argues that "civic nationalism places its emphasis on maintaining the community's civic values, such as freedom and democracy, as well as free association."[116] The determining factor for belonging as a citizen of Hong Kong is then not one's race or ancestry, but rather acceptance of and adherence to the local values that distinguish Hong Kong's culture and history.[117] As a result, moving beyond the overly simplistic racialized constructions of one country as well as Stalin's dusty four characteristics of a nationality, Wong announces that "anyone who is willing to become part of Hong Kong can do so, regardless of their race or the color of their skin, so long as they identify with local civic values, are loyal to Hong Kong, and place Hong Kong's interests first."[118]

Just as Stalin's outdated standards for a nationality are redeployed to affirm a previously unrecognized Hong Kong nationality, so civic nationalism redeploys the law that marginalized the people of Hong Kong in the *Kong* case to affirm the same people's say in their own future. Lee points out that "in international society, nationalities have the right to form independent, sovereign nations," thereby recapturing the law as a tool for liberation rather than oppression.[119] This right to self-determination is featured prominently in the first article of both the International Covenant on Civil and Political Rights and the International Covenant on Economic, Social, and Cultural Rights: "All peoples have the right of self-determination. By virtue of that right they freely determine their economic, social, and cultural development."[120] Both of these international covenants have been ratified and are still in effect in Hong Kong, at least in theory.

Beyond these covenants, the United Nations has also maintained a list of non-self-governing territories entitled to self-determination in accordance with the 1960 General Assembly Resolution 1514: Declaration on the Granting of Independence to Colonial Countries and Peoples.[121] Hong Kong was featured on this list from 1946 to 1972, as it was a colony of the United Kingdom. Yet soon after the People's Republic of China entered the United Nations, the city was removed at Beijing's initiative without any discussion or debate, depriving the Hong Kong people of their right to self-determination.[122] As Carole Petersen points out in her analysis of the legal bases of self-determination claims, to assert that Hong Kong under British rule did not qualify for recognition as a colony (and thus does not qualify for self-determination) is really to stretch the limits of logical argumentation.[123] In the same sense that deploying the term "democratic," as in the phrase "the people's democratic dictatorship," does not actually make a dictatorship democratic, so removing Hong Kong from a list of internationally recognized colonies does not make the city any less of a colony, and thereby only obscures but does not erase the city's still unfulfilled right to pursue self-determination. Adherence to the law then not only serves as an example of the Hong Kong nationality's distinct civic values but also leads naturally to an affirmation of the Hong Kong people's right to put those same civic values into action through self-determination.

Jack Lee closes the final version of his essay in *Hong Kong Nationalism* by envisioning how these values can be fully realized via an open and legally binding referendum on the city's future:

> Today, as the framework of One Country Two Systems under the Basic Law approaches its breaking point with all progress toward democratization stalled indefinitely, granting our people a chance to make a decision via a referendum will make Hong Kong's future considerably clearer. Regardless of whether the final vote opts for independence or the continuation of One Country, Two Systems, the

future will be clearer. We may have missed our opportunity in the 1980s, but now in the 21st century we should be able to become the masters of our own fate.... The most pressing matter today is for the Hong Kong people to step out of our old mindset, recognize our own identity and our position on the global stage, and seek new possibilities for Hong Kong's future.[124]

Inverting the situation described in Leung's opening essay, wherein the law is binding yet also disempowering, self-determination envisions the Hong Kong people recapturing the law and using it for their own empowerment and freedom. Exercising the right to self-determination then becomes an exercise in civic values, which in turn manifests the Hong Kong community through a lasting social contract affirmed by the law: an outcome that the Hong Kong people as active participants in an engaged civil society deserve yet have been repeatedly denied.

The only question remaining is how to make this eminently reasonable proposal a reality within an increasingly unreasonable political and legal context.

A Law unto Itself

Self-determinationism's meticulously argued legal reasoning has made it one of the most influential schools of thought in the ongoing debate about Hong Kong's future, with advocates of this idea having made their way into the city's Legislative Council (albeit in most cases only very briefly) as well as being prominently represented in international media coverage of Hong Kong politics.

One of the more controversial organizations advocating self-determination was Youngspiration, whose Baggio Leung ran as a proxy for disqualified independence advocate Edward Leung in New Territories East in the 2016 Legislative Council election.[125] Youngspiration ran in the 2016 election on a platform of "Hong Kong nationality, self-determination of our future" (*Heunggong mahnjuhk, chihntouh jihkyut*), echoing the title of the aforementioned *Undergrad* issue. The influence of *Undergrad*'s work was further reaffirmed by Youngspiration's advocacy of civic nationalism, welcoming anyone who embraced Hong Kong's civic values as part of the Hong Kong nation. Youngspiration vowed to use its seats in the Legislative Council to promote national thought, building a solid foundation for a referendum on the city's future. This unofficial referendum, according to the group's proposal, would be held online in 2021, with the explicit goal of applying public pressure on the selection of the chief executive in 2022. In accordance with its embrace of civic values, Youngspiration promised to keep all options open in this referendum, including the full range of possibilities from independence to internal self-determination to the continuation of One Country, Two Systems to full integration with China.[126]

The 2016 Legislative Council election also witnessed the deployment of self-determinationist rhetoric by Lau Siu-lai of the Labor Party and Eddie Chu Hoi-Dick of the Land Justice League.[127] Yet the political party best known for advocating self-determination is undoubtedly Demosistō, which grew out of the anti-national education protest group Scholarism. Founded in 2016 and disbanded on June 30, 2020, Demosistō proposed replacing the outmoded idea of "democratic return" first criticized by Chin Wan with a vision of "democratic self-determination." The group's name, derived from Greek, means roughly "standing for the people" or alternately "standing for democracy," evoking the links between constituting a people and building democracy articulated by Brian Leung in his *Undergrad* introduction. Demosistō was home to such influential political figures as Joshua Wong and Agnes Chow, both of whom were leading figures in the Scholarism protests against national education and the 2014 Occupy protests, as well as Nathan Law, who briefly became the city's youngest legislator after winning a Legislative Council seat in the 2016 election representing Hong Kong Island. Wong, the subject of extensive global media coverage that has made him without a doubt the most recognizable figure in Hong Kong's youth protest culture, outlines what self-determination means to him in his book *Unfree Speech,* arguing that "self-determination is an established concept in international law and is a recognized human right in the United Nations International Covenant on Civil and Political Rights. But it was a new concept in Hong Kong."[128] Facing the same 2047 deadline for One Country, Two Systems that Chin Wan sought to resolve with Eternal Basic Law, Demosistō proposed a decade of discussion and debate on the city's future through the 2020s, leading to a referendum in 2030.[129] As with Youngspiration, in a demonstration of the party's embrace of civic values and commitment to the democratic process, all options for the city's future would be on the table in this referendum.

It is imperative to note that all of these proposals are fully in accordance with the Basic Law. In a 2019 article in the *Hong Kong Law Journal* examining the legal basis for Hong Kong self-determination, Carole Petersen argues that the Sino-British Joint Declaration and the Basic Law that governs Beijing's rule over Hong Kong originally had the potential to satisfy the requirements for internal self-determination, a form of self-determination internal to a nation-state that can still guarantee a people's rights when a competing territorial claim makes full self-determination impractical.[130] These founding documents granted the Hong Kong Special Administrative Region numerous powers of the type normally associated with an independent state, and most importantly, by guaranteeing civil and political rights along with the promise of universal suffrage in fair and open elections, promised the Hong Kong people the right to determine their own fate.[131] Had these guarantees been fulfilled, Hong Kong would have realized its own internal self-determination under Beijing's sovereignty, and there would accordingly be no need to advocate this ideal today.

The Hong Kong people's legal right to internal self-determination has however been unsurprisingly denied by the centralizing PRC state. In attempting to right this wrong, self-determinationists make recourse to the law, clearly demonstrating Hong Kong's unique culture relative to China, yet in this act also ironically reproducing the core dilemma: Beijing's complete refusal to abide by the law with regard to its commitments to Hong Kong. In a system that does not respect the power of the law to constrain those in power, working within the system to realize change is rarely rewarded; more often, it is a path to self-destruction. Rights lawyers in China, for example, who have laudably attempted to work peacefully within the current political and legal system to realize the rights promised to citizens in the country's constitution, have been met in reality with extralegal detention, torture, and even disappearance.[132] Similarly, self-determination advocates' mindful attention to working within the law has not spared them Beijing's wrath.

After winning Legislative Council seats via direct election in 2016, Baggio Leung and Yau Wai-ching of Youngspiration were removed from office for uttering vulgarities and pro-independence slogans while taking their oaths, setting a precedent for "disqualification" that subsequently led to the removal of Nathan Law of Demosistō for critical comments delivered prior to taking his oath.[133] Youngspiration largely disappeared from the Hong Kong political scene after these disqualifications. Demosistō by comparison remained active, but did not have an easier time participating in Hong Kong's political system. Agnes Chow was disqualified from a Legislative Council by-election in 2018 due to Demosistō's platform of self-determination.[134] The same excuse was used to disqualify Joshua Wong from the 2019 District Council elections.[135] Standing for democracy in Hong Kong today is not easy. Demosistō subsequently announced in January 2020 that it was dropping the call for democratic self-determination from its party platform.[136] Whether this change would have enabled full participation in elections is a moot point, insofar as the party itself disbanded immediately prior to the enactment of the National Security Law in late June 2020. Despite this disbandment, in August 2020, Agnes Chow was detained under the recently enacted National Security Law, and although currently out on bail in late 2021 still faces a number of serious charges. When I initially finalized this chapter for submission in September 2020, Baggio Leung was serving time in prison for attempting to enter the Legislative Council chambers after his disqualification, but as of late 2021 he has now served his time and fled to the United States, where he has called for stronger US sanctions against the Chinese and Hong Kong governments. As a globally recognized symbolic figurehead of one wing of the self-determination and protest movement, Joshua Wong's fate under the National Security Law was always uncertain; while this book's manuscript was under review, Wong was sentenced to thirteen and a half months in prison for a June 2019 protest outside of the city's police headquarters. While in prison on these 2019 charges, Wong was charged along with fifty-two others in January 2021 with violating the National Security Law for his participation in July 2020 pan-democratic primaries for the subsequently canceled 2020 Legislative Council election.

Just as Brian Leung's analysis of the *Kong* case summoned a revealing metaphor of a new arrival unbound by obligations, a similarly evocative metaphor can be found in the extralegal detention of activists calling for recognition of their legally guaranteed rights: both tell the story of Hong Kong today. And herein lie both the promise and the risk of the self-determinationist vision: abiding by the authorities' interpretation of the law in a context in which the authorities interpret the law such that they do not have to abide by the law tragically transforms the civic duty of lawfulness into perpetual compromise with authoritarian lawlessness, a very different and indeed destructive form of Eternal Basic Law.

The measured and meticulously argued reasoning behind self-determinationism thus remains at once its greatest source of appeal and its greatest weakness. There remains to this day no plausible timeline for the Hong Kong people to decide their own fate as supported by both local and international law: self-determination in the political context of Hong Kong today presents a promising yet perpetually unrequited social contract.

HONG KONG INDEPENDENCE

Anyone who has picked up this book about Hong Kong independence and read to this point will be relieved to learn that there are some activists who do in fact advocate this idea. Unlike city-state theory, Eternal Basic Law, or self-determination, Hong Kong independence is not a completely new idea: since at least the mid-2000s there have been websites and small anonymous groups promoting the city's independence. The introduction of this concept into mainstream political discussion is, however, very new. Prior to 2016, independence remained a decidedly fringe idea in Hong Kong, treated largely as taboo in polite political company. Small groups of protesters advocating independence were regularly ostracized as "CCP agents," suspected of using a toxic and impractical ideology to fracture the democracy movement, which consciously worked within the scope of the city's legally protected rights for progress toward the legally guaranteed endpoint of democratization.

We all know how that ended. To understand how independence transitioned from a largely fringe concept to a central topic in political debates, we need to turn again to *Undergrad*, which in September 2014 published an issue titled "Hong Kong, Democracy, Independence" (*Heunggong, mahnjyu, duhk-laahp*), reframing independence advocacy as the logical next step in Hong Kong's fight for universal suffrage.[137] Yuen Yuen-lung opens this collection of essays with a quotation from an unexpected source: pro-establishment politician James Tien. Defending the central government's 2014 control-focused political reform proposal, Tien had commented that genuine universal suffrage without prescreening of Chief Executive candidates "would be equivalent to Hong Kong independence."[138] For the many Hong Kong citizens who had been hoping and working peacefully for decades for genuine democratization and universal suffrage within the prevailing legal framework that ostensibly guarantees these final outcomes, this comment was rightly shocking, insofar as it treats the promised and legally guaranteed endpoint of Hong Kong's political reform, a fair and open vote, as just as unacceptable to Beijing as the most taboo of ideas: Hong Kong independence.

Yuen argues that the attempt to group legally guaranteed universal suffrage together with the forbidden idea of independence necessitates nothing less than the shattering of all taboos: independence advocacy can no longer be the third rail of Hong Kong politics from which the democracy movement must keep its distance.[139] After all, no matter how much distance you maintain from this concept for the sake of respectability and compromise, you will always already be labeled an independence activist, and your work within the law for legally guaranteed democratization will be placed outside the scope of respectability and even legality by Beijing. Hong Kong independence as an act of transgressing the confines of polite political activism and the law itself is in fact, Yuen tells us, the greatest fear of the central state and can thus no longer be a taboo for the democracy movement. Rather, it must become this movement's logical next step: "Unless our generation is willing to abandon our desire for democracy, we need to break the taboo on discussing independence, promoting the ideas of democracy and independence together, and shouting out 'democratic independence for Hong Kong!'"[140]

Between the moment Yuen wrote these words in the summer of 2014 and the moment that they were published that September, Beijing's August 2014 decision ruling out free and open elections in Hong Kong provided the strongest evidence yet for his argument. Decades of legal efforts and peaceful activism left, in the end, everything fundamentally unchanged. Any enthusiast of independence would have always known that an independent Hong Kong would need to be democratic; enthusiasts of democratization, Yuen tells us, needed to recognize that in order to be democratic, Hong Kong would need to be independent.

The Hong Kong National Party

A year and a half after the publication of this *Undergrad* collection, on March 28, 2016, a young man by the name of Andy Chan Ho-Tin walked up to a podium crowded with microphones, adjacent to a crimson red flag that read "Hong Kong National Party." Chan had called a press conference to announce the establishment of the Hong Kong National Party, the city's first political party openly calling for an independent Republic of Hong Kong. Introducing the party, Chan declared that the Hong Kong people needed to be awakened to their national consciousness; he asserted that the "Hong Kong colonial regime," which served the interests of China rather than Hong Kong, needed to be overthrown; he proposed independence as the only path forward for Hong Kong's future; and he announced that the Hong Kong National Party would embrace any and all effective forms of struggle against the city's occupiers.[141] At the end of Chan's introduction, photographers gathered around to snap photographs, with hundreds of flashes suddenly illuminating the scene. In a context in which radical changes in political thought were already occurring at lightning speed, this press conference and the ideas articulated therein still managed to be uniquely and daringly new.

The Hong Kong National Party was completely unlike anything that Hong Kong had seen previously and is also unlike anything that the city will likely see again in the near future. If, as Yuen Yuen-lung asserted, the increasingly dire political situation in Hong Kong necessitated breaking the democracy movement's taboo on discussing independence, the Hong Kong National Party seemed to relish every opportunity to shred this taboo beyond any chance of repair. Whereas city-state theory sought its foundations in a revitalized Chinese (*wah-hah*/*huaxia*) culture, and supporters of self-determination sought the foundations of freedom in the law, the Hong Kong National Party found its calling in overthrowing all preexisting foundations of culture and law and starting over. The National Party (1) explicitly modeled its work on the insights of revolutionary parties, (2) developed a comprehensive theory of Hong Kong nationalism, (3) applied the language and aesthetics of anticolonial struggle to the Hong Kong-China relationship, and (4) advocated the use of any and all means necessary to realize its goal of overthrowing the CCP and obtaining independence. Each of these features of the party and its politics is analyzed in turn here.

The Hong Kong National Party was explicitly modeled on earlier revolutionary parties, such as the Revolutionary Alliance or, admittedly somewhat ironically considering the current political environment, the Chinese Communist Party. While the Hong Kong National Party had two public faces in the form of its convenor, Andy Chan, and its spokesperson, Jason Chow, all other members were anonymous. This meant that, like the Revolutionary Alliance whose anonymous members infiltrated the Qing dynasty's New Army to initiate the 1911 Xinhai Revolution, members of the Party theoretically could never all be tracked down and detained at once. To maintain this anonymity, party members communicated primarily through the Telegram app, which would a few years later become the cornerstone of real-time anonymous organizing and information sharing in the 2019 anti-extradition protests.

The National Party furthermore promoted intellectual innovation to develop a complete theoretical system for Hong Kong independence. Similar to the role of *New Youth* in the New Culture Movement in China, the Hong Kong National Party journal *Comitium* provided a forum for open discussion and theory building. The editor's introduction to *Comitium* reads as follows:

The Hong Kong National Party is not only committed to overthrowing the Hong Kong communist colonial regime but is also looking ahead to envision life after the founding of the Republic of Hong Kong. This journal explores matters related to building and defending a Republic of Hong Kong, covering such topics as political organization, elections, national defense, diplomacy, social policy, welfare, education, livelihood issues, and other factors in the construction of an ideal republic. We also consider various means to push for the establishment of an independent Hong Kong, as well as developing political theory suited to Hong Kong's current situation. The Hong Kong National Party hopes that *Comitium* will guide everyone hoping to realize genuine change in Hong Kong society today by providing inspiring visions for our future, as well as guiding the people of the Hong Kong nation in making these ideals a reality. We welcome all to join this discussion, sharing your thoughts, and learning from one another. These ideas will eventually be put into practice, laying the foundations of our republic, and protecting the welfare of the Hong Kong nation and its future generations.[142]

These are admittedly high aspirations. Although *Comitium* only survived for little more than a year, with its third issue being considerably abbreviated and a fourth planned issue never seeing the light of day, the journal did in its brief existence cover an impressive breadth of topics in a way that has left a deep and lasting impression on how people talk about politics and ethnic identity in Hong Kong.[143]

Articulating an Anti-colonial Community

Comitium developed the most systematic theorization of Hong Kong nationalism of any of the schools of thought engaged in this ongoing discussion. Three articles on this topic from its first two issues demonstrate how this conversation developed and how *Comitium* provided an answer to the question initially posed by Brian Leung in his *Undergrad* introduction a few years earlier: the question of the Hong Kong people's identity.

In *Comitium*'s inaugural issue, an author writing under the pen name Kai Keih contributed an article titled "Disrupting China's Ever-Expanding Colonial Hegemony: Insights from Shih Shu-mei's Sinophone Theory."[144] Kai begins his discussion from a situation raised in chapter 1: the increasingly deeply felt conviction that "Hong Kong is not China" is increasingly commonly rebutted by cynical reference to Hong Kong citizens' Chinese heritage and use of "Chinese language and characters" as indications that they are undeniably "Chinese," and that Hong Kong is thus undeniably China.[145] This Chineseness is presented as a fact, beyond any possibility of change or even debate: insofar as one cannot simply stop speaking the language that one speaks or writing the characters that one writes, one then cannot by this logic stop being Chinese. Developing a rebuttal to this simplistic will to nationalist possession, Kai draws upon Sinophone theory, which in its rearticulation of various Chinese languages (so-called dialects) as "Sinitic" and their speakers as "Sinophone" rather than simply "Chinese," "disrupts the chain of equivalence established . . . among language, culture, ethnicity, and nationality."[146] Just as one can speak English in America and Australia or have a line of descent from people of British heritage anywhere around the world without owing loyalty to the United Kingdom, one can also be a Sinitic language speaker or have Chinese heritage without being Chinese. This is a jarringly simple yet also notably underappreciated fact obscured by the simplistic equation of language, race, and nationhood in the ideologies of the Chinese centralizing state.

Beyond questioning the burdensome assumptions of possessive Chineseness, Sinophone theory also breaks new ground by addressing the underexamined issue of Chinese imperialism. China is typically presented, both in its own national narratives and in academic theory, as a victim of Western imperialism. Yet the Chinese empire has historically been a colonizing power on the East Asian mainland and beyond and continues this colonizing Hancentric project in the modern era in (1) a territorial mode, targeting "minorities" within borders that the state inherited from the Qing empire, as well as in (2) an extraterritorial racial mode, targeting so-called overseas Chinese beyond China's borders regardless of their time abroad and self-identification.[147] Such racial colonization is apparent in the declaration that Hong Kong is "Chinese," yet is also obscured by the state cult of pan-Chinese victimization, which ideologically eludes differences and conflict among those labeled Chinese while overemphasizing difference and conflict across the constantly ideologically reinforced Chinese-foreign binary. The establishment of the colony of Hong Kong, which provided the opportunity for millions to live a better life, is presented as a moment of national shame because "foreigners" were involved, while the establishment of the Hong Kong Special Administrative Region, which has enabled Beijing to repress the city's political and cultural dynamism, is presented as a redeeming conclusion to this humiliation via a false racial unity. For Kai, the novel perspectives developed in Sinophone theory break the false equation between Sinitic linguistic heritage and racial identity that provide the basis for PRC claims of natural sovereignty over all whom it imagines to be Chinese, as well as deconstructing the state narrative of eternal victimization that obscures China's own acts of imperialism in Tibet, Xin-jiang, Hong Kong, and beyond.[148]

Having differentiated a Hong Kong nation from a colonizing Chinese-ness, party spokesperson Jason Chow (the only author contributing under his real name) proceeds in "Constructing the Hong Kong Nationality" in the same *Comitium* issue to articulate the distinct historical path of and future prospects for this nationality.[149] Whereas *Hong Kong Nationalism* based its discussion of self-determination on a Stalinist framework that primarily did the symbolic work of invalidating the central Party-state's contradictory nationality theory, Chow draws explicitly upon constructionism to argue that nationalities are the self-constructing products of both objective and subjec-tive elements. In his words, "Nations are not eternal realities. The essence of a nation is the product of both subjective and objective economic, cultural, and political processes. A nation can be born from gradual changes over a lengthy historical period, and the conditions of its formation can also be consciously or unconsciously produced."[150] In the gradual process of refining a theory of a Hong Kong nation, we move here beyond Chineseness, and even beyond a one-dimensional checklist of national characteristics (and its deconstruction), to a dynamic, historically informed vision of a nation constructed in the inter-action between objective conditions and subjective identifications.

For Chow, the objective condition that initiated the still largely unrecog-nized self-construction of a Hong Kong nationality was the official establish-ment of Hong Kong in 1841.[151] Chow's brief history of the colony presents the Sinophone people resident there as gradually developing their own culture, life-style, and history "in organic interaction" with the social institutions, political and legal systems, and customs of their British colonizers.[152] These subjective interactions with objective conditions produced a culture and society that were influenced by yet also distinct from Great Britain, while also being notably distinct from the Chinese nation taking shape to the north, where social and cultural production was a matter of central planning.[153] The product of these experiences was thus a society and culture uniquely Hong Kong's own.

Although one can trace the origins and history of a nationality, Chow argues that nationalities are always dynamic, living processes without any final point of completion: the future is always open. The only precondition for this openness, Chow argues, is that a nationality must be in control of its own fate: "A nationality's development can only be overseen by itself.... Only the Hong Kong people can build their own nation."[154] Such openness and inconclusiveness can in turn only be guaranteed by correspondingly open and inconclusive political and cultural institutions that allow people to have a regular say in directing their own future; nation-building and democratization are thus one and the same. By this logic, the central government is not only denying the Hong Kong people a say in their political process by denying the territory democracy; China is in fact, in Chow's analysis, manipulating the open process of identity formation in Hong Kong to realize its own prede-termined and closed vision.[155] In the name of national integration, increasing economic reliance on China, large-scale immigration from China, the promo-tion of Mandarin Chinese, and the increasingly widespread use of simplified characters are all examples of Beijing's colonizing attempts to exercise control over what should be an open and always incomplete process.[156] Quenthai, another contributor to *Comitium*, argues that Hong Kong has in fact been doubly colonized since 1997, with conventional territorial colonization supple-mented by ideological colonization in the concepts of "pan-Chineseness" and Chinese victimization, leaving the majority of residents fundamentally unable to recognize colonizing processes as such.[157] An important part of recapturing control of Hong Kong's fate, Chow argues, is recognizing this colonization, articulating it, and then resisting it.[158]

In the second issue of *Comitium*, Quenthai articulates how such resis-tance can in fact contribute to the process of identity formation in "A Cri-tique of *Hong Kong Nationalism* from an Anti-colonial Perspective."[159] Quenthai begins by expressing his support for the vision proposed in *Hong Kong Nationalism*, the book developed from the influential 2014 *Under-grad* issue, which he lauds as the most sophisticated school of nationalist thought in Hong Kong.[160] Yet precisely because of its sophistication and its corresponding potential for advancing Hong Kong's political development, Quenthai argues that this framework needs to be improved by criticism and reflection, modeling therein the open-ended nature of nation building artic-ulated by Chow.[161]

Quenthai focuses his critique of *Hong Kong Nationalism* on its deployment of "civic nationalism," a concept originally inspired by Ernst Renan, developed by Anthony Smith, and given one of its most sustained treatments in Rogers Brubaker's comparative study of national identities in *Citizenship and Nation-hood in France and Germany*.[162] To provide an extremely brief summary of Brubaker's argument, he posits that notions of national belonging in Germany are based in ethnic or racial ideas, whereas notions of belonging in France are based in identification with civic values. The former is representative of ethnic nationalism, while the latter is representative of civic nationalism. Although Brubaker was making a broader argument in his analysis about the challenges presented to European integration by contending visions of citizenship—an argument with useful insights for the conflicted integration of Hong Kong into China—the main lesson often taken away from these concepts is that ethnic nationalism is dangerous and exclusionary, while civic nationalism is considerably less so. Although the theoretical distinction of particular national types of belonging may not be quite so absolute in reality, in practice this binary preemptively does the work of constructing an obvious good/bad framework within which commentators forced to acknowledge the nation-state as the current mode of organization around the world, a mode of organization unlikely to fade away anytime soon, can comfortably place themselves on the "right" side of nationalism.[163]

Quenthai, however, argues that this safe analytical concept of civic nationalism with its abstract values is completely impotent for progressing toward the endpoint that he envisions: the awakening of national consciousness and the establishment of a Republic of Hong Kong.[164] If, as Benedict Anderson noted while examining the "colossal sacrifices" of recent centuries, the core conundrum raised by nationalism is precisely how people become willing to die for a nation, it is worth remembering Heidegger's parallel observation that "no one dies for mere values."[165] The eagerness to promote civic nationalism over ethnic nationalism apparent in *Hong Kong Nationalism* is then in Quenthai's analysis a preemptive critique of a potential mistake in the necessary event of establishing a nation that has not yet occurred and toward which this overly eager critique provides no clear path.[166] Civic nationalism is then not the key to Hong Kong's future, Quenthai argues, but rather a residual concept, meaning that its primary function is in stating what it is not: it is, primarily, a declaration that citizenship and belonging are not to be defined racially.[167] Yet in declaring what it is not, civic nationalism fails to provide a clear articulation of how these concepts are to be defined and thus how Hong Kong might break out of its current political dilemma; civic values are far too vague and amorphous to mobilize people for the cause of nation building.[168]

Readers may have begun to note that a defining characteristic of the Hong Kong nationalist discussion is always taking an argument one step further than expected, and Quenthai does so by positing that civic nationalism would be insufficient not only for nation building but even for defending the city's freedoms in an established Hong Kong republic. Insofar as civic nationalism is a residual concept, it is also in many senses an empty signifier: powers with influence in society can promote their particular visions to fill in the blanks of these civic values.[169] Quenthai sees a particular risk with regard to the concept of "Chineseness," which Sinophone theory shows is a mode of identification that equates language, culture, and national sovereignty in a colonizing mode. Whereas the perceived "Chineseness" of Hong Kong has played a central role in obscuring the colonial nature of Beijing's rule over the city, this concept would again, by right of the city's heritage and the powers promoting this idea, inevitably find a place among the civic values defining belonging in a Hong Kong republic.[170] Yet this eternal return of Chineseness would thereby reintroduce one of the core anchoring points of Chinese colonization within the Hong Kong nationalist project, reinforcing rather than overcoming the city's subjugation.

Civic nationalism's residual nature thus makes it insufficient for the cause of nation building, and its potential openness to recolonizing concepts would also be insufficient for maintaining independence in the aftermath of the founding of a republic.[171] Yet how, then, are citizenship and belonging to be constructed? How can the goal of building and defending a nation be realized while at the same time maintaining a reasonable distance from racial nationalism, which would after all be inconsistent with Hong Kong's multiethnic and multicultural society?

Quenthai here retheorizes the open process of national identity formation articulated by Chow from an anti-colonial perspective, combining in this process elements of both ethnic and civic nationalism, which he reimagines not as mutually exclusive opposite types but rather as complementary and indeed equally integral components of any nationalism.[172] First, the ethnic element of Quenthai's anti-colonial nationalism is found in collectively recognizing the People's Republic of China as a colonizing other that oppresses and threatens Hong Kong's distinct culture and way of life.[173] Insofar as ethnic identity is constructed relationally across a boundary, ethnicity here is initially formed in reinterpreting the PRC's political, economic, and cultural policies as an other, seeing its rule as colonial, and thereby constructing a Hong Kong identity in explicit opposition to this other and its rule.[174] Within such a colonial context, Quenthai asserts, ethnic nationalism and anti-colonial resistance are two sides of the same coin: one cannot realize the goal of nation building without resisting the other's colonial oppression, and one cannot truly bring an end to such colonial oppression without working toward building a nation independent from the other.

This shift toward an ethnic nationalism, however, also does the necessary work of clarifying the amorphous concept of civic nationalism. Civic values are, in Quenthai's analysis, concretized in the process of resisting colonization, constructing what he calls an "anti-colonial community" fusing ethnic boundary thought with civic values.[175] The process of resisting colonial oppression develops a communal experience of recapturing basic freedoms denied, thereby producing and consolidating a community dedicated to protecting these freedoms and resisting the other taking them away: a particularly prescient argument, in the light of the anti-extradition protests of 2019.[176] The experience of anti-colonial resistance then not only contributes to the construction of a republic founded in concrete national identity and civic values, but will also make these ideas salient as objects of potential loss, thereby enabling their lasting defense after the future establishment of a Republic of Hong Kong.

Comitium, the journal of the Hong Kong National Party, thus made significant progress in its short life span toward a considerably more nuanced theorization of the idea of a Hong Kong nation than any previous contributions to this discussion. Rebutting the simplistic equation of Chinese language, culture, and nation that entrapped Hong Kong as naturally Chinese, the Hong Kong nation is instead revealed as an open process developing in dialogue with both objective and subjective elements.[177] The key matter is to ensure that the people of this nation exercise control over these open processes through correspondingly open political and cultural institutions, a control that is notably lacking in post-1997 Hong Kong.[178] Reclaiming such control through anti-colonial resistance will not only facilitate independent nation building but will also, by providing a foundation for communal ethnic identity and civic values of resistance, help to maintain this independence.[179] By developing a comprehensive theory of Hong Kong nation building, drawing upon the dual processes of logically analyzing the prevailing political situation and provocatively expanding the boundaries of politically acceptable speech, the Hong Kong National Party's Comitium journal built a new foundation for reimagining Hong Kong's future.

By Any Means Necessary

What does "anti-colonial resistance," the term employed by Quenthai in his Comitium article, actually mean? Which modes of resistance are effective and ethically acceptable, and which are not? These were without a doubt the most controversial of the many very controversial questions raised by the Hong Kong National Party, and the answers developed in the resulting dialogue have left an indelible mark on Hong Kong's protest culture.

There was from the start something aesthetically striking about the Hong Kong National Party and its unrestrainedly resistant style that is nearly impossible to put into words: the dark crimson flags fluttering in the wind, one after another, at the party's politically contentious weekend street stands; the jarring slogans including "Hong Kong independence" and "freedom from Chinese colonizers" plastered across retro-style posters and echoing off the city's endless rows of skyscrapers; the calm and quiet outrage of its gatherings; and even the blunt brevity of its social media presence, responding with an inimitable and unforgettable combination of placid calm and utter contempt to each attempt by the local government to suppress its activities. There was a certain aesthetic of pure unapologetic resistance that, particularly when combined with the party's daringly unrestrained disdain for conventional activism, embodied a completely novel and hopefully revolutionary vision of Hong Kong politics and indeed identity.

The jarring novelty of this aesthetic style was reflected in the party's new and often controversial modes of spreading the word of independence. For example, soon after its formation the National Party announced its "middle school political enlightenment scheme," citing a quotation from Liang Qichao's "Young China" (also quoted in Xi Jinping's *Governance of China*, vol. 1): "If the youth are strong, the country will be strong; if the youth are independent, the country will be independent; if the youth are free, the country will be free."[180] Hong Kong National Party members stood outside middle schools at the end of the school day, handing departing students flyers promoting Hong Kong independence, so as to help them "understand the necessity of Hong Kong independence and the conditions required to realize this goal."[181] This program also promoted the establishment of underground Hong Kong National Party branches in middle schools across the city. After years of baseless accusations from the establishment camp about students in the city being indoctrinated with foreign liberal thinking that denied their Chinese roots, the National Party openly went to the gates of eighty schools across Hong Kong to promote the most taboo of political ideas directly to students. Giving voice to the shock value inherent in such political activity, one school principal interviewed by *Mingpao* simply commented that "their targeting these kids is immoral."[182]

Returning to James Tien's comments equating the legally guaranteed end-point of democracy and the taboo of Hong Kong independence from which Yuen Yuen-lung's 2014 reflections on independence began, there is a certain transgressive power to be found in refusing to play safe and proactively doing that which one's opponents will after all accuse one of doing anyway. This logic is again apparent in the National Party's decision to join hands with other critics of PRC imperialism globally, contributing to the construction of an international anti-colonial alliance with Hong Kong as one of its core members. After decades of false allegations of collusion between Hong Kong activists and "overseas anti-China forces," the National Party proactively embraced the opportunity to work with said overseas anti-China forces. Andy Chan and Jason Chow traveled on multiple occasions to Taiwan, where they explicitly evoked Taiwan's model of an independent nation resisting Chinese invasion as worthy of emulation by Hong Kong.[183] Chan traveled to Japan to discuss the establishment of a Free Indo-Pacific Alliance, including representatives from Mongolia, East Turkestan, Tibet, Taiwan, India, Japan, and Vietnam, forming a coalition of countries under Chinese occupation (or the threat thereof) for the explicit goal of defeating the Chinese Communist Party.[184] Rather than basing Hong Kong's future on its reliance upon China, the Hong Kong National Party explicitly reversed these assumptions to reimagine the city's future as the cornerstone of an international alliance against PRC colonization.

One of the most controversial policies pursued by the Hong Kong National Party was its repeated appeals for the United States to revoke the Hong Kong Policy Act: a step that was taken in July 2020 as this manuscript was being finalized.[185] The 1992 Hong Kong Policy Act mandated the treatment of post-1997 Hong Kong as an independent tariff region distinct from China for trade purposes, exempting the city from various tariffs and restrictions on the transfer of technologies to which the People's Republic of China is subject. These exemptions were explicitly premised on the continuation of Hong Kong's pre-1997 system of rule of law, judicial independence, and other robust rights protections after 1997. The People's Republic of China did not fulfill its promises in this regard, but for years the United States did little more than express the usual concerns about the city's diminishing autonomy. The Hong Kong National Party began to change this dynamic in August 2017, when Andy Chan penned a letter to the US Consulate General in Hong Kong, requesting the cancellation of the city's special status under the Hong Kong Policy Act in response to China's repeated infringements of the city's autonomy. Chan delivered the letter in person to representatives at the consulate, followed by a crowd of journalists filming the entire spectacle. In August 2018, Chan wrote another letter directly to US president Donald Trump requesting the cancellation of the Hong Kong Policy Act and the enforcement of sanctions against both the Chinese and Hong Kong governments.[186]

The idea of a political party calling for its own territory and government to be sanctioned by another may at first seem puzzling but becomes considerably more legible when one recognizes that the boundary-building processes within this exercise thereby label the government to be sanctioned as not in fact one's own. Highlighting the deep ironies of the accelerating unraveling of One Country, Two Systems, those who hoped for a Hong Kong distinct from China in the future argued that the United States needed to treat Hong Kong today as part of China, facing the same sanctions and trade restrictions. Meanwhile, establishment figures who considered Hong Kong to be an eternal and inalienable part of China argued that the United States in fact needed to treat the city as distinct from China. Activists who envisioned a future Hong Kong separate from China wanted the United States to declare that Hong Kong is China and treat it accordingly, while establishment figures who argue that Hong Kong always has been and always will be part of China wanted the United States to continue to treat Hong Kong differently from China.

Yet of all of its boundary-shattering innovations in political thought and activism, the National Party's most controversial legacy is undoubtedly its insistence on endorsing any and all forms of effective resistance against what it called the "Hong Kong colonial regime," an approach first articulated by Andy Chan at the press conference announcing the party's establishment.[187] The party's public statements on this topic were always brief and vague for understandable legal reasons, alluding only to the need to move beyond the notably ineffective modes of resistance that had been employed in recent decades, a point highlighted in Lewis Loud's article discussed in the preceding chapter. In the second issue of *Comitium*, however, in "The Use of the Useless: On Civil Disobedience," a National Party member writing under the pen name Jilaahn Yuhngyihp developed the most systematic theorization of the use of force in Hong Kong's anti-colonial resistance.[188]

Jilaahn Yuhngyihp begins by stating that civil disobedience, in his interpretation, takes peaceful protest to its most confrontational extreme: civil disobedience as a method is located in between peaceful demonstrations and violent revolution, attempting to force concessions from the state.[189] Yet such measures, according to the author, can only work in a society that is imperfect (and thus in need of change) yet also nearly just (and thus able to be pressured to change).[190] Hong Kong under PRC rule certainly fits the bill of an imperfect society that would benefit from a change in the relationship between state and society. Yet, the author adds, Hong Kong is not a nearly just society. Nearly just, he clarifies, means a society that either has a fully democratic system or robust constitutional protections for civil rights.[191] If civil disobedience could be imagined as an antibiotic against state abuses, it can provide a cure for mild cases with the support of a robust immune system of democratic accountability and legal constitutionalism. Yet in severe cases without these immune supports, the state simply builds up antibiotic resistance, decreasing both the frequency and the extent of its concessions and boosting the strength of its abuses, responding to the nonviolent confrontation of civil disobedience with escalating violence.[192]

There is indeed a lengthy and laudable tradition of nonviolent civil disobedience realizing meaningful change in societies around the world; there is, however, also a lengthy tradition of nonviolent civil disobedience failing to realize any change under CCP rule. How are the people of Hong Kong supposed to use their moral strength, and only their moral strength, to realize freedom and democracy in a struggle with a regime that looks down on moral strength? How can one be nonviolent with a state that does not hesitate to use the most extreme and cruel forms of violence against people exercising their constitutionally guaranteed rights? The use of civil disobedience's uselessness, according to Jilaahn Yuhngyihp, is its serving as a wake-up call to Hong Kong civil society of the need for more forceful means of resistance.[193] The author's analysis foreshadows discussions and tactical shifts that unfolded in the protest movement of 2019 and are likely to become a lasting legacy in an increasingly repressive Hong Kong.[194]

Although the Hong Kong National Party was disbanded in September 2018, a little more than two years after its founding, its effects on Hong Kong politics and the city's struggle against Beijing's continually escalating control remain apparent. A genuine diversity of independence-supporting groups has emerged in the wake of the Hong Kong National Party's demise. One prominent group was the Students' Independence Union led by Wayne Chan, who played a significant role in protests against the extradition proposal in 2019 before fleeing into exile in June 2020. Another was Studentlocalism, founded by Chan's friend Tony Chung, who was detained under the National Security

Law soon after its passage.[195] In November 2021 as this book went to press, Chung pled guilty to charges of secessionism. Facing a potential sentence of life in prison, after announcing his plea Chung calmly added, "I have nothing to be ashamed of." The Chinese and Hong Kong governments have been particularly aggressive in suppressing the independence wing of the Hong Kong nationalist movement, banning parties, arresting prominent advocates, and handing out lengthy prison sentences. Yet in their eagerness to silence these activists, they have ironically provided the best evidence yet to support these activists' main thesis: that the city's freedom was always already doomed under Chinese rule.

RETURNISM: PARTY LIKE IT'S 1997

On July 1, 2017, the twentieth anniversary of Hong Kong's handover, two people initially standing in silence outside the pro-Beijing "Space Dreams" celebratory display in Victoria Park were suddenly surrounded by more than a dozen journalists snapping photos. One waved an oversized British flag back and forth in the oppressively still summer heat. The flag sagged despondently whenever he paused, unable to rely on any hope of a breeze for support. Another held a banner that read "celebrate the 119th anniversary of the British extension to the New Territories," referring to the Convention between the United Kingdom and China Respecting an Extension of Hong Kong Territory, signed on July 1, 1898. Below this, with a map of Hong Kong emblazoned with the British flag, the banner read: "The Chinese outrageously breached the Sino-British Joint Declaration. Resume British sovereignty over Hong Kong." The banner identified the two lone protestors as members of the Hong Kong-UK Reunification Campaign, which promotes Hong Kong's reunification not with China, but rather with the United Kingdom.

Speaking briefly with the protesters before they walked away, I asked why they had chosen this cause. One responded that she felt a deeper cultural tie to the United Kingdom than to China. When I enquired about how they might envision Hong Kong rejoining the United Kingdom, the other protester told me that because China had repeatedly breached the Sino-British Joint Declaration, and because the Joint Declaration is an international treaty governing Hong Kong's handover that has been registered at the United Nations, the question of Hong Kong's fate was no longer solely for China to decide: this was an international matter that needed to be handled in accordance with international law. As they began to walk away to another engagement, I asked how people on the streets generally responded to their protests. They told me "some people agree with us but are afraid to say so in public. Many other people just think we are crazy."

This exchange raises an unexpected question: Why would anyone promote the idea of Hong Kong's recolonization by the United Kingdom? The political phenomenon that I here label returnism is a thought-provoking example of Hong Kong nationalism, taking provocation against Chinese nationalist doctrine to completely new levels, while at the same time combining the cultural, legal, and revolutionary logics of the preceding three schools of thought (city-state theory, self-determination, and independence) into one highly unlikely but also uncannily reasonable proposal, revealing the unreal nature of reality under One Country, Two Systems.

Culture and Colonization

Returnists promote a novel interpretation of culture and colonization, arguing that Hong Kong today in fact has considerably more in common culturally with the United Kingdom than with China.[196] The fact that this statement requires such effort to think through and understand is a powerful testament to the ideological influence of pan-Chinese racial nationalism on our assumptions. For returnists, a core cultural legacy of Hong Kong's colonization by the United Kingdom is its existence as an internationalized and multicultural city that is open to multiple cultures, religions, and political stances. Such openness can be seen in the city's language, music and film, and cuisines, often described as "hybrid," as well as in its rule of law system and respect for freedom and human rights.[197] These are all healthy legacies of Hong Kong's colonial era, and this positivity and the resulting cultural affinity produced within the colonial process are of course where things start to become complicated.

In academia, the discourse on colonialism is reliably flattened into little more than total denunciation. Bruce Gilley's 2017 article "The Case for Colonialism," highlighting "significant social, economic and political gains under colonialism," was clearly designed as a provocation against this flattening discourse, and it certainly succeeded in this regard by becoming the target of two petitions calling for its withdrawal from *Third World Quarterly* and eventually triggering the collective resignation of fifteen members of the journal's board.[198] Beyond all the hype, however, Gilley made at least one significant contribution by highlighting the ubiquity and persistence of a singular "colonialism bad" discourse.[199] Yet Gilley's counterconstruction of a "colonialism good" discourse did not succeed in significantly enriching the discussion; it strikes me more as a counterprovocation overlooking the complexity inherent within the sheer diversity of colonial situations. The point should be, then, to think through the complexity of situations in which the good can arise even from the bad; the twentieth century, after all, has amply demonstrated how reliably the bad can arise from ostensibly good intentions.[200]

A comparative analysis of lived political experiences of colonization and ostensible noncolonization may then facilitate moving beyond simplistic labeling and attendant moralizing, or perhaps beyond simplistic moralizing and attendant labeling. If we consider Hong Kong's history exclusively through its binary relationship with the United Kingdom, there were undoubtedly grave injustices in the colonial era that no reasonable person can deny: the ban on people of Chinese descent living on the Peak, or the long-standing failure to implement full democracy.[201] Yet such a perspective fails to explain why people in China proactively chose to flee their homes to move to a colonial state and willingly become colonial subjects, nor does it explain the widespread feeling of anxiety about the end of British rule in the 1980s and 1990s.[202] Such phenomena can only be understood through a tripartite comparison that also considers the political and socioeconomic context in China. In comparison to China at the time, the colonial system in Hong Kong, despite its injustices, nevertheless endowed residents with considerably more rights and freedoms than those available to citizens of China, who ostensibly lived beyond colonization yet in fact faced a considerably greater degree of unjustifiable domination, which continues to this day.[203] This stark reality also explains the anxieties surrounding Hong Kong's handover in 1997: the cultural legacies of openness and tolerance are precisely what citizens of Hong Kong have hoped to preserve, as well as being precisely what Beijing seems increasingly determined to erase.

If a "colonialism bad" perspective cannot represent the full complexity of Hong Kong's history, returnists also argue that a counterdiscourse describing Chinese rule as "colonial" makes the mistake of flattening distinct colonial regimes under a single descriptor. Returnists see the former remote metropole of London facilitating the expansion of freedom, rights, and rule of law in the city, while also taking an increasingly hands-off approach to the management of local affairs over the course of the colony's history. Returnists then contrast this model of rule with that of another considerably more proximal metropole, joined by an assumed racial-cultural link, which has only ever taken an increasingly interventionist and controlling approach against the liberalizing trends fostered by the former. The point here is that the Chinese colonization of Hong Kong is not simply a "continuation" of the pre-1997 colonial situation, as a singular discourse of colonization would suggest. Rather, these are two vastly different colonial metropoles, and a significant part of the problem with Chinese colonization in the eyes of returnists is precisely that China has not continued the United Kingdom's colonial style.[204] Chinese nationalist narratives casually ostracize such observations as a certain slavishness to the foreign, but they are in many senses simply a reflection of lived political realities.

Returnists thus highlight the multidimensional nature of colonization's effects on culture. First, colonization is not in all cases simply and uniformly bad, as it is precisely in the process of colonization that Hong Kong was able to develop a culture that respects human rights, personal freedoms, and multiculturalism distinct from the oppressive political culture in the People's Republic of China. Second, returnists emphasize that not all colonization is created equal: China's rule over the city since 1997, according to returnists, is in fact considerably more colonial in the sense of "bad" than British colonial rule ever was, insofar as this rule is attempting to introduce an oppressive foreign political culture into Hong Kong. One could then say that Hong Kong's freedoms have been fostered as well as destroyed by colonization. Rather than Gilley's inversion of the standard discourse of bad colonization in an attempt to recapture the "good" therein, a comparative perspective that recognizes the multidimensional experiences of colonization, as well as the diversity of regimes incorporated under this label, provides a more fruitful approach for thinking through colonization's legacies and working through its aftermaths or continuations.

The Legal Argument for Returnism

Returnists are not, as a standard and unimaginative reading would suggest, simply arguing for the "recolonization" of Hong Kong. Rather, they are arguing for the revitalization of the political, social, and cultural systems that the people of Hong Kong built under British rule and with which they feel a greater sense of identification compared to Chinese rule.[205] Foremost among these systems is Hong Kong's legal system, which in its general soundness (at least, until 2020) diverges sharply from the legal system in China even today, four decades into the overhyped process of reform and opening. As we saw earlier in this chapter, the law formed the cornerstone of the self-determinationist vision, providing an orderly and legally sound path for the people of Hong Kong to have a say in their own future: a path to nationhood that at the same time highlighted the distinct cultural features of this nation. Returnism pursues a similar albeit different legal path to Hong Kong's self-determination, developing a novel legal argument that is in many respects, despite its unlikely nature, surprisingly coherent.

This path begins from the Sino-British Joint Declaration, a legally binding international treaty between the United Kingdom and the People's Republic of China, signed in December 1984 and registered with the United Nations in 1985. The Joint Declaration is designed to manage Hong Kong's handover to China and China's subsequent administration of the city, guaranteeing Hong Kong "a high degree of autonomy" with "executive, legislative, and independent judicial power, including that of final adjudication."[206] The declaration explicitly prevents China from interfering in the territory's freedom of speech, press, assembly, association, and academic research: Hong Kong's systems are, according to this declaration, to remain unchanged for a period of fifty years, extending until 2047.[207] As Carole Petersen notes, the Sino-British Joint Declaration is a robust agreement that provides all the conditions necessary for Hong Kong to realize genuine self-rule.[208] The only issue with any agreement of this type is whether it would in fact be implemented as promised. Unfortunately, any reasonable reading of the first two decades of the twenty-first century can only conclude that the People's Republic of China has not honored this promise.

Because the Sino-British Joint Declaration provided the legal foundation for Hong Kong's handover to and rule by China, and because China has been repeatedly in open breach of this internationally recognized legal agreement, returnists call on the United Kingdom to request a UN review of the Joint Declaration's implementation.[209] A major shortcoming of this plan is that the United Kingdom will most likely never do this. Yet one returnist has told me, in a statement that succinctly summarized the hopefully imaginative nature of the many discussions reviewed in this chapter, that if one is going to be caught up in the fact that this is an unlikely scenario, then one might as well simply give up, sit back, and watch the most likely scenario of Hong Kong's complete disintegration unfold. Setting aside one's doubts momentarily, one can say with a fair degree of certainty that should such a review be held by the United Nations, the only reasonable conclusion would be that China has violated the Joint Declaration on multiple occasions. And as a result of these breaches, the

Sino-British Joint Declaration would be judged to be no longer valid, a conclusion that, according to returnists, would mean a return to the status quo as of June 30, 1997: the resumption of UK rule over Hong Kong, which was after all to continue "in perpetuity" on Hong Kong Island and Kowloon (excluding the ninety-nine-year lease on the New Territories) according to the Treaty of Nanking (1842) and the Convention of Peking (1860).[210]

Scholars of international relations and international law may comment in more depth on the overall legal soundness of this proposal. Yet as a scholar of political thought and social movements, I must give returnists credit for having one of the most detailed plans for resolving the city's current dilemma of any of the new schools of political thought in Hong Kong today. They provide a cultural argument for their affinity with the United Kingdom, as well as a legal argument mapping out their return to UK sovereignty. Despite the apparent impossibility of their roadmap for Hong Kong's future, returnists argue convincingly that their vision is the most practical plan of any of the schools of independence thought.[211] Striking a deal with China, as envisioned by city-state advocates, is unlikely to succeed due to the power differentials between the two parties. Using the same legal systems that Beijing is intent on destroying to realize self-rule, as proposed by self-determinationists, seems even more unlikely. And considering the shocking endurance of the Chinese Communist Party, envisioning a path to Hong Kong independence born from the Party's collapse would require a wait of indeterminable length that could extend even well beyond 2047.[212] Combining a sound legal argument with the prospect of international legal support, returnists see the unlikely idea of returning to the United Kingdom as the most likely path to genuine self-rule for Hong Kong.

This path would also, returnists argue, provide the most secure guarantee for the preservation of the city's freedoms and way of life. Returnists tell us that neither a Hong Kong city-state, a self-determined Hong Kong, nor an independent Republic of Hong Kong could escape China's threat to this new nation's way of life. Any of the preceding schools of thought would thus face formidable political, economic, diplomatic, and military challenges even after achieving the already extremely daunting goal of establishing a self-ruling polity.[213] The resumption of UK sovereignty, returnists argue, would provide the strongest protection against such pressures: Hong Kong would find economic partners and diplomatic allies among the democracies of the world, who could support the newly independent city in pushing back against the pressures and threats that China would undoubtedly deploy.[214] Such alliances would also have significant defense implications: as part of the United Kingdom, Hong Kong would be protected by an alliance with the strongest militaries in the world.

Colonial Anti-colonial Resistance

Beyond incorporating and superseding the cultural and legal arguments of other schools of Hong Kong nationalist thought, returnism's promotion of recolonization also paradoxically embraces the revolutionary anti-colonial arguments of independence supporters. In doing so, returnists argue that the genuine autonomy enjoyed by various British Overseas Territories today is in fact the most realistic path to Hong Kong independence: recolonization would in fact be an express train to independence.

As with their legal arguments, returnists provide ample evidence to demonstrate that recolonization would ironically provide stronger protections for independence than China's ostensible decolonization. One returnist article, "Gibraltar and Hong Kong," compares the current status of these two territories, both historically linked to the United Kingdom.[215] Culturally, the author argues that the people of Gibraltar have Spanish roots and live a Mediterranean lifestyle considerably divorced from British culture. Despite these cultural ties to Spain, however, the people of Gibraltar have repeatedly demonstrated their desire to maintain UK sovereignty over their land.[216] A 1967 referendum with 95.8 percent voter participation resulted in a 99 percent vote in favor of maintaining British rule.[217] A 2002 referendum on shared sovereignty between Britain and Spain, with 87.9 percent voter participation, again resulted in a 99 percent vote in favor of maintaining British rule.[218] Why has a region with clear Spanish heritage so resiliently refused to embrace Spanish sovereign rule and instead embraced its status as a British Overseas Territory? The answer, according to returnists, is to be found in the same reason that a city with Sinitic heritage is now refusing Chinese rule: the deeper universal culture of democracy, transparency, and good governance that both Gibraltar and Hong Kong share with the United Kingdom and many other countries the world over. As one of the few remaining British Overseas Territories, Gibraltar's diplomacy and defense are managed by the United Kingdom, while the remainder of its internal affairs are managed on its own within a parliamentary democratic system.[219] Hong Kong was similarly promised complete control over its internal affairs within a democratic system, with China only overseeing matters of diplomacy and defense. The primary difference, however, is that Gibraltar's ruler has kept its promises, even proactively granting its people a choice, not only once but indeed twice, to redefine their relationship with the United Kingdom and thereby determine their own future.

This element of choice is crucial for understanding the returnist argument. Returnists are not seeking recolonization but rather proper decolonization, based in the relative freedom, autonomy, and indeed right to self-determination enjoyed by colonies of the United Kingdom as compared to colonies of the People's Republic of China. It is one of the great ironies of history that the ostensibly proudly decolonized and "returned" Hong Kong today feels much more like an oppressed colony than places that have actually remained under unambiguous colonial rule.[220] In the returnist vision, returning to the United Kingdom through the legal voiding of the Sino-British Joint Declaration would transform Hong Kong into a British Overseas Territory with genuine autonomy on a par with Gibraltar.[221] Such autonomy, combined with military and diplomatic protection from the democracies of the world, would provide Hong Kong with an opportunity to rebuild its political institutions and develop its democracy, before eventually holding a referendum on the city's future.[222] Such paths to determining one's own future are completely impossible under Hong Kong's current framework under Chinese rule, yet would be eminently realistic as part of the United Kingdom.

Returnists thus complicate the discourse on culture and colonization by highlighting positive colonial legacies and questioning the overly simplistic labeling of two distinct outside regimes as simply "colonial." Returnists furthermore appeal to international law to argue that the People's Republic of China's repeated violations of the Joint Declaration and the Basic Law mean that Hong Kong should be returned to the United Kingdom. And in one of the greater ironies of the entire deeply ironic discussion surrounding One Country, Two Systems, returnists see the recolonization of Hong Kong by the United Kingdom as the most direct path to decolonization and self-rule. Returnism thus incorporates the cultural, legal, and anti-colonial logics of the preceding three schools of nationalism toward the commonly shared goal of giving the Hong Kong people a say in their own future. Returnists, however, envision realizing this choice via a proposal even more thrillingly paradoxical than One Country, Two Systems: colonial anti-colonial resistance.

CONCLUSION: HONG KONG'S POLITICAL ENLIGHTENMENT

This chapter presents an overview of the main schools of political thought in Hong Kong today imagining a future for the city distinct from China. Chin Wan's initial intervention via city-state theory in the early 2010s highlighted Hong Kong's cultural distinctiveness relative to China, while also reimagining the Hong Kong-China relationship and the power differentials therein in a way that forever changed how people think and talk about this relationship. Building on Chin's paradigm-shifting intervention, the University of Hong Kong Undergraduate Student Union journal *Undergrad* took these ideas a step further by promoting self-determination in accordance with Hong Kong's rights under international law and the Basic Law. The legal basis of self-determinationism again reaffirmed the cultural distinctiveness articulated by Chin Wan, while at the same time embodying this distinctiveness through its vision of an orderly and open referendum on the city's future resolving Hong Kong's political dilemma. Rather than operating optimistically within the restrictions of the law, the Hong Kong National Party envisioned a new form of anti-colonial resistance beyond the law, articulating a vision of a distinct Hong Kong nationality tasked with the mission of building a Republic of Hong Kong by any means necessary. Finally, returnists incorporated the culturalist, legal, and anti-colonial logics of the preceding schools of thought to make the unlikely idea of Hong Kong's return to the United Kingdom seem like an eminently reasonable proposal.

These intellectual developments do not constitute a singular "Hong Kong independence movement," but rather a diverse range of schools of thought based in radically different political philosophies that accordingly promote radically different visions for Hong Kong's future. Their sole point of commonality is their shared awakening to the fact that One Country, Two Systems is an irreparably failed model. Speaking with people involved in each of these schools of thought over the years, and sometimes with people whose thinking has evolved from one school to another, I came to realize that there is often almost as much animosity between the various schools of thought as there is toward Beijing. What we see in these intellectual developments is not a singular movement but rather a series of increasingly open and heated debates about the future of Hong Kong and its relationship with China. Do we envision Hong Kong as a city-state that forms the cornerstone of a Chinese federation, revitalizing the lost tradition of feudalism? Do we envision

Hong Kong recapturing the law and using it for the purposes of the city's self-determination and thus liberation from a lawless state? Do we envision Hong Kong's liberation operating beyond the restrictions of the law, resisting the colonizer's control by any means necessary? Or do we find the path to anti-colonial resistance in recolonization by a state that embodies the same universal values that residents of Hong Kong embrace? The possibilities are endless and will undoubtedly continue to evolve, whether in dialogue in Hong Kong or abroad, based in the awakening from and unmasking of the optimistic mythologies of Hong Kong's fate under Chinese rule.

As Peter Sloterdijk highlights in his reflections on the Enlightenment, enlightenment can be, in its ideal form, "the free dialogue of those who, under no external compulsion, are interested in knowledge."[223] One can certainly see echoes of this ideal in the constantly evolving Hong Kong nationalist discussion, a free and open exchange of ideas seeking answers for an uncertain future. Sloterdijk's analyses, however, also show how enlightenment is far too often "a losing battle."[224] Speaking honestly and thoughtfully in and of itself is resented by hegemonic powers who promote a counter-enlightenment of antireflection: celebrating One Country, Two Systems as a resounding success, while representing all other dialogue beyond One Country, Two Systems as a malevolent plot to destroy China that must be crushed at any cost. Sloterdijk points out, in a comment that resonates with Hong Kong's fate today, that "hegemonic powers cannot be addressed so easily; they do not come voluntarily to the negotiating table with their opponents, whom they would prefer to have behind bars."[225] Yet such a near instinctive turn to repression, rather than suppressing these intellectual developments, has in fact provided the most definitive evidence yet for these theories' underlying thesis that there is no hope for Hong Kong's distinct way of life under continued Chinese rule: the central government's repressive response to the city's political enlightenment in fact all too uncannily echoes Hong Kong nationalists' predictions.

As shown in the final chapter of this book, Beijing's frantic eagerness to track down, discredit, marginalize, and even imprison the "black hands" behind the rise and spread of independence thinking in Hong Kong leaves it completely unable to recognize its own hand in these developments, thus unknowingly reproducing, in response to political tensions, the very sources of these tensions.

CHAPTER 3

Seeing (Exactly) Like a State

Knowledge/Power in the Hong Kong-China Relationship

Abstract: "One Country Two Systems" is a success, but foreign enemy forces have provided a breeding ground for "Hong Kong independence" thought. Confronting the emerging trend of abuse by these independence forces, this article by a member of the democratic wings of China's political system proposes policy responses in step with the times. The author argues for the necessity of drafting stability maintenance policies, strengthening Chinese patriotic education, as well as providing more opportunities for Chinese youth with Hong Kong residence to play a role in politics in Hong Kong.

—Chen Hao, "Keeping Up with the Times in Responding to Abuse by 'Hong Kong Independence Forces'"

The preceding abstract introduces one of the earliest articles on the idea of Hong Kong independence in an official academic journal in the People's Republic of China.[1] Featured in the *Journal of the Fujian Institute of Socialism*, the piece is extremely brief, coming to only two and a half pages of cliché-laden prose. At the time of its publication in 2014, the author Chen Hao was a Fuzhou-based graduate student, and in the years since Chen has not published any further research. "Keeping Up with the Times in Responding to Abuse by 'Hong Kong Independence Forces'" also has never been cited by fellow academics, according to its China National Knowledge Infrastructure (CNKI) record. In researching this chapter, I had decided to read the entire rapidly expanding corpus of PRC academic studies of the idea of Hong Kong independence in chronological order, but there was at first glance no reason to take this early, two-page article particularly seriously.

However, having subsequently reviewed the entire corpus of official academic literature from the People's Republic of China on Hong Kong independence, altogether nearly sixty articles published over a period of six years,

I found that Chen's brief early intervention stands out as prophetic: although Chen's title refers to "keeping *up* with the times," his work was in fact very much *ahead* of the times.

First, Chen was prophetic in writing about Hong Kong independence in mid-2014 when this idea was still largely marginal even in Hong Kong political culture: the issue of *Undergrad* that eventually became *Hong Kong Nationalism* had only been published a few months earlier. Second, Chen was uniquely prescient in unknowingly setting the tone and modes of argument for all subsequent analyses in this academic literature in China. Chen portrayed participants in the debate about Hong Kong's future not as representatives of diverse philosophical perspectives, as shown in the previous chapter, but rather as a singular entity: "the Hong Kong independence movement." Chen furthermore portrayed this movement as not only singular but also singularly wrong and fundamentally pathological. According to this narrative, the new visions put forward by activists and political theorists are not the products of critical reflection on the failures of One Country, Two Systems, but rather a sign of Hong Kong's fundamental unfitness to manage its own affairs. Finally, Chen presciently sees a cure to this pathology in the further expansion of state power in Hong Kong, precisely the solution that every subsequent official Chinese academic analysis has proposed, as well as precisely the policy approach that Beijing has taken. In his underappreciated, genre-defining piece, Chen's analysis of the origins of the idea of Hong Kong independence, as well as his proposed solutions, already articulated the conclusions proposed by Chinese academics more than half a decade and dozens of journal articles later.

Chen's article begins with a notably immoderate narration of China's place in the world today:

A kind, friendly, and civilized lion has awakened in the East! Just as the spring breeze brings dew, reform has brought this millennia-old magnificent and great nation of ours back to life, lifting its head and flying high, leaving the world in awe! Since the establishment of the new China, the people of every region, nationality, and party have found themselves standing together with the Chinese Communist Party, their hearts bound together as one, building up the old China from a weak and poor semi-colonized impoverished nation where warlords battled with one another into an independent nation standing on its own, taking its first steps into flourishing prosperity, building a socialist great power with a moderately prosperous society and rapidly rising national strength.[2]

Chen does not leave much space for nuance here: from his word choice, to his lengthy run-on sentences, all the way down to the gratuitous exclamation points, any reader can feel his boundless excitement at the idea of China's rise. Yet it is not enough to merely acknowledge this excitement. Chen wants everyone to share it:

> Witnessing the glorious rise of socialist China, the people of every nationality of our nation, our compatriots in Taiwan, Hong Kong, and Macao, and our overseas Chinese unanimously feel a sense of pride and joy. This strong and prosperous mother is a blessing for the billions of sons and daughters of the Chinese nation scattered across the globe.
> Yet just at this moment that the people of various nationalities, regions, and parties that make up our big Chinese family are joining hands to charge forward toward the Chinese dream of a strong and prosperous nation, a certain group in a certain corner of our little brother Hong Kong, the so-called "pan-democrats," are constantly and incomprehensibly disrupting our moment of glory.[3]

Those who do not share Chen's excitement about the rise of the People's Republic of China are in this discourse not only missing out on a moment of glory but actually hindering China's rise and thus "threatening the harmony of our big Chinese family," a kinship metaphor that captures both the ideal of familial affection and the all too real confines of inescapable familial bonds. Building upon these metaphors that emphasize both innate closeness and disapproval of any "disharmony," the solution is simple. Chen tells us that the actions of such "spoiled children" are simply "intolerable" and require a resolute policy response: which is, after all, precisely how Beijing was always already going to respond.[4]

This chapter critically examines official Chinese research on Hong Kong independence, the body of scholarship that Chen's humble but affectively hyperbolic contribution initiated, building upon my reading of fifty-seven academic articles on the topic published between 2014 and 2020 drawn from the Chinese academic database CNKI. Chen's article adroitly predicts the entire subsequent corpus of official Chinese scholarship on Hong Kong independence. First, Chen constructs this phenomenon as inherently pathological: whereas he uses the metaphor of the spoiled child, which has emerged as a central trope in this genre of writing, other scholars deploy the metaphor of the hysteric trapped in the past, the fugitive existing beyond the law, or the virus threatening the downfall of the Chinese nation-state. In response to this pathology, Chen proposes numerous interventionist policies for the Chinese state to adopt in Hong Kong, including reasserting the central government's powers to interpret the Basic Law, resurrecting an aborted patriotic education program, and promoting vague stability maintenance measures.[5] These are all precisely the types of policies that official scholars are still recommending to this day, as well as the types of policies that the central state is currently enforcing in Hong Kong. They are also, one must note with a pessimistic sigh, precisely the types of policies that first produced rising political tensions in Hong Kong, as analyzed in chapter 1.

Chen's article closes with the following run-on sentence: "Let us learn from the teachings of Chairman Xi, firmly establishing national consciousness, motherland consciousness, and civic consciousness, perpetually enhancing every nationality and every region's identification with our mighty motherland, the Chinese nationality, Chinese culture, and socialism with Chinese characteristics, so that all can make their contribution to realizing the Chinese dream of the grand rejuvenation of the Chinese nation!"[6] This chapter ponders how official researchers could look at (or rather perhaps not look at) recent developments in Hong Kong and propose such a solution, as well as thinking through what the future could hold for Hong Kong when the central Chinese state insists on seeking solutions to unfolding crises precisely in these crises' roots.

TOWARD A STRUCTURALIST ORIENTALISM

The fact that the insights of Edward Said's *Orientalism* have not been applied to China's rule over Hong Kong is a stark testament to the limits of the postcolonial imagination. Such evasion foregoes not only an opportunity to interpret this troubled colonial situation through a potentially revealing framework, but also an opportunity to further develop this framework through its application to novel manifestations of colonization and oppression. In his influential book, Said employs a Foucauldian framework of knowledge/power to argue that the academic study of "the Orient" created the conditions for and even enabled European colonization of "the East." Said defines Orientalism as a discourse that "places things Oriental in class, court, prison, or manual for scrutiny, study, judgement, discipline, or governing" toward "dominating, restructuring, and having authority over the Orient."[7] A central component of this discourse is the presumed "ineradicable distinction between Western superiority and Oriental inferiority": the assumption, in sum, that the other is not only essentially different but also in this difference essentially inferior.[8] These ideas of inferiority originally have no correspondence with reality, but in turn play a determinant role in shaping reality: strength is a matter not only of military or technological dominance but also of knowledge and the production thereof, such that the hegemony of particular ideas in turn actually shapes reality itself.[9] Knowledge/power, in constructing this binary distinction of a strong and dynamic West and an inferior and unchanging East, justifies colonization of the Orient in advance and in turn reproduces this distinction over time by framing thought and thus reality.[10] In Said's phrasing, Orientalism creates a situation in which "the Orient was not (and is not) a free subject of thought or action."[11]

For all of his original contributions to our understanding of global power relations and representations of the other, Said's exclusive interest in the relationship between West and East produces a certain myopia that has hindered the development of a broader understanding of relations of domination beyond this particular binary. His analytical framework, as implied by its highly geographically specific name, is in fact ripe to be read in an essentializing mode that constructs an inherently benevolent and perpetually victimized East in relation to an always colonizing and victimizing West. Ironically, Said's seeming deconstruction of the East-West binary then promptly reconstructs this binary in the assumption that power relations have only ever involved the West dominating the East, generating an ontological Orientalism in reverse.[12] Doubly ironically, Said's myopic vision of Orientalism as operating solely along the East-West binary has played a determinant role in limiting the imagination of anti-Orientalist critique, such that the relevance of Orientalism for China is all too often assumed to be little more than the study of Western representations of China, thereby neglecting China's own colonial practices.

Noting the pitfalls of Said's geographically bound approach, in "Grammars of Identity/Alterity: A Structural Approach," Gerd Baumann develops a structuralist framework of selfing/othering, wherein relations of domination are detached from the genuinely arbitrary signifiers of East/West. Baumann declares his intention to expand what he calls Said's "baby grammar," which "only uses the simplest of oppositions and exploits them to maximum contrast," proposing instead three distinct structures of relations between selves and others: (1) orientalizing, (2) segmentation, and (3) encompassment.[13]

Orientalizing, in Baumann's analysis, is not a phenomenon that emanates solely from the West, directed solely toward the East. Rather, orientalizing is one of the primary structural grammars through which people across the world imagine and in turn relate to others, and it can exist across infinite axes unbound from the geographical area known as "the Orient."[14] The primary feature of orientalizing as a structure is a binary relationship characterized by imagined characteristics and hierarchy. Baumann emphasizes that the dynamics of imaginary relations across this binary can be considerably more complex than Said's portrayal indicates, even allowing for potential inversions of hierarchies in different fields: "the Orient" can then be imagined not only as a site of inferiority, but also as an imaginary object of desire for what has been lost in "modern life."[15] One can see such reversible binary relations in, for example, Han imaginings of Tibetan primitivism, which are split between racialized denigration and spiritual romanticism.

Segmentation recognizes identity as a multilayered process, including such components as national identity, race, ethnicity, class, age, gender, sexual orientation, local identity, political leanings, and personal experiences. Different levels or segments of one's sense of self become salient in different contexts, determining who one is or who one is perceived to be at particular moments. One can share commonalities with others, such that the line between self and other is blurred, while at the same time having differences with these same others that enhance the perception of distance.[16] Segmentation is particularly apparent in the rise of Hong Kong identity against a broader possessive Chinese identity over the past two decades, to the point that this once local identity as a segmental subset of Chineseness is now perceived by ever more subjects to have become a national identity distinct from Chineseness. Segmentation is however also apparent in official Chinese academic studies' constructions of Hong Kong nationalism, which highlight the general youthfulness of activists as not just a fact but rather a loaded symbol of such childlike characteristics as impracticality or impulsivity, constructing the central government by contrast as a mature adult who needs to step in and apply discipline firmly.

Encompassment, by contrast, is an act of forced selfing by co-optation.[17] Like segmentation, encompassment also recognizes distinct levels of identity. However, rather than emphasizing different aspects of the self in different contexts, encompassment subsumes lower-level differences into higher-level commonalities, thereby expressing ownership over that which is encompassed. Encompassment is thus always hierarchical: "The self-styled others are but a subordinate part of an encompassing Us."[18] One can see such encompassing processes in, for example, the all too familiar declaration that the people of

Hong Kong are inherently and undeniably Chinese: "We are all, after all, Chinese" (*dajia dou shi Zhongguoren*).

Baumann's elaboration of these grammars of selfing/othering reveals processes of identity construction as considerably more complex than envisioned in Said's framework. At the same time, a structuralist unmooring of these grammars from Said's unidirectional geographical assumptions has the potential to shed significant new light on colonial situations whose discussion had been previously foreclosed. China, although undeniably part of "the Orient" and a historical victim of Western colonization, is at the same time an expansive colonial power with its own deployments of orientalizing knowledge/power to rationalize its domination of others: ethnic minorities (including minorities who were once part of nations like Tibet), citizens of Hong Kong, citizens of Taiwan, and the broader so-called Chinese diaspora. The most easily recognizable orientalizing representations in the service of Chinese state domination are to be found in its stereotypical portrayals of minority others: from the costumed performance of ethnicity by minoritized representatives at the National People's Congress to exotic dance performances for tourists in so-called minority regions, both official and popular representations of ethnicity in China today produce an Orientalist binary between the Han majority and the so-called minority nationalities, with the latter constructed as the norm by relation therein.[19]

There are certain tropes in these portrayals that will be immediately familiar to anyone who has been exposed to these representations: (1) the ethnic other as child, in need of guidance from the mature and rational Han majority; (2) the ethnic other as underdeveloped or primitive, embodying an earlier stage of history in the present, in need of guidance from the modern and developed Han majority; (3) the ethnic other as different and uncivilized, not yet fully inducted into the glory of Han Chinese culture; and finally, a discourse that has become increasingly prominent in recent years, which sees (4) the ethnic other as a potential biological threat to the body politic, requiring constant monitoring, confinement, and even elimination, as we see in occupied Xinjiang today.[20] These images are unrelated to the actual existence of those purportedly described therein, determined in advance by Han nationalist orientalizing (premised on a binary of exoticism and normalcy, primitivism and modernity) and encompassing (forcefully incorporating the exoticized other to play a particular predetermined role in the narrative of the Chinese nation) perspectives, thereby imagining those represented therein as invariably benefiting from their forced incorporation into a Han-led nation.

The central state's relationships with ethnic minorities and with Hong Kong are both colonial relationships, yet they are also distinct types of colonial relationships that accordingly produce sometimes overlapping and at other times divergent identity binaries. Whereas majority-minority relations in China are framed within Han nationalist narratives of a civilizing mission, relations between the central state and Hong Kong are primarily framed within the Han nationalist narrative of a rising China, as seen in Chen Hao's pioneering contribution.[21] Although the framing narratives of the relationship are thus different, the tropes through which these relationships are articulated are strikingly similar. In the following sections I examine four core discourses of Hong Kong in official Chinese narratives that echo official constructions of the ethnic other: (1) Hong Kong as child, lacking the maturity and self-control of the newly powerful central state; (2) Hong Kong as underdeveloped hysteric, driven crazy by being left behind by China's rapid economic development; (3) Hong Kong as uncivilized outlaw, needing the central state's strong-arm intervention in order to return to its defining characteristic of a rule of law society; and (4) Hong Kong as virus or cancer, presenting a potentially fatal threat to the otherwise inevitable rise of China.

Another common point in the construction of these discourses, which I discuss in more detail at the end of this chapter, is the role of official Chinese academia therein, in the form of either anthropological study of "the minorities" or the political, social, and legal studies contributing to Beijing's Hong Kong-ology. *Orientalism* was first and foremost a critique of Western academia's contribution to Orientalism and thus colonialism, but in the four decades since its publication, its teachings have been fully incorporated into the target of its critique, with the same disciplines and institutions that Said targeted actively promoting critical reflection on problematic assumptions about the other and the power dynamics therein. By contrast, in state-controlled academia in China, Orientalism as a geographically bound concept perpetually caught in the East-West binary circuit has primarily served the purpose of reinforcing state power and its attendant colonizing perspectives, presenting the Han-dominated central state as a bastion against unilocal "Western imperialism." The ideology of the century of humiliation portraying China as perpetual victim, when fused with Said's myopic focus on "the West" that portrays "the East" as eternal victim, ideologically obscures considerably more lasting trends of humiliation and injustice perpetrated by the Han central state on its colonies and indeed its own people even to this day.

Louis Althusser once said that ideology has no outside, such that we are always already inside ideology.[22] This notably imprecise assertion has had a certain resonance in academic discourse, framing critical analyses of ideologies as being just as ideological as what they critique. This seemingly meta-ideological stance is however itself ideologically burdened, producing a flattening relativism that far too often forecloses critical analysis and indeed thinking. First, not all ideologies are created equal: if we take ideology simply to mean that our access to the world is never direct and unmediated, Althusser's statement may make a certain degree of sense, but would at the same time sadly lose sight of the fact that an innate characteristic of humanity is the ability to work toward stepping outside of these ideologies and reflecting upon them, such that some indirect and mediated representations and understandings of the world are indeed better, in the sense of being more critically reflective or revealing, than others.[23] Second, this inevitable inequality can be traced to many potential causes, but foremost among these is their conditions of production.[24] One could certainly argue that intellectual work within spaces of academic freedom and unfreedom is invariably suffused with ideology, or even that the idea of academic freedom is itself an ideology, but the primary point to emerge from such a claim would be to draw a false equation between systems in which one is largely free to take the admittedly sometimes difficult step outside of prevailing ideologies without the threat of punishment and another in which the state exercises direct control over one's publications and actively threatens deviations from ideological dictates with life-destroying punishment. If ideology is indeed a universal affliction, we cannot at the same time lose sight of the fact that some forms of thought and writing are shaped considerably more by "ideology," in the sense of a misrepresentation of the world, than others. Beijing's Hong Kong-ology is, I propose, considerably more burdened by ideological controls and distortions than most.

The following four sections summarize and critically evaluate the ideological frameworks through which official academic studies represent Hong Kong and recent political and intellectual developments there. I draw upon yet also expand insights from *Orientalism* through an analysis of four central tropes in this corpus which, to paraphrase Said, place China in a whole series of possible relationships with Hong Kong without ever losing the relative upper hand.[25] In the figure of the spoiled child, the maladjusted and impoverished hysteric, the fugitive from the rule of law, and the biologized virus or malignant growth within the national body politic, official academic representations of Hong Kong construct the city as founded upon a pathology that only the central government can cure. Although the centralizing state and its controlling political initiatives are the source of the city's crisis today, the reassertion and intensification of such control comes to be seen as the only possible solution.

HONG KONG AS CHILD

No matter whether we are talking about strengthening young people's knowledge of Chinese history and culture, or striking against and containing 'Hong Kong independence' activities and maintaining social stability, we need everyone to step forward and do all that they can. Sometimes we will face pressures, but we must not waver.
—Chairman Xi Jinping, speech on the twentieth anniversary of Hong Kong's handover to China, July 1, 2017[26]

The majority of advocates of Hong Kong independence are young people. The most vocal proponents of this idea come from a new generation of younger activists, and polling has shown that as much as 40 percent of young people (ages fifteen to twenty-four) support independence.[27] These are empirical facts. These facts are, however, a point of particular focus in official Chinese academic studies of Hong Kong nationalism, moving in this focus beyond the realm of acknowledging a fact to developing this fact into a trope. In focusing on this aspect of identity and the associations linked to this idea, Hong Kong is constructed in these official studies as unrealistic and stubborn: a spoiled child certain that it needs something that would actually only do it harm, and that simply does not know better. This orientalizing construction, in turn, presents the central government as the sole mature political force in the relationship, thereby tasking the Chinese state with enforcing discipline on its unruly child.

Youthfulness is an inherently polyvalent symbol: one can see positive associations of open-mindedness and exploration, breaking out of tired old ways of thinking, as well as negative associations of ignorance or impulsivity. Capturing this polyvalence, the common metaphor of the ethnic minority as child in official Han portrayals of ethnic relations operates on two levels. On the one hand, minority figures are imagined as primitive and thus lacking in basic knowledge of modern politics, economics, and culture; as a result, this child minority figure has much to learn about modernity from its elder brother nationality, the Han. On the other hand, precisely by right of this condescending assumption of primitivity, ethnic minority cultures are imagined to possess significant liberating potentials that are lost in the cruel realities of adulthood: the Han thus also has much to learn from these nobly naïve figures, just as a jaded adult can begin to see the world anew through the eyes of a child. Susan Blum's fascinating study of Han imaginaries of "primitive" ethnic minorities powerfully captures this tension between haughty condescension and yearning admiration.[28]

The portrayal of Hong Kong as youth in official academic research is by contrast starkly one-dimensional. Tian Feilong, in a 2019 article in the *Journal of the Guangzhou Institute of Socialism*, articulates six features of what he calls the "youth localism" in Hong Kong, all of which are negative.[29] These six features are (1) failing to understand One Country, Two Systems and the Basic Law; (2) embracing an anarchistic populism and a radical political urgency; (3) shattering Hong Kong's respect for the rule of law by promoting armed resistance; (4) tricking people into taking increasingly radical stances; (5) naively embracing interactions with Taiwanese political figures and foreign powers; and (6) lacking interest in constructive dialogue, cooperation, and policy planning, and instead engaging solely in resistance, vetoes, and struggles.[30] The kids, Tian Feilong warns us, are not alright. These six characteristics are not only negative but one-dimensionally negative: there is, one must note, no potential upside to young people failing to understand the Basic Law or tricking people into taking increasingly radical stances. A simultaneously empirically accurate and polyvalent symbol, youthfulness, is thereby deployed in these studies to represent Hong Kong's current political culture in a one-dimensionally negative light.

In these portrayals, the impressionability characteristic of a child is always already misused, making the Hong Kong child impulsive and spoiled, devoid of the innocence that characterizes the ethnic other. At the time of Hong Kong's 1997 handover from the United Kingdom to the People's Republic of China, state media made constant references to the idea of Hong Kong as a lost child finally returning home.[31] Yet after the celebratory tone of the reunion had faded away and everyone was forced to live together under one roof, the imaginary parent in this structure was left to ponder precisely what this moody and impulsive adolescent had been exposed to while away from home. Sang Pu has succinctly expressed this dynamic in his study of Hong Kong as "China's orphan," perpetually blamed not only for having lived beyond the controls of the central state, but indeed for having lived all too well.[32] From the reunited parent's perspective, this lost child's immersion in colonial pollution as a result of its being raised by a despised foreign stepparent, as well as its premature exposure to the crises of modernity as a result of Hong Kong's early economic boom relative to China, mean that its entire childhood environment, a moment of ideal innocence, was fundamentally corrupting. In contrast to the figure of the minority child, cultivated in an imagined natural and unadulterated environment not yet impacted by modernity, there is no purity or innocence in the figure of Hong Kong as child, whose impressionability has always already been exposed to far too many negative influences. This singularly negative portrayal of the child in the figure of Hong Kong could be read as a product of official status anxiety with regard to the city: it is precisely because China obviously still has so much to learn from Hong Kong and its system that official narratives must repress this reality by pretending that there is absolutely nothing to learn and that the hierarchy that it proposes is fixed and irreversible.

Following Hong Kong's "return" to its imagined proper national family, the parent in this metaphor needs to process and respond to emerging behavioral challenges but has been inconveniently prevented by policy constraints from applying the tried and tested tough love that it knows its child needs. Tian Feilong, for example, characterizes One Country, Two Systems, supposedly the legal basis of Chinese rule over Hong Kong, as an obsolete policy of "isolation."[33] This policy has in his telling guaranteed Hong Kong a high degree of autonomy, but it has also left the city isolated from its reality as part of China. Huang Chenpu sees the constraints of One Country, Two Systems as allowing many of the negative influences of the colonial era to live on as legacy institutions in the present: Hong Kong schools, in Huang's telling, operate as Western "brainwashing centers" driven by "anti-communist" and "anti-China" thought.[34] Huang articulates the Chinese state's very particular vision of an ideal educator perhaps all too bluntly when he states that "a number of professors and teachers in Hong Kong are incapable of setting a positive example for youth by loving China and loving the Chinese Communist Party."[35] The city's formerly free media are furthermore portrayed by Huang as a lingering bad influence whose maniacal demonization of the Chinese Communist Party has been aided and abetted by One Country, Two Systems.[36] Meanwhile, these narratives claim, the supposed overpoliticization of Hong Kong's main political parties has left them inattentive to basic livelihood issues, such that Hong Kong youth in general face a dead-end situation with their incomes stagnant and real estate perpetually beyond their reach, leaving them unable to even begin to aspire to their ideal of success.[37] Unhealthy influences from the child's time away, in this telling, have been allowed to linger through burdensome constraints, leaving the imaginary parental figure summoned in this metaphor unable to act like a proper parent.

Indulgence of unhealthy trends has reinforced the bad behavior of what Chen Hao in his pioneering study called the "spoiled children" of Hong Kong, whose minds are filled with delinquent ideas.[38] Such legally protected liberties as freedom of speech, press, and assembly are invariably portrayed as fundamentally "Western" and impractical for China's "national conditions" in PRC propaganda. Traded off at gunpoint in China's post-1989 shift toward an ideology of economic development as the driving force of history, these freedoms are imagined not only as the impractical, frivolous concerns of foreigners but also as potential hindrances to China's rise. As these corrupting ideas continue to circulate freely in Hong Kong, aided and abetted by colonial legacies and the educational and media systems, Tian Feilong sees a process of radicalization escalating into calls for Hong Kong independence.[39] The idea of Hong Kong independence, from this perspective, can only ever be based in a fundamental misunderstanding of the law, of Hong Kong's relationship with China, and indeed of reality, misunderstandings that have been fostered and encouraged by One Country, Two Systems' constraints on the central state's disciplining powers.[40] The idea of the Hong Kong people determining their own future just as many colonized people around the world have done is transformed in these discourses into little more than an overpriced and impractical toy that a spoiled child impulsively demands. The child has no understanding of what he or she is demanding, nor of whether the demand is practical; there is simply an overwhelming and stubborn impulse, based in a misunderstanding of reality, to obtain this unrealistic ideal. No matter what inventive narratives a child may spin together to justify such a purchase, there is little purpose in listening carefully, weighing the logic of the argument, or earnestly rebutting each point. When its demands are not met, the child throws a tantrum, screaming and thrashing around on the floor. Such irrationality is manifest in Tian's reference to increasingly militant forms of protests among youth and the inability to engage in dialogue and compromise.[41]

The stubbornness of the child figure is matched only by the stubbornness of the legal constraints of One Country, Two Systems preventing the exercise of authority. The founding conundrum of the Hong Kong-China relationship since the negotiation of the 1997 handover has been the fact that Hong Kong is considerably more politically advanced than China, the "adult" metropole that manages its affairs. This conundrum was acknowledged but not fully resolved by One Country, Two Systems and its promise that the central authorities, perpetually unbound by laws, would be bound by law not to intervene in the city's autonomy. This conundrum is, however, erased in the reversal of this hierarchy through the figure of the ignorant and impulsive child, portraying Hong Kong's dynamic and at times admittedly unpredictable political discursive field as an indicator of the city's fundamental inability to manage its own affairs, constructing China by contrast as the adult in the room. The noninterference dictated by One Country, Two Systems then becomes not a legal guarantee to protect Hong Kong's unique lifestyle and mature civil society but rather a dereliction of duty, allowing Hong Kong to maintain a childish and dysfunctional way of life that is pushing the city to the brink of self-destruction in the name of "autonomy." Intervention is then not to be understood as an unaccountable dictatorship destroying a robust legal and political system, but rather as a parent proactively intervening for the benefit of a misguided child on the path of self-destruction. As Tian Feilong notes in his reflections on "youth politics," continued indulgence is no longer an option. There is a paradoxical need to set all rules aside to allow the adult in the relationship to step in and apply the rules.

One can see reflections of this structural imaginary of unruly children in the controversy surrounding the 2016 disqualification of Legislative Council candidates and lawmakers. In July of that year, under pressure from China, the Electoral Affairs Commission announced an unprecedented requirement for all candidates for the Legislative Council to sign a statement confirming their understanding of three articles of the Basic Law.[42] These were (1) Article 1, which states that "the Hong Kong Special Administrative Region is an inalienable part of the People's Republic of China"; (2) Article 12, which states that "the Hong Kong Special Administrative Region shall be a local administrative region of the People's Republic of China, which shall enjoy a high degree of autonomy and come directly under the Central People's Government" and (3) Article 159, which gives the National People's Congress the sole and final right to interpret or amend the Basic Law.[43] In justifying this new requirement for candidacy, the chairman of the Electoral Affairs Commission, Justice Barnabas Fung Wah, commented: "The EAC notices that there have been comments and proposals in the public arena which have deviated from 'one country, two systems' and the constitutional status of Hong Kong as prescribed in the Basic Law. In this regard, there are public concerns on whether candidates fully understand the Basic Law, in particular Article 1, Article 12 and Article 159(4)."[44] The suggestion here that candidates may not fully "understand" the law and as a result may not be eligible to participate in elections is an infantilizing attempt to represent a diverse array of political perspectives as misunderstandings of reality: always, of course, perfectly understood by the authorities. In turn, requiring candidates to undergo a test of their "understanding" of the law in the form of a confirmation statement is a fundamentally disciplining process, forcing candidates to submit to the authorities' ostensibly objective but in fact very particular interpretation of the law in order to be able to exercise their own legally guaranteed right to stand for office.

Such condescension was further compounded by the revelation that unelected representatives on the Electoral Affairs Commission would be the final judges of the sincerity of candidates' declarations. Simply signing the statement confirming one's understanding of the law was not enough; one furthermore had to convince the assigned civil servant that one was signing sincerely, without however having any clear guidelines as to how precisely to prove one's sincerity beyond the act of signing.[45] Andy Chan of the Hong Kong National Party unsurprisingly refused to sign a statement endorsing these articles of the Basic Law and was accordingly the first Legislative Council candidate to be disqualified in July 2016.[46] Nakade Hitsujiko and Alvin Cheng Kam-mun, both advocates of city-state theory, signed their confirmation statements but still had their candidacies disqualified.[47] Edward Leung of Hong Kong Indigenous originally questioned the legal basis for the statement and refused to sign, but later changed his mind and signed. Despite yielding to these demands, however, Leung still had his candidacy for the Legislative Council denied.[48] Such pseudoscientific deciphering of "sincerity" by the Hong Kong government only makes sense within an imagined natural hierarchy wherein the adult authorities not only know the law better than the childish candidates, but indeed know the candidates and their beliefs better than they know themselves.

After numerous candidates were disqualified on this thin legal pretext, other approved candidates who actually won their elections were removed from office on even flimsier legal pretexts. Baggio Leung and Yau Wai-ching of Youngpsiration, who ran as substitutes for disqualified activist Edward Leung, won seats as legislators in the Sixth Term of the Hong Kong Special Administrative Region's Legislative Council. At their oath-taking ceremony on October 12, 2016, as discussed in chapter 2, Leung and Yau sprinkled their oaths with various insults and profanities while displaying flags that read "Hong Kong is not China."[49] The Legislative Council president declared that their oaths were invalid, and while proceedings were still underway in Hong Kong on the legality of this decision, Beijing intervened with an interpretation of Article 104 of the Basic Law declaring that any lawmaker whose oath was declared invalid would be disqualified from assuming public office.[50] Insofar as Beijing's goal was clearly to banish Leung and Yau, democratically elected by the people of Hong Kong, the interpretation was to be applied retroactively. Beijing knows best, after all.

There is not sufficient space here to think through the full legal implications of the National People's Congress's intervention in Hong Kong's political and legal systems in this case. There is a growing legal literature on this topic, and it will suffice to say that the majority of researchers seem notably unimpressed with Beijing's legal reasoning.[51] Rather, applying the analytical framework developed here to official representations, I would like to bring readers' attention to an article published in the Liaison Office–owned newspaper *Ta Kung Pao* three weeks after Beijing's decision, "Investigation: Revealing Yau and Leung's Path to 'Independence.'"[52] The article portrays Yau and Leung as delinquent youth who "lacked a proper home environment and did not receive a quality education," resulting in "these two youth proceeding down a path of self-destruction" that eventually led to their embrace of Hong Kong independence. Although *Ta Kung Pao* claims that Leung and Yau's story demonstrates "an educational crisis in Hong Kong and the negative impacts of the over-politicization of society," the report does not in reality present much evidence to support these claims.[53] According to one interviewee, Yau Wai-ching's family was overly lax with her as a child, producing an adult who in *Ta Kung Pao*'s portrayal lacks any "sense of responsibility."[54] The brief sketch of Baggio Leung mainly focuses on the fact that his father passed away when he was nine, after which he was raised by his mother. In both cases, according to this narrative, a lack of parental guidance led both Yau and Leung down the dangerous path of embracing Hong Kong independence, with deep and disturbing implications for Hong Kong politics.

The details in this report are notably scarce and unconvincing yet also at the end of the day insignificant. Beijing-owned *Ta Kung Pao* was not actually conducting an investigation but rather writing into a preestablished trope based in a crude form of psychoanalysis that assumes that enthusiasm for a Hong Kong identity distinct from China could only ever be the muddled musings of a misled child. Through these metaphors, the central state, whose impulsive interventions in Hong Kong have greatly escalated political tensions, is presented as the sole levelheaded adult in the room, who needs to intervene yet again to resolve these tensions produced by misguided and impulsive youth. In a pattern repeated in other hierarchical structures examined in this chapter, the spoiled child trope finds the solution to the ongoing political crisis in Hong Kong precisely in its origins: intervention by the central authorities.

HONG KONG AS HYSTERIC

Based on the laws of economic development, the laissez-faire allocation of resources is a double-edged sword. For talented people with a competitive advantage, it naturally means more opportunities and ever more space for growth. But for those who are weaker, there will be ever greater pressures and increasingly limited resources available. If they are not able to improve themselves and adjust to change, they run the risk of being marginalized.

—Han Shanshan, "Thoughts on the Radical Hong Kong Independence Movement Based on the Intrusion into the PLA Barracks: Characteristics, Causes, and Risks," 2014[55]

The narrative is by this point painfully familiar, a seemingly indispensable feature of any Chinese study of Hong Kong nationalism. As I turn the page and begin to see the first hints, I know before even making my way through a few sentences that I could write the rest on my own from memory: the vicissitudes of economic development in East Asia have reshaped the dynamics of the Hong Kong-China relationship, leaving the city's residents unable to adjust to new realities, such that they attempt to flatter themselves with an anachronistic form of local supremacism that pathologically denies the very core of their selfhood.

As discussed at the start of this book, the first authors to articulate this narrative were Zhu Jie and Zhang Xiaoshan of Wuhan University, who initially sketched its general outlines in a 2016 article in *Hong Kong-Macao Studies*, the official journal of the Chinese Association of Hong Kong and Macao Studies, titled "A Historical Narration and Restoration of 'Hong Kong Native Identity,' with a Review of the Formation and Evolution of 'Hong Kong Independence' Thought."[56] Zhu and Zhang further elaborated this narrative in a strikingly similar article in the exact same journal the following year, "A Psychosocial

Perspective into the Radical Nativism in Hong Kong."[57] The narrative has subsequently been recycled, generally without citation, in dozens of articles in the years since then, becoming a veritable cornerstone of official academic writing on Hong Kong politics today.[58]

Zhu and Zhang tell us that in the nineteenth and early twentieth centuries very few residents of Hong Kong identified with this city as their permanent home. People generally viewed Hong Kong as a place of temporary residence, providing a refuge from the disorderly political situation in China: a borrowed place on borrowed time. Residents thus saw themselves primarily as temporary visitors who expected to return to their homeland, China, when the situation there stabilized.[59] If we accept Zhu and Zhang's claim, we must also note that these temporary residents had quite a lengthy wait ahead of them. Zhu and Zhang see a shift toward a more prominent Hong Kong identity only emerging after 1949, a development they attribute to limited cross-border interactions after the closure of the Hong Kong-China border, as well as to a colonial education system that in their interpretation downplayed Hong Kong people's Chinese identity.[60] In contrast to such equally plausible explanations as the development of a distinct local culture with the passage of time, the authors portray these trends as forced and thus artificial, finding at the core of the very idea of Hong Kong as a home a certain unshakeable inauthenticity that contrasts unfavorably with a far more natural Chinese identity.[61]

The growing sense of local identity emerging in the post-1949 era coincided with a period of rapid economic development in Hong Kong extending from the 1950s through the 1980s.[62] The newfound wealth of Hong Kong, according to Zhu and Zhang, meant that residents in this period not only began to feel less Chinese, but also began to feel "better" than the Chinese: what the authors call Hong Kong chauvinism (da Xianggang zhuyi).[63] Such chauvinism, they claim, was only further bolstered when China's reform and opening program in the 1980s mimicked Hong Kong's economic utilitarianism and strove to attract Hong Kong capital, technology, and management expertise.[64] Zhu and Zhang imagine, in very broad yet always confident strokes, the effects of these developments on Hong Kong residents' identity: "For Hong Kong residents, the 1970s and 1980s were a period of self-confidence, everything was getting better each day, and everyone had an opportunity to succeed: Hong Kong's local consciousness and identity took shape in this type of context. On account of the contrast with the Mainland and the admiration for Hong Kong's accomplishments, the people of the city began to overestimate their own importance."[65] Insofar as the specter of comparison has always been a matter of the utmost importance for Chinese nationalist thinking about Hong Kong, it is impossible to decipher whether this chauvinism that Zhu and Zhang cite is an actually existing phenomenon (at least to the degree that they portray) or rather the product of the authors' embarrassedly imagining the Hong Kong people seeing the China that they themselves saw in the early reform era.[66] As always, Zhu and Zhang's analyses are less about Hong Kong than about the official Chinese imagination of Hong Kong, from which they derive the structure of their narrative and which they in turn reproduce and reinforce in their own narratives.

Whether this chauvinism was real or imagined, marginal or widespread, Zhu and Zhang know that Hong Kong's superior position relative to China was destined to change. Whereas China had much to learn from Hong Kong in the 1970s and the 1980s, "since Hong Kong's return, the gap between Hong Kong and the Mainland has shrunk."[67] Pursuing a solely quantitative perspective that grants a certain innate advantage to a country of 1.4 billion people, the authors assert that the Chinese economy has grown rapidly in recent decades and is now the second largest economy in the world; at the same time a number of cities across China are as always right on the verge of replacing Hong Kong as Asia's financial center. Zhu and Zhang explain: "Since Hong Kong's return, due to some historical shifts, Hong Kong's economic growth has slowed. Although this has no direct relationship with Hong Kong's return to China, the feeling that things are not quite what they used to be, or even a feeling of nostalgia for lost golden years is unavoidable. Hong Kong as an economically developed city will naturally have different growth rates from a still developing China, but the sheer speed of China's rise nevertheless cannot help but bring into stark contrast Hong Kong's decline."[68] Whereas official propaganda emphasizes racial commonality based in innate blood ties in the Hong Kong-China relationship, Zhu and Zhang's comments show just how large a role hierarchy and comparison also play therein. Yet this is not only a matter of hierarchy but rather the construction of a particular type of seemingly natural hierarchy: the inversion of this hierarchy from the Maoist era to today, such that China's power relative to Hong Kong is now apparent for all to see, is portrayed by the authors as at once an unprecedented development of the type that the world has never seen before as well as a predestined return to a natural state of affairs.

Although the times are rapidly changing, Zhu and Zhang tell us, Hong Kong is not. Here the authors have appropriated for academic purposes a common nationalist trope in the discussion of Hong Kong: the idea that this city, imagined as modern and advanced from a distance, in fact fails to impress when experienced firsthand, seeming upon closer inspection to be more like a once-modern city trapped in the past. Zhu and Zhang develop a slightly more complex version of this narrative, claiming that the commonly cited markers of a fading modernity are little more than externalized reflections of the internal minds of residents, who in their failure to adjust to the new era remain mental captives of the now long-lost hierarchies of the 1970s and 1980s. This idea of the past lingering in the present can be usefully compared to the trope of the "living fossil" commonly deployed in discourses of ethnic relations in China. Whereas the living fossil minority can be a "noble savage" from a simpler and more innocent stage of history, Hong Kong is imagined to remain trapped in an earlier but still modern and thus polluted era, unable to adjust to new realities, possessing all of the primitivity but none of the purity. And accordingly, the Hong Kong people are imagined, in contrast to the imaginings of ethnic minorities, to hold no rare insights into a simpler way of life that has been lost, but rather carry within themselves the burdens of an anomalous and now irrelevant past pride that leaves them fundamentally maladjusted to the realities and hierarchies of the present.

Having constructed a historical narrative of inverted hierarchies, Zhu and Zhang proceed to incorporate this narrative into a crude psychoanalytical framework such that the emergence of the idea of a Hong Kong nation is reframed as an angry and mistakenly self-glorifying reaction to the city's growing marginalization relative to China. According to this narrative, insofar as the city's gradual quantitative eclipse by China does not accord with Hong Kong's ego ideal, residents feel compelled to present an ever more falsely inflated self-aggrandizement so as to rescue their collapsing self-image: "Scholars have pointed out that 'Hong Kong chauvinism' has not disappeared. Rather, with the dramatic rise of China's economy, this chauvinism is left with a little less pride and a lot more ostracism and fear [. . .] due to the continued assaults against their sense of self."[69] The Hong Kong nation is then, in Zhu and Zhang's construction, not just an imagined community. It is a delusional community, produced via an angry and irrational act of self-aggrandizement to repress a nagging sense of inferiority. In another study, Wang Wanli puts forward the imaginative hypothesis that thinkers and activists committed to Hong Kong independence have been particularly attracted to Benedict Anderson's theory of imagined communities precisely because they want to avoid objective realities and instead envision the nation as a purely subjective and thus imaginary matter: a quite exceptional misunderstanding of both Anderson's theory and Hong Kong politics, in one fell swoop.[70] Yet despite his miscomprehensions, Wang still manages to arrive at the same conclusions as Zhu and Zhang: strengthened local identity in Hong Kong is in fact solely a sign of weakness, to which Beijing must respond with a show of real strength.

Whereas Zhu and Zhang imagine themselves as capable of mining the psyches of the average Hong Kong resident, their framework in fact provides abundant materials for analyzing and understanding official narratives of Hong Kong-China relations. Said defines Orientalism as a discourse that "places things Oriental in class, court, prison, or manual for scrutiny, study, judgment, discipline, or governing" toward "dominating, restructuring, and having authority over the Orient."[71] In the discourse analyzed here, Zhu and Zhang first place the people of Hong Kong in a subordinate relationship relative to a rising China, before in turn throwing the entire city onto the psychoanalyst's couch, a framing that affirms in advance the authors', and by extension Beijing's, sanity and stability. The analysts are destined to find their patient mentally ill, not because he or she is, but rather because their goal from the start is to reaffirm the fundamental rationality and indeed infallibility of the system that they represent. Such sanity is, we must note, not a conclusion that could be plausibly reached by any analysis of the system itself, but rather must be achieved through the pathologizing construction of its other. It is only through the binary representation of Hong Kong as lost in delusional bouts of envy that one could conclude that Beijing is a sane and reasonable ruler.

The policy implications of this construction of Hong Kong as a mentally disturbed living fossil are articulated all too clearly in a *Hong Kong-Macao Studies* article, "Consolidate a Hong Kong Consensus via Economic Development and Livelihood Improvement."[72] The authors, Chen Guanghan and Li Xiaoying of Guangzhou's Sun Yat-sen University, manage to simplify the arguably overwhelming complexity of sociopolitical developments in Hong Kong in recent years, difficult to fully represent even in a book-length study, into a one-dimensional dilemma with a correspondingly one-dimensional solution, covered impressively concisely over six pages of text. They begin from the now all too familiar narrative of Hong Kong's descent from a rapidly developing economy in the twentieth century to an economy in a new era still trapped in its long-gone heydays; from a politically stable global financial center to a politically divided city that has scared away investors; and from a central investor in and beneficiary of China's rise to an increasingly marginal player in this process which now proceeds regardless of Hong Kong's involvement.[73] Things have changed, they tell us, and as a result of this change Hong Kong needs a "new consensus" for the new era. And because supreme ideological confidence is a basic qualification for any PRC-based Hong Kong-ologist, the authors do not shy away from telling us all precisely what this consensus must include: setting aside political disputes to focus on the people's livelihood, enhancing regional cooperation to provide "more space" for Hong Kong's development, employing Hong Kong's strengths in finance to support the Belt and Road Initiative, and expanding Hong Kong's role as a global Renminbi (RMB) trading center.[74]

It may seem all too easy to laugh off such obviously wrongheaded and shamelessly Sinocentric analyses, but this would be the wrong response: the Chinese Association of Hong Kong and Macao Studies is, after all, an official organization that plays a prominent role in shaping perceptions of and formulating policy toward Hong Kong. There are thus two points about this self-declared new Hong Kong consensus, drafted conveniently from across the border in Guangzhou, that merit closer examination. First, every element of this new consensus is focused on economics, ignoring the social and political controversies that have been at the forefront of concern in Hong Kong for at least the past two decades. Zhu and Zhang's figure of the underdeveloped hysteric has been so warmly received and repeatedly invoked in official Chinese narratives, in my reading, because it simplifies all of Hong Kong's complex issues down to matters of economics, making these issues easy to explain and to resolve. If political strife is simply a result of resentment about Hong Kong's fading economic power relative to China, then all that Beijing needs to do to resolve this problem is to further integrate Hong Kong into its own economic development plans. Such a transformation of political, ethnic, or social issues into an economic issue is a common tactic in official Chinese narratives, precisely because the economic realm is an area in which the state is eager to take action (as opposed to developing new political or social policies) and in which it has the resources and will to make an impact. One can see a similar economic salvationism in Tibet, where leaders remain confident that just a little more development will finally resolve tensions, or in Xinjiang, where the unjustifiable arbitrary detention of millions in concentration camps has been perplexingly rationalized as some type of "vocational education."[75] When all problems are flattened into economics, economic development becomes the solution to all problems. Chen and Li's study of Hong Kong is not actually talking about Hong Kong, but rather using Hong Kong to talk about pre-formed official ideologies.

This brings us to the crucial second point: the solutions to all of Hong Kong's issues in this framework are to be found not in Hong Kong but rather solely in China. This solution precisely inverts the logic of Hong Kong nationalism: counter to Chin Wan's paradigm-shifting call to abandon all hope in China and instead seek local solutions to Hong Kong's challenges, Chen and Li instead tell residents to abandon all hope in Hong Kong and find all solutions in China, whether this takes the form of expanding the city's role as a Renminbi trading outpost or playing a supporting role in the Belt and Road Initiative.

Nowhere is this type of illogical logic more apparent than in the much-hyped yet also perpetually vague and meaningless Guangdong-Hong Kong-Macao Greater Bay Area proposal that both the central and local governments have been promoting in recent years. Based in such massive infrastructure projects as the Hong Kong-Zhuhai-Macao Bridge, the Express Rail Link between China and Hong Kong, and the Shenzhen-Zhongshan Corridor highway system, the Greater Bay Area concept is intended to facilitate the flow of capital, goods, and people through an integrated space extending from Hong Kong and Macao through Guangdong Province, further intertwining the economies of this region as well as the lives of its residents. Official commentators have been quick to point out that the proposal is not intended to belittle Hong Kong but rather to prevent its marginalization by incorporating the city into China's rise.[76] Yet already within this claim we can see Zhu and Zhang's logic of inverted hierarchies: whereas migrants once fled to Hong Kong to escape the poverty and chaos of Maoist China to find a new life, the Greater Bay Area now provides a chance for Hong Kong residents to flee the perceived economic malaise and political chaos of the city to build a new life in a newly rising and stable economic center. Coming full circle in the cycle of history as traced by Zhu and Zhang, there will yet again be no ties to nor identification with the local space of Hong Kong, much less any idea of a Hong Kong nation, but rather simply a determinant economic pragmatism driving people to wherever the money is.

Everyone with whom I have spoken in Hong Kong thinks of the Greater Bay Area as a joke and sees the idea that they might identify as a "Greater Bay Area person" as utterly laughable. Anyone who has spent even a few moments outside of the confines of the Liaison Office will rightly be highly skeptical of such a formula. Yet Beijing's Hong Kong-ology is after all not about understanding the actually existing dynamics of politics and identity in Hong Kong. It is about ignoring and indeed erasing these realities, so as to replace them with preformed narrative constructions through which the central state can exercise imaginary mastery over the city. In this sense, while the Greater Bay Area may in many senses be little more than vapid nothingness, it is at the same time also a very real policy to which the central and local governments are deeply committed, and in which billions will undoubtedly be invested. Its impact will also be very real, continuing the processes of economic centralization reviewed in chapter 1: processes which, we must remember, have only produced ever greater feelings of difference rather than integration.

For Zhu and Zhang, the economic dynamism that has long been a prominent feature of Hong Kong's identity is now to be found only in China. Therefore, against the mutually isolating assumptions of One Country, Two Systems, Hong Kong not only *needs China* in order to be itself again but in fact *needs to be China* in order to be itself. Such a logic of replacement is also found in the newly emerging discursive structure of Hong Kong as a lawless land, which needs Beijing's firm hand in order to restore the rule of law, a topic to which I turn in the next section.

HONG KONG AS OUTLAW

"Hong Kong independence" has never been legal.

—Feng Qingxiang and Xu Haibo, "Origins of the 'Hong Kong Independence' Phenomenon and Its Elimination," 2017[77]

Nothing epitomizes the distinctiveness of Hong Kong quite like its legal system. The exceptionality of the city's rule *of* law system becomes ever more apparent when contrasted with China's rule *by* law system, wherein the CCP exercises obsessive control over the courts, sees itself as the law, and is thereby able to operate above the law. Official Chinese academic studies of Hong Kong, however, paint a very different picture of the city's legal culture. Hong Kong is orientalized therein as a society slipping into lawlessness due to the recent discussions of Hong Kong independence, before being encompassed as requiring urgent intervention from the center to restore law and order. Hong Kong, in this telling, needs China in order to be more like itself again: a rule of law–based society.

Before proceeding into the narrative construction of Hong Kong as a lawless land, it is advisable to review basic legal realities actively obscured in the narratives that follow. The ideas and debates around Hong Kong's political future and its relationship with China introduced in chapter 2 are best understood not as symbols of wanton lawlessness but rather as manifestations of Hong Kong's mature political culture and rule of law system. There is of course no doubt that these discussions are deeply controversial and are obviously strongly disliked by the Chinese authorities and even by many citizens of the city. The legal protection of free speech, however, is intended precisely to protect controversial and even unpopular speech. After all, speech that is noncontroversial or that simply reproduces prevailing political assumptions needs no such protection. The ongoing discussions and debates on Hong Kong nationalism and the city's relationship to China as outlined in chapter 2 do not violate any laws by any reasonable rule of law–based interpretation, and any attempt to silence these discussions would in fact constitute a violation of the free speech guarantees enshrined in the Basic Law.

These simple truths are, however, wrong, according to official Chinese academics: very, very wrong, in fact. Official studies begin from the predetermined conclusion that there is an urgent need for the Chinese state to cast aside the restrictions of One Country, Two Systems in order to step in and restore order in Hong Kong, before proceeding to build a legal argument to legitimize this conclusion. The law here is not something to be respected and carefully interpreted in the light of existing case law, but rather something to be arranged in such a way as to give an aura of respect to the interventionist compulsions of the central state.

One of the most straightforward arguments enabling such a conclusion is derived from a very particular reading of the Basic Law. Article 27 of the Basic Law unambiguously states that "Hong Kong residents shall have freedom of speech, of the press and of publication; freedom of association, of assembly, of procession and of demonstration; and the right and freedom to form and join trade unions, and to strike."[78] Meanwhile, Article 1 of the Basic Law states that "the Hong Kong Special Administrative Region is an inalienable part of the People's Republic of China."[79] Numerous official scholars have argued that Article 1 overrides Article 27, such that the discussion of Hong Kong as anything but an inalienable Special Administrative Region of the People's Republic of China cannot be legally protected free speech: the primacy of Article 1 is even cited in support of its cardinal importance, as if the Basic Law was written in descending order of significance. In his 2018 piece "Detection and Legal Regulation of 'Hong Kong Independence' Speech: A Perspective from

Article 23 of the Hong Kong Basic Law" in *Hong Kong-Macao Studies*, Li Yiyi cites Article 1 to make the not so obvious argument that any "proposal to split China in 'Hong Kong independence' speech obviously violates Hong Kong's Basic Law."[80] Wang Fuchun, in his 2018 article "On Establishing an Anti-secession Law for the Hong Kong Special Administrative Region," proposes that the freedom of speech guaranteed in Article 27 of the Basic Law can only protect speech that is in accordance with all other articles of the Basic Law, and thus cannot be used to protect any "illegal speech" that goes against other articles, in particular Article 1.[81]

The sheer directness of this argument reveals its own logical fallacies all too directly. The Basic Law is not criminal law, but rather a constitutional document for managing the Hong Kong Special Administrative Region. Because it is not criminal law, the Basic Law naturally lists no penalties for thoughts or statements that disagree with or imagine an alternative to current political arrangements. Yet even if the Basic Law were criminal law, is the expression of an opinion that differs from current laws illegal? There is an undeniable distinction between discussing a crime and committing a crime: I can say that I am going to steal all of the chicken nuggets from the fast-food restaurant down the street, but unless I actually do so, nothing illegal has in fact happened. The issues at hand here, however, have far deeper implications than chicken nuggets, relating to matters of politics and thus to matters of freedom and social development. For example, the criminalization and eventual decriminalization of marijuana in the United States is a useful point of comparison. I distinctly remember being impressed as a teenager in the 1990s that while marijuana was illegal, publications like *High Times*, which advocated legalization, were able to operate without legal sanction, eventually leading to a considerably more open approach to this mind-altering substance in American society. The transformation of the definition of marriage in recent decades is another significant example: even when US law explicitly stated that marriage only applied to the bond between a man and a woman, activists were able to promote the idea of a more open vision of marriage without legal sanction, which has in turn redefined the meaning of this institution. A legally protected space for difference of opinions with regard to current political, legal, and social frameworks is then not only an essential component of freedom of speech but also a facilitator of progress in political, legal, and social matters, ensuring that laws and thus society do not remain perpetually frozen in the thought patterns of the past. Similarly, the ongoing debate over

Hong Kong's political future outlined in chapter 2 is not illegal but rather an example of human self-reflection breaking through the ideological constraints of the past to imagine an alternate future.

Another official scholar, Luo Weijian, pursues a considerably more circuitous path to the predetermined conclusion of illegality, convolutedly constructing a novel definition of freedom of speech in such a way as to specifically exclude the discussion of independence. In his 2016 article in *Hong Kong-Macao Studies*, "Analysis of Illegality about Statements and Actions of 'Hong Kong Independence' and the Legal Regulations: Enlightenments from the Case of Macao Courts," Luo develops a memorably idiosyncratic definition of free speech.[82] He begins by declaring, perhaps a bit disingenuously, that free speech is great. This greatness, which makes the ideal of free speech worth defending, is to be found in the fact that it (1) enables citizens to judge with which politicians and policies they agree, as well as to provide oversight on political matters; (2) helps in discovering truth, particularly in seeking out the objective rules behind phenomena; and finally, (3) facilitates personal development and creativity.[83] All of these phenomena, Luo asserts, are of benefit both to individuals and society, and it is as a result of these benefits that freedom of speech is a legally protected right.[84]

In any other context, Luo's proposal might be easily forgotten as a peculiar attempt at defining free speech, seemingly completely insulated from the literature on this topic. Yet Luo's aim here was never to impress readers with an innovative perspective on free speech matters. Rather, his goal is to develop a plausible definition of free speech that can then be used to make restrictions on speech plausible: an admittedly difficult maneuver that necessitates some elaborate mental gymnastics. The next step in Luo's routine is thus to redeploy his very particular definition of free speech so as to present the specific benefits around which he constructed his definition as limiting preconditions for speech's protection as free. Suddenly shifting his tone to declare that "freedom does not mean being able to just do whatever you want," the initial proposal that free speech is protected because speech can be of benefit to society is inverted to declare that only speech that is of benefit to society can be legally protected.[85] By this logic, speech considered to be "not beneficial" is not only not protected by free speech guarantees but also becomes illegal. Who, then, decides which forms of speech are beneficial or not? According to Luo, this is a matter for the government to decide. The fight for free speech over the span of centuries, a history of resisting governments' monitoring

and suppression of speech, ironically culminates in Luo's vision in subject-
ing speech to state monitoring and suppression in cases that the government
judges to be "nonbeneficial."

It may not come as a surprise to readers that the discussion of Hong Kong
independence, in Luo's view, falls definitively into the category of nonbeneficial
and thus illegal speech. Official studies reliably present a highly sensationalized picture of Hong Kong society today, wherein the decidedly "nonbeneficial" political debates of recent years have pushed the city to the precipice of
complete chaos. Wang Fuchun tells readers that economic activity in Hong
Kong has been thrown into turmoil and that people's daily lives have been
greatly disrupted.[86] Han Shanshan declares that the activities of Hong Kong
independence enthusiasts have openly challenged the authority of the central
government and done great damage to social harmony in Hong Kong.[87] Chen
Yijian and Huang Tong argue that so long as discussions of Hong Kong independence continue, the city will be unable to achieve prosperity and stability,
official talking points that official academics assume are naturally the primary
goals of all Hong Kong citizens.[88] The fact that illegal speech can be uttered
openly in Hong Kong without legal sanction thus undermines Hong Kong's
status as a rule of law–based society. Our official Hong Kong-ologists tell us
that the time for cautious rebuttal has long passed, and that the state needs to
take immediate action to restore order.[89]

As with the preceding examples, the final destination of every one of these
discussions of the rule of law is a strident call for the Chinese state to cast aside
all restrictions so as to intervene directly and return Hong Kong to normalcy.
This particular argument is, however, especially unique insofar as it attempts
to construct a binding legal basis for the central state to abandon its binding legal responsibilities, using the law to work around the law. Li Yiyi works
toward this paradoxical endpoint when he argues that all of the legal responsibility for One Country, Two Systems since 1997 has been unfairly placed on
Beijing's shoulders: the central government, Li claims, can be found guilty of
violating two systems, but no one in Hong Kong has ever been found guilty
of violating one country.[90] The point here is not to take this claim seriously
and wonder to oneself when the central government has ever been held in any
way responsible for any of its violations of the Basic Law, of which there have
been many. Rather, a statement like this should be read as a reinterpretation
of Beijing's legal responsibilities to include not only restraining itself to protect
two systems, but also unrestraining itself to protect one country, the natural

outcome of the fatal underlying flaws in the Basic Law discussed in chapter 1. In this line of argument, Luo Weijian asserts:

> First, the government is legally required to protect behavior that is in accordance with the law. Second, the government is legally required to restrict behavior that is in violation of the law. Third, if the government not only fails to restrict behavior that is in violation of the law but even goes so far as to protect it, the government is then in violation of the law. Fourth, a government legally restricting illegal behavior is a manifestation of abiding by the law, so any court should support it. Only by correctly understanding the SAR's Basic Law and other relevant laws can we restrict and sanction all behavior that violates or challenges the law.[91]

It is then not Hong Kong's status as a rule of law society that protects people's rights to discuss Hong Kong independence. Rather, the discussion of Hong Kong independence is illegal and threatens Hong Kong's status as a rule of law society. If the central government fails to act to restrict such illegal behavior, it is in fact violating the law, which is of course unacceptable. Shredding its legal guarantees to be a responsible and law-abiding power that will refrain from intervening in Hong Kong then becomes the only way that the central government can be a responsible and law-abiding power.

This vision of overriding legal constraints to restore a supposedly more genuine law and order is apparent in numerous policy developments in Hong Kong in recent years, with one of the most prominent examples being the 2018 ban on the Hong Kong National Party. Established in March 2016 (as narrated in chapter 2), the Hong Kong National Party was blocked from official registration for years.[92] Its convenor, Andy Chan Ho-tin, was also the first Legislative Council candidate to be disqualified from running for office in the 2016 elections, as also discussed in chapter 2.[93] In July 2018, Secretary for Security John Lee notified Chan that the government was planning to ban the Hong Kong National Party. Just two months later, the ban had been confirmed, declaring the National Party an "unlawful society" under the Societies Ordinance designed to deal with underground criminal organizations.[94]

Assessing the basis for this ban in the *Hong Kong Law Journal*, Carole Petersen highlights numerous legal and procedural issues that raise significant questions about the ban's legal basis.[95] The Security Bureau claimed that the National Party posed a threat to national security, public safety and order, and the rights of others. These sound like quite serious charges, but their coherence dissolves upon closer inspection. As Petersen notes, the claim that the Hong Kong National Party presents a threat to national security was based on the Security Bureau's assertion that the party had taken "concrete steps" toward achieving Hong Kong independence. These "concrete steps" however, consisted solely of "speech acts and other peaceful activities, such as printing leaflets, giving radio interviews, raising funds and attempting to register the HKNP."[96] All of these acts are, we must note, legally protected political activities that cannot become targets of suppression simply because the central government dislikes the messages conveyed therein. The claim that the Hong Kong National Party presents a threat to public safety and order was partly based on the possibility that the party could organize assemblies that might block traffic, yet as Petersen points out, this is a purely speculative possibility that does not provide sufficient grounds for banning a political party.[97] Finally, the claim that the party presented a threat to the rights of others was based on Secretary for Security John Lee's assertion that the National Party "spreads hatred and discrimination" against Chinese people, which Petersen notes is an "absurd characterization" of the party's speech acts, which have been primarily focused on the topic of Hong Kong independence.[98] In its essence, the ban was based on the same predetermined conclusion that I analyzed earlier: discussion of Hong Kong independence is (for reasons to be determined) illegal and needs to be stopped.

The flawed legal basis for the ban was not subjected to legal review. Rather, precisely because of the weakness of the legal argument, the government also failed to afford the Hong Kong National Party the type of procedural protections that should be expected in any case, not to mention a case with such a profound and lasting impact on basic freedoms in the city. Andy Chan, as the convenor of the Hong Kong National Party, did not receive publicly funded legal assistance to defend the party against the authorities' charges.[99] The government failed to provide Chan with documents that he requested to build his case.[100] Chan's request to make an oral rather than written submission in response to the government's claims was denied, and the time span between the initial proposal and the final decision affirming the ban was so limited, granting only one brief extension, that Chan lacked sufficient time to complete the required written submissions.[101] Finally, nine members of the Executive Council that made the final decision on the ban had previously made public statements about the Hong Kong National Party that very clearly indicated they were not in any way disinterested parties with regard to the decision.[102] This flawed procedure was not a mere coincidence but rather, in connection with the flawed legal argument, a sign of the government's eagerness to cast aside legal reasoning and procedures to achieve a predetermined conclusion, using the law not as a guide but rather as a cover for their own conduct.

If the 2018 decision to ban the Hong Kong National Party was only about one party, it would have already been a grim development: a political party was erased and the lives of two young activists who had started the party were forever changed. Yet the ban on the Hong Kong National Party was in fact about far more than this. The ban was an unprecedented step to restrict freedom of expression and association, freedoms that are ostensibly guaranteed in Hong Kong by the International Covenant on Civil and Political Rights.[103] The only semicoherent argument that the authorities could develop to justify this ban was the same flawed logic: Hong Kong independence is illegal according to a deliberate misreading of the Basic Law, so permitting the discussion of this idea is illegal, so banning such discussion is not only legal but indeed the very definition of the rule of law itself. Any evidence-based rebuttal of these claims, asserting the legally protected freedoms of speech and association, was not acknowledged by the authorities, who remained steadfast in their preemptive determination of the party's illegality. Therefore, while the ban was portrayed as a defense of the legal system, it was in reality a case of official discrimination based on political opinion, taking the unprecedented step of depriving people of their legally guaranteed rights to speech and assembly solely on account of their association with a concept that the central government dislikes: Hong Kong independence. This step set the tone for relations between the Hong Kong/PRC governments and Hong Kong civil society in the years that followed, culminating in the 2020 implementation of the National Security Law.

Lawlessness and the law are thus literally two sides of the same coin in Beijing's vision. Just as youthfulness constructs Beijing as the adult in the room, and just as the supposed jealous insanity of independence advocacy constructs the PRC as sane, so the portrayal of Hong Kong as outlaw constructs through binary opposition an image of the central government as protector of the law. The orientalizing function of this portrayal is readily apparent, yet its encompassing function here is even more significant: insofar as rule of law is a defining feature of Hong Kong, this narrative presents the city as needing Beijing to intervene not only to restore an elusive ideal of order but indeed simply to be itself again. The most effective way to protect Hong Kong's rule of law system is then not to observe the restrictions on Beijing's power enacted via One Country, Two Systems but rather to abandon these restrictions altogether, obliterating the rule of law in the name of its defense: precisely the conclusion that the One Country, Two Systems arrangement was supposed to prevent, yet toward which it was always already proceeding. The strident insistence of the mantra that the authorities know what is legal or not belies the authorities' own anxiety in this regard, as a rule of law system that determines these matters through deliberation, a defining feature of Hong Kong, is slowly eclipsed by an arbitrary, politicized system that has decided these matters in advance and will rule all contrary evidence inadmissible.

HONG KONG AS VIRUS: ONE BODY, TWO SYSTEMS

Andy Chan is not a human being.
—Arthur Shek, *Hong Kong Economic Times*, August 2018[104]

The most disquieting tropes through which official academic studies discuss independence activism are the ideas of a virus, cancer, or other biologically toxic formations. In 2016 Zhu Jie and Zhang Xiaoshan, always in the avant garde of official narrations of Hong Kong politics, described the still quite novel concept of Hong Kong independence as spreading like a "virus" among young people.[105] Li Qin, writing in *Hong Kong-Macao Studies* in 2019, characterized Hong Kong independence as a cancer: "In recent years, the 'Hong Kong independence' issue has gradually developed from the problem of a few individuals' behavior to a political problem with its own parties and organizations. It has grown from a passing localist trend to a full-blown theoretical system advocating 'city-state rule.' It has grown into a cancer that is destroying Hong Kong's prosperity and stability."[106] Playing on the homophonous nature of "independence" (*duhk/dú*) and "poison" (*duhk/ dú*), Chinese state media in the city frequently refer to the idea of Hong Kong independence as "Hong Kong poison." For example, I have been portrayed in a cartoon on the Beijing-owned online news portal dotdotnews declaring "Hey, I'm here to spray some poison (independence)!" In these analogies, political judgments are naturalized in the language of biology, which at once orientalizes thinkers and activists as manifestations of a toxic disorder within the national body, while also encompassing these same figures as problems that need to be urgently fought against and eliminated by the state's immune system. Yet at an even deeper level, these biological metaphors express the lingering tensions between interior and exterior, essentialism and change, and regeneration and degeneration inherent within China's imaginary relationship with Hong Kong.

Identity and difference, always inherently social relationships, are nevertheless ripe for representation through biological metaphors. Just as human beings tend to envision our self-identity as a reflection of an internal essence, so we also tend to imagine relations between social groups, premised on the idea of difference, as the result of essential biological distinctions. Race is one of the most common metaphors through which such essentialized difference (and assumed sameness) is imagined, and it remains a notably underexamined topic in China-Hong Kong relations. Beijing's claim to Hong Kong, as analyzed in chapter 1, is based on a racial essentialism of imaginary blood ties that envisions people of Sinitic descent around the world, regardless of their place in their respective societies, as inherently Chinese by right of the belief that they have "Chinese blood" flowing through their bodies.[107] The idea that Hong Kong is an indivisible part of China, an idea taken for granted for far too long, is precisely such a racialized construct.

Although presumed within this imaginary to be undeniably Chinese by right of unbreakable blood ties, the people of Hong Kong are also presumed to be less than fully Chinese in the proper sense. From at least the early years of the reform era, the PRC Party-state has promoted an official identity characterized primarily by a constructed political and social difference in opposition to the idea of "the West," which is imagined as a source of disorderly pollution.[108] Through this binary oppositional structure, officially constructed identity and its politically limiting vision are endowed with the value of racial-ideological purity and accordant pride.[109] Although this construction primarily serves the domestic political purpose of enhancing state-society relations through an image of the self cast against the other, thereby ideologically minimizing internal differences, it nevertheless also has deep implications for the center's relationship with Hong Kong, insofar as Hong Kong was colonized and in many senses shaped by this other. Many of the distinctions that make the city what it is have in fact been othered in official central state constructions as "non-Chinese" and thus unnatural. Hong Kong's presumed inherent racialized Chineseness is as a result also presumed to have been misshaped by history into an anomalous and degenerative Chineseness, characterized foremost by its distance from the norm.[110]

Insofar as Hong Kong's history demonstrates that this norm is constructed and that biology determines neither one's identity nor one's politics, the city's distinctiveness, even in its othering as not purely "Chinese," still subverts the Party-state's essentialist vision of the current political system as the sole natural outcome of five millennia of Chinese history. After all, official constructions of culture and identity in the People's Republic of China are, we must remember, no more authentic and no less historically constructed than the supposedly anomalous state of today's Hong Kong. Although the rise of China on the global stage has facilitated the equation of the state's hegemonic image with Chineseness itself, those of us familiar with the anthropological literature will remember that New Territories culture was in recent history considered a most authentic vision of Chineseness in contrast to life to the north. Such imaginings invariably shift with time, yet the central state's deployment of identity relies on the idea that such things do not change, envisioning instead a myth of invariable authenticity extending from the Yellow Emperor to the present. There is thus a need to marginalize the anxiety-inducing variability (constructionism) inherent within Hong Kong's historical experience so as to restore homogeneity and invariability (essentialism), a task achieved by rein-scribing Hong Kong's difference within metaphors that present such differ-ences as dangerous mutations.

Cheng Siwei, former vice chairman of the National People's Congress Standing Committee, did precisely this when he bluntly told a group of chil-dren at Heung To Middle School in 2004 that some Hong Kong people were "bananas."[111] By this Cheng meant that they were "yellow" and thus "Chinese" on the outside but "white" and thus "Western" on the inside. In this metaphor, the colonial experience is mapped into people's bodies via a crude binary color scheme, such that a distinct sociopolitical tradition emerging from historical experience becomes an anomalous splitting presence within the self: One Body, Two Systems. This invasive internal mutation lying beneath citizens' skin will not lie dormant; rather, it naturally expands outward like a cancerous growth, threatening to consume its hosts. Cheng furthermore claimed that such "sin-ners of the Chinese nation" would eventually find themselves trapped in a futile mission of whitening their skin. The compulsion for wholeness and consistency extending from the inside out is an underlying assumption of this framework.[112]

Such a denial of one's own essence is in fact so futile that one's biological roots are revealed even in the very act of denial. In her article "An Exploration of Hong Kong's Colonial Complex in the Process of Reconstructing Chinese Identity in the City," published in the *Journal of the Party School of Xinjiang Production and Construction Corps of the Chinese Communist Party* in 2017, Li Youkun analyzes this pathological internal whiteness denying one's own Chi-neseness as in fact little more than an inferior form of "feudal" Chineseness erased in China proper on account of the mighty, glorious, and correct rule of the Party.[113] According to Li, "the worship of power in Chinese feudal culture led some Hong Kong people to worship Western political and economic models, while also believing Western images of China constructed to make them hate the Mainland. Power is a certain strength and authority that drives people to obey."[114] Counter to Chin Wan's assertion that Hong Kong is home to the best of Chinese culture untarnished by the Chinese Communist Party's cultural policies, Li argues that Hong Kong is in fact home to the worst forms of Chineseness precisely because its culture has not been purified by the ostensibly anti-feudal Chinese Communist Party. There are two highly significant implications for Hong Kong-China relations in this viewpoint, featured in an officially sanctioned and tightly controlled academic journal. First, the sociocultural change that produced Hong Kong's distinct culture and identity is envisioned here not as an example of progress but rather of degeneration. Second, Hong Kong's innate Chineseness is so undeniable that the more one denies one's Chineseness, the more one's Chineseness, albeit in an inferior, degraded form, becomes apparent.

A person who attempts to deny his or her own undeniable essence is doomed to become a nonentity, a nonperson. Prominent pro-Beijing figure Arthur Shek, former vice president of the *Hong Kong Economic Times*, wrote an opinion piece in August 2018 with the provocative but also revealing title "Andy Chan Is Not a Human Being" (*Chan Ho-tin mh haih yahn*).[115] In order to reach this troubling conclusion, Shek reviews a list of essential human categories only to find that Chan cannot fit into any, thus rendering him a nonentity. First considering the category of Hong Kong people, Shek says that Chan's calls for the US government to sanction the city would ruin the economic livelihoods of seven million Hong Kong people, which means that he could not be a "Hong Kong person."[116] Then, considering the category of Chinese people, Shek notes that while Chan speaks Chinese and uses Chinese characters in his writing, he advocates Hong Kong independence, which means that he could not be a "Chinese person."[117] Finally, however, Chan could not be an American person because he does not drink American water or eat American fruits, vegetables, chickens, and ducks, but instead "drinks water from Guangdong's East River and eats fruits, vegetables, fish, chicken, and ducks from China."[118] If Chan cannot logically fit within any of these human categories into which people must fall, Shek argues one can only conclude that he is in fact a nonperson. Shek's biopolitical musings on humanity and the lack thereof here resonate with Roberto Esposito's analysis of the "non" within the Third Reich's thanatopolitics: the non is, like Shek's portrayal of Chan, "not a true man, but has human features. He does not have an image, but continually changes appearance. He is not a type but a countertype. He belongs to the world of the 'non.'"[119] Hong Kong independence is then no longer just a problem of misguided youth or the disintegration of law and order; it becomes a problem of nonhuman entities hiding in plain sight among humans, thereby blurring the boundaries between the human and the nonhuman. We all know all too well the troubling implications of such dehumanizing language.

The shifting power dynamics of China's relationship with the world have made these anomalous creatures only more anomalous. According to Li Youkun, whereas identification with the power of "the West" once provided the people of Hong Kong with a false sense of pride relative to China, the emptiness of this pride is rapidly becoming apparent on account of China's rise: "Hong Kong's development has fallen behind in recent years, in stark contrast to the Chinese mainland's rapid rise since the implementation of reform and opening, a fact that has agitated some Hong Kong people's blind colonial complex."[120] Following Zhu and Zhang's analytical lead, this is where Li sees the veritable "poison" of Hong Kong independence turning deeply toxic, embracing a false self-glorifying identity to cover over one's weakness: "[Hong Kong independence activists] hysterically declare to the world that Hong Kong is more advanced and outstanding than the Mainland, but their nostalgic wading in an already long-lost colonial experience is really just a desperate attempt to repress reality and maintain their fading sense of superiority. To a certain degree, one could say that Hong Kong independence advocates' pathological nostalgia for the colonial era is really just nostalgia for their pathological sense of superiority relative to the Mainland."[121] Hong Kong-China relations are shifted in this view from the reunion of a parent and a lost child to a struggle between an undeniable essence and a degenerative mutation, between inside and outside, and between the rise of China and the fall of "the West."

In contrast to power, which takes effort to maintain as seen in this narration of the shifting power dynamics between China and the West, degeneration is self-reproducing and thus always has the potential to expand infinitely.[122] The maintenance of One Country, Two Systems, which essentially preserves Hong Kong's degenerative mutations, is then not only unhealthy for Hong Kong but also presents a risk to the rise of China as a whole: as is always the case in these biopolitical visions, there is a risk of the inferior potentially infecting the superior.[123] The weak link of Hong Kong within China thus becomes an entry point for Western powers aiming to infect the body politic and hinder China's rise. According to Li, "Hong Kong has always been an important card for Western countries to play in their strategy toward China."[124] The Hong Kong independence discussion here cannot be the product of the city's open political culture or reflection on the failures of the One Country, Two Systems model, but rather must be an externally manufactured conspiracy forced into the national body to undermine the nation's eagerly awaited rise. Seeking evidence to support this claim, Li lists a number of examples of prominent Hong Kong activists who have personal or family ties to pre-1949 "feudalism" in China, the pre-1997 colonial Hong Kong government, or the West. Li names Benny Tai, Chan Kin-man, and Reverend Chu Yiu-ming of Occupy Central; Emily Lau and Martin Lee of the Democratic Party; former civil servant Anson Chan; and Jimmy Lai of *Apple Daily*, adding various defamatory comments about their families and educational backgrounds.[125] Astute readers may note one major problem with Li's analysis: this is the first and last time any of these names are mentioned in this book, precisely because most have nothing to do with the idea of Hong Kong independence that Li claims to be explaining. Despite the obtuseness of Li's argument, its implications are significant: there are underlying anomalous biological phenomena threatening to infect and undermine the nation itself. After proceeding through these manifold analytical constructions of the child, the hysteric, the outlaw, and the virus, we find ourselves back at the point from which this chapter began: Chen Hao's indignant discovery that a Hong Kong–based cabal is attempting to disrupt China's otherwise inevitable rise, which they should be celebrating rather than undermining.

Just as biological metaphors are essential to understanding China's claim to Hong Kong, so these metaphors of biological anomaly fundamentally change the narration of this relationship. Whereas Hong Kong's handover from the United Kingdom to China in 1997 was supposed to be a defining moment in the country's regeneration, this moment is reimagined here as incorporating degenerative mutations into the body politic, undermining the once stable sense of the self and threatening the nation's long-term rise. The accusatory framework developed in these analyses echoes the disciplining mode of psychoanalysis critiqued by Deleuze and Guattari in *Anti-Oedipus*, wherein desire is always already guilty of the most horrendous of crimes and thus needs to be disciplined and controlled. Revealingly, Deleuze and Guattari speak of the decoded flows of desire within the unconscious as an "orphan," the lost child of official narratives, who is blackmailed by the Oedipus complex's guilt-inducing accusation that one wants to murder one's father and marry one's mother: "That's what you wanted!"[126] Similarly, the open-ended flows of political thinking and debate beyond the law of pan-Chinese racial-national unity are recoded here in official studies as a fate even more horrid than that of Oedipus: killing one's genetic motherland and engaging in incestuous union with one's adopted parents. The solution in both cases is to submit to the Law of the Father, the law that exists beyond all laws, manifest here in the National Security Law into whose control Hong Kong descended late in the evening of June 30, 2020.

Niklas Luhmann has characterized the law as the protective immune system of society, an evocative metaphor in light of the biopolitical constructions analyzed in this section.[127] Days after the implementation of the National Security Law in late June 2020, a piece in the Liaison Office–controlled *Wen Wei Po* referred to the law as "anti-virus software" that would eliminate the "political viruses" that had thrown the city into chaos and threatened to drag all of China down with it.[128] By rendering such legally protected phenomena as the discussion of sovereignty and independence as illegal activities proscribed by the law, the 2020 National Security Law epitomizes Luhmann's characterization of such immune systems as "operat[ing] without cognition, knowledge of the environment, or analysis of disturbing factors; they merely discriminate things as not belonging."[129] These ideas and the discussions surrounding them were judged to be always already "not belonging" according to the law, regardless of what the law actually said. The implementation of a law that officially renders these legally protected activities illegal can only be based on the type of operation without cognition, lacking knowledge of the environment, or devoid of analysis of contributing factors that Luhmann highlights: it is the logical conclusion of the illogical analyses examined here, seeking to repress rising concerns about the preservation of freedoms and rule of law under One Country, Two Systems by completely abandoning the freedoms and rule of law system that One Country, Two Systems was supposed to protect, all in the name of One Country, Two Systems.

The self-reproducing destructive processes observed in degeneration also have their parallel in the immune responses intended to eliminate degenerative elements: autoimmune illnesses, wherein the protective apparatus of the immune system becomes so aggressive that it attacks the very body that it is supposed to be defending.[130] This self-destructive attempt at protection, operating without cognition, knowledge of the environment, or analysis of disturbing factors, is eventually unable to decipher what belongs and does not belong, attacking without discretion and thereby leading to the death and dis-integration of the body that it is supposedly protecting. Such a fate seems, in my initial reading, to be the most likely outcome of Hong Kong's National Security Law.

FROM KNOWLEDGE/POWER TO IGNORANCE/POWER TO KNOWLEDGE VERSUS POWER: THE NOT-SO-HIDDEN SCRIPT OF HONG KONG POLICY

The National Security Law forced on Hong Kong in mid-2020, in its complete refusal to engage with the real dynamics of Hong Kong politics and attendant choice to envision critics as infections of the body politic in need of elimina-tion, is the logical conclusion of the official studies analyzed here. If the criti-cal reflections on Hong Kong-China relations presented in chapter 1 and the new pathways analyzed in chapter 2 represent a political enlightenment from the mythologies of pan-Chinese racial identity and national unity, the official studies analyzed in this chapter represent a determined counter-enlightenment wherein the state aims to discredit its critics and reassert its hegemony.[131] The four metaphors of Hong Kong independence analyzed here all construct a sim-ilar structural vision of the Hong Kong-China relationship, orientalizing Hong Kong as suffering from a lack that requires supplementation, before encom-passing the city as only ever able to be completed and thus saved by China. This counter-enlightenment produces a narrative wherein Hong Kong, whether it realizes it or not, needs China simply in order to be itself. The PRC Party-state embraces this narrative, which it has itself produced, and within which its offi-cial academics work, seeking solutions to ongoing political dilemmas precisely in their origins: ever-expanding hegemonic power.

In the imagining of Hong Kong as an impulsive youth, the city's mature and lively political culture is portrayed as immature and irrational, led astray by negative historical influences. The stubbornness of the ignorant children of Hong Kong is matched only by the stubbornness of the legal constraints of One Country, Two Systems on the central government. Yet when faced with a child proceeding down the wrong path, a parent needs to do what is right. The central government tells us that regardless of legal constraints, it must step up, apply discipline, and guide this unwise and impulsive city back onto the path of reason. Hong Kong's crisis is, then, a matter of discipline.

In the imagining of Hong Kong as a newly impoverished hysteric, the city is portrayed as an economic failure and living fossil trapped in lost glory days, lashing out angrily at its newly successful motherland. Having laid Hong Kong out on the psychoanalyst's couch, a solution is found in giving the city the economic and mental support that it needs to leave the past behind and move into the future, located unambiguously in China. The central state is ready to provide what is necessary, but the people of Hong Kong need to set aside their pride to embrace China's economic rise and their peripheral place therein. Hong Kong's crisis is, then, a matter of economics and pride.

In the imagining of Hong Kong as outlaw, its rule of law–based culture is presented as rapidly slipping away as a result of legally protected free discussions of the city's future. Hong Kong thereby requires active intervention by the Chinese central government not only to restore law and order but indeed to even begin to be like itself again. In an appropriately paradoxical construction, the legal constraints of One Country, Two Systems need to be set aside in order to allow the central state to restore law and order in Hong Kong. Hong Kong's crisis is, then, a matter of law and order.

Finally, in the imagining of Hong Kong as virus, cancer, or poison, the city's culture produced within the historical experience of British colonization is reimagined as an infectious disease undermining China's body politic. Although Hong Kong always has been and always will be Chinese, its Chineseness is as a result of this mutation characterized by a degenerative distance from the central state's norm. Insofar as this degeneration could undermine China's racial regeneration, the central government needs to step in to eliminate this infection. This is a matter of concern not only for the city of Hong Kong but indeed for the entire nation of China. Hong Kong's crisis is, then, a matter of infection and a resulting immune response.

Through each of these official constructions framing Hong Kong-China relations, the causes of Hong Kong's rapidly unfolding political crisis are obscured to a point beyond recognition. In each case, the source of Hong Kong's problems is to be found solely on one side of the binary: in Hong Kong's impulsivity, delusion, lawlessness, or toxicity. And in each case, the solution is accordingly always to be found on the other side of the binary: China will provide Hong Kong with all that it needs in order to be itself again, whether this means discipline, economic aid, law and order, or purification. Through each of these metaphors, a fundamentally political problem, produced by Beijing's inability to abide by its legal commitments and refrain from interfering in Hong Kong, is transformed into literally anything but a political problem. The purpose of these constructions is then not to present an actual solution, but rather to halt the processes of reflection and exploration beyond the orthodoxies of the Chinese nation-state initiated by the enlightenment of the Hong Kong nationalist discussion: the state presents a counter-enlightenment, constructing critics as fundamentally unworthy of dialogue and confidently finding all solutions precisely in the origins of problems. Yet in producing and reproducing these narratives, we must not overlook the fact that the state also reproduces and reinforces a fundamental misunderstanding of the sources of tension in Hong Kong: ignorance/power under the guise of knowledge/power. Trapped within and indeed thriving on its own misunderstandings, the state's reassertion of hegemonic power also undermines this same power by confirming the arguments of Hong Kong independence activists.

We can see Beijing's reassertion of power in accordance with this model in recent years, seeking solutions in disqualifying naughty children, guiding Hong Kong into the future in the Greater Bay Area, setting aside legal constraints to enforce law and order, and finally integrating the city into the PRC's national security network to eliminate infectious threats, now safely cordoned off in prisons. All are premised on the expansion of state power from which these tensions began in 2003 and toward which official studies lead. Those who take the time to wade through the sea of orthodoxy that constitutes the corpus of official academic studies of Hong Kong independence can thus find revelatory hints of future policy directions. To provide a personal example from research for this book, I will never forget reading Wang Fuchun's "On the Establishment of an Anti-secession Law in the Hong Kong Special Administrative Region" one evening in May 2020. Just a few days earlier, Beijing had announced that it would be taking the unprecedented step of using Annex III of the Basic Law, within which PRC laws can be applied in the Hong Kong Special Administrative Region, to force a new National Security Law directly onto the city. Reading through Wang's quite tedious legal argument about the importance of opposing secession, I suddenly came across the following passage: "After our country legislated a National Security Law in 2015, and after we spent years reminding the Hong Kong Special Administrative Region that it has a responsibility to join in the protection of national security, Hong Kong still has not passed a National Security Law, resulting in potential holes in our national security efforts. Correspondingly, in order to fill in these holes, the central government could insert the National Security Law into Annex III of the Basic Law, such that the law would then take effect in Hong Kong."[132] Wang had thus, in an article published in May 2018, told us precisely what the Party-state would do in May 2020: use the Annex III loophole to force the National Security Law on the city of Hong Kong.

How should we interpret such synergies between official analyses and policies? Is there a cause-effect relationship between these official studies and Hong Kong policy? Did the Politburo Standing Committee read Wang Fuchun's commentary in *Local Legislation Journal* and decide that his proposal was the best path forward? The actual relationship is at once far simpler and considerably more complex. Rather than academic studies shaping the direction of policy, I see the conclusions of both official studies and state policies shaped in advance by a prewritten ideological script that is both hidden and easy to see. This script always already assumes and indeed affirms the need for a firmer hand from the central government in Hong Kong and has guided both policy and the analysis that rationalizes these policies since at least the rise of Xi Jinping if not earlier. Both are reading from the same circular and self-reproducing fore-structures of understanding: the prewritten script of China's rise and the need for a firmer hand.

According to this script, the One Country, Two Systems framework is the product of a particular historical moment that has now passed.[133] Initially proposed in the early years of the reform era, this framework reflects China's weakness at that particular historical moment relative to Hong Kong and the West. The power dynamics have, however, shifted since those times, such that a proposal that was once a guarantee reassuring the Hong Kong people is now a disservice to these same people, depriving them of the benefits of China's rise under direct CCP rule, while at the same time potentially disrupting China's rise by proscribing direct rule. The logical conclusion of this hidden script, reading One Country, Two Systems as primarily a matter of lost historical hierarchies of power that have now been inverted, is then to allow the CCP to abandon two systems and exercise direct rule over Hong Kong: disqualifying candidates and democratically elected legislators, banning political parties, forcing further economic and cultural integration, and even integrating the city into the Party-state's national security system.

The problem with such a prewritten script, however, is precisely that it is prewritten and thus cannot engage with real developments, while nevertheless having very real effects. It does not operate on the level of reflection and thus knowledge, but rather on the level of pure power and insistent circular repetition, attempting through an endless expansion of studies and policies to force Hong Kong in all of its complexity into a preformed narrative. The body of official academic studies on Hong Kong independence is characterized first and foremost by confidence in knowing by the authors and a corresponding complete dismissal of the thoughts of anyone in Hong Kong. According to this official perspective, they do not understand China, nor Chinese history or culture, nor even their own society.[134] In its power politics of antireflection, the central state fails to notice that the society with which it is interacting is not in fact the society that it imagines. Official academic studies can portray Hong Kong as an undisciplined child, an underdeveloped hysteric, an outlaw in need of the restoration of law and order, or a virus in need of elimination, and can repeat these tropes endlessly. Beijing's official policies can even treat the city as such. Holding determinedly to this script, however, does not produce the society imagined therein.

From the other side of this relationship, insofar as Beijing's anti-intellectual script of ignorance/power affirms the intellectual insights of Hong Kong's political enlightenment, the city's activists are indeed interacting with the state power with whom they think they are interacting, and they understand this state far better than it understands them and indeed itself. The central state's search for a solution in the cause of the problems, fueling the eternal return of controlocracy as both problem and solution, thus ironically provides the best evidence yet to support Hong Kong independence activists' argument: that One Country, Two Systems is fundamentally broken and unable to protect the city's autonomy and liberties.

Knowledge and power then are not mutually intertwined and reinforcing in this colonial relationship, but are rather separate resources distributed unevenly on either side of this binary. This contrasts markedly with the vision of knowledge/power articulated in *Orientalism*, the book from which our reflections on these official studies began. In *Orientalism*, Said presents knowledge not simply as a reflection of reality but rather as playing a determinant role in the shaping of reality. Drawing upon Foucault, knowledge for Said is intertwined with power, such that power relations produce fields of knowledge, and such knowledge itself also constitutes a power relation. Building on this fusion of knowledge and power, Said defines the discourse of Orientalism, characterized by a self-other binary and marked internal consistency, as "the corporate institution for dealing with the Orient—dealing with it by making statements about it, authorizing views of it, describing it, by teaching it, settling it, ruling over it: in short, Orientalism as a Western style for dominating, restructuring, and having authority over the Orient."[135] In this process, the Occident "was able to manage—and even produce—the Orient politically, sociologically, militarily, ideologically, scientifically, and imaginatively during the post-Enlightenment period."[136] The relational outcome of this knowledge-based production and management is the discursive yet also real placement of the Orient in subordination, at once producing and perpetuating unequal power relations. Said is thus not only arguing that colonial domination employed the analyses of Orientalist scholars for its own purposes, but rather that Orientalist scholarship was an intrinsic part of the power of colonial domination. In Said's vision of knowledge/power, because of Orientalism, the Orient is never a free subject of thought or action.

This is without doubt an evocative theoretical framework, yet the sheer resonance of this theory far too often excuses its glaring imprecisions. Beyond the dramatic declaration of the mutual imbrication of knowledge and power, a declaration that tellingly grants an otherwise unattainable degree of imaginary power to its academic disciples (as producers of knowledge) and is thus unlikely to provoke disagreement among its readers, how exactly does knowledge contribute to power? How exactly is Orientalism, according to Said's analysis, able to render the Orient an unfree subject of thought and action? We can begin to find answers to these underexamined questions by rereading Said's framework through the example of Hong Kong's colonization by the People's Republic of China.

The Hong Kong-ology analyzed in this chapter features all of the characteristics of Orientalism as articulated by Said: these studies construct a discourse based in a binary of self-other, premised on the idea of dealing with Hong Kong, whether by describing it, authorizing views of it, analyzing it, ruling over it, or proposing solutions for it, and characterized first and foremost by a marked internal consistency. We would then seem to have, as I proposed at the beginning of this chapter, a novel example of an Orientalist knowledge/power construction that would then, according to Said's framework, produce Hong Kong as a fundamentally unfree subject of thought and action. And yet that is the opposite of what we have seen happen here: during the 2010s, as these policies and their accompanying analytic rationalizations drawing from the same script were constructed, Hong Kong became an increasingly difficult place for Beijing to rule. The self-affirming constructions of official Hong Kong-ology do not transform Hong Kong through the confluence of knowledge/power, nor do they make the city more suited to domination in accordance with the hidden script discussed earlier. Rather, these constructions simply mean that China misunderstands Hong Kong and the dynamics of social and political developments in the city.

Power and knowledge are thus not mutually intertwined in this colonial relationship. Rather, power and knowledge are distributed unevenly therein: power shaping the dynamics of this relationship is primarily concentrated in the central state, while knowledge and understanding of the dynamics shaping this relationship are primarily concentrated on the side of Hong Kong civil society and its newly emerging analyses, free from the restrictions of past orthodoxies. Rather than being part of a feedback cycle of provocation and counterprovocation between powers as envisioned in the cyclical sociological analysis in chapter 1, the city of Hong Kong faces a cycle of knowledge-based enlightenment and power-based counter-enlightenment between vastly mismatched powers, increasingly brought into direct conflict with one another by escalating political tensions. As new knowledge and understanding produced by critics increasingly lay bare the power dynamics of Beijing's rule, Beijing increasingly relies on its power to strip away legally guaranteed rights and repress the insights of Hong Kong's political awakening. Yet in doing so, the central state's bare display of antireflective power only further affirms the knowledge-based insights of its critics.

As the two sides of this dispute are pulled ever further apart, they are also ironically coming together in agreement on the end of One Country, Two Systems. The enlightenment revelations analyzed in chapter 1 unmasked this protective framework as insufficient to preserve Hong Kong's distinct political, sociocultural, and economic systems from the Chinese Party-state's controlocratic tendencies, such that the only realistic path forward for the protection of Hong Kong's liberties and distinct way of life (two systems) is to be found beyond the limits of one country, as articulated in the proposals for two countries reviewed in chapter 2. The counter-enlightenment constructions analyzed in chapter 3 also portray One Country, Two Systems as a failure, but from this perspective its failure is to be attributed not to a lack of checks on central power, but rather to a surplus of such checks: with China's rise and the resulting shift in power dynamics, limits on the power of the central government are not protecting Hong Kong but rather permitting the city to perpetuate its unhealthy habits, leading down a path of degeneration that could endanger China's national regeneration. From vastly different perspectives, both the Hong Kong nationalist enlightenment and the official Chinese nationalist counter-enlightenment are reaching agreement on the failure of One Country, Two Systems, while proposing diametrically opposed solutions: One Country, One System or Two Systems, Two Countries.

As we helplessly watch the political situation in Hong Kong deteriorate under the National Security Law and the collapse of One Country, Two Systems toward One Country, One System, it is easy, indeed far too easy, to say that Hong Kong civil society miscalculated by developing these proposals for Two Systems, Two Countries. Yet if we view these unfolding events from the long span of history, is it not far more likely that the Chinese Communist Party and its enablers in Hong Kong have miscalculated? Repressive situations of the type that we see in Hong Kong today not only indicate a complete miscomprehension of the society with which Beijing is dealing but have also been shown throughout history to be fundamentally unsustainable. And as Eric Tsui has noted, "Once ethnic thinking emerges, it is impossible to erase."[137]

In the endlessly unfolding and continually escalating political crisis within which the city of Hong Kong finds itself, knowledge and power are not intertwined; rather, power stands on one side, while knowledge stands on another, diametrically opposed. Hong Kong's ongoing political crisis will see no resolution until the day when either power obtains knowledge, or knowledge obtains power.

Conclusion

Knowledge versus Power

This escalating showdown between knowledge and power, between new political visions and anachronistic orthodoxies, and indeed between democratization and dictatorship, continued to accelerate at unprecedented speeds over the eighteen months during which I was writing this book in 2019 and 2020.

I was in Hong Kong on June 12, 2019, when protests began against the government's proposal to revise its extradition law to allow suspects to be extradited to any jurisdiction in the world, including China. Over the next six months, a new movement overtook and fundamentally reshaped this city in ways that few ever could have imagined.

I must admit that it was a bit awkward to be giving talks on Hong Kong independence during the protest movement of 2019. Because the Chinese state had employed its usual, highly predictable allegation that the protests were a nefarious, internationally backed attempt to "split the motherland," many protesters and supporters went to great lengths to argue that the protests had nothing to do with Hong Kong independence. And there was genuine truth in these arguments. If we review the five demands that eventually became protests' rallying cry, namely withdrawing the proposal to amend the extradition law, withdrawing the label "riot" from the protests of June 12, granting amnesty to protest detainees, holding an independent inquiry into police brutality, and implementing universal suffrage, it is apparent that none of these demands promote independence.

Yet if we take a closer look at the details of the protest movement, it also becomes apparent that many of the intellectual and methodological innovations of the Hong Kong independence discussion reviewed in this book have been taken up by protesters, highlighting the impact of Hong Kong nationalism on the protest movement and indeed on broader political culture in the city. Yuk-man Cheung has even argued, in a powerful analysis of the 2019 protest movement, that "nationalism is the most important motive force behind the revolution."[1]

Take for example the movement's leaderless structure, which has been a topic of much discussion. In one sense, this structure was a practical response to the government's persecution and imprisonment of the figureheads of the 2014 Occupy Central and 2016 Mongkok protests. The most obvious practical benefit of a protest movement without a leader is that there is no way for the government to detain the movement's leader. There was, however, a deeper philosophical element in the protests' rejection of leaders, which can be traced back to the dissatisfaction with conventional activism and particularly the role of mainstream political figures in moderating activism, as articulated in Lewis Loud's comparison of Hong Kong's political system and the imperial examination discussed in chapter 1. In an opinion piece in the *New York Times* in the early stages of the protest, Loud himself highlighted the "liberating effect" of this leaderless structure, commenting that "without the old elites, a massive gathering can rapidly splinter or spin off into small, nimble side operations."[2] Tactically, without leaders, there is not only no one telling one what to do, but there is also no one telling one what not to do, allowing for the bottom-up application of novel tactics.

Such leaderless action and methodological innovation have been facilitated by the use of the Telegram app in the planning and execution of protests. I had first learned about the Telegram app in my interactions with the Hong Kong National Party, who used it as an anonymous and supposedly end-to-end encrypted means of communication beyond the monitoring of the authorities, as discussed in chapter 2. In my interactions with the many groups associated with the independence wing of the Hong Kong nationalist discussion over the years, I invariably found Telegram to be the preferred means of communication. Yet I almost never used the app for any other purpose until June 2019, when Telegram suddenly became the protest movement's primary communication platform. Drawing upon the same strengths of anonymity and security that had made the app appealing to independence supporters, protesters used Telegram to have encrypted conversations with contacts, as well as to contribute anonymously to perpetually active public protest discussion groups, some with tens of thousands of participants, in which people broke news, proposed new tactics, shared information on developments on the ground in real time, and even notified one another of the current location of police in order to evade arrest. Telegram, once primarily a communication platform for independence activists, thereby suddenly became one of the most widely used apps in Hong Kong in the summer of 2019.

The 2019 protests were also unique, in contrast to the "peaceful, rational, and non-violent" (*woh leih fei*) approach to protest that had dominated Hong Kong activism for decades, in their employment of the use of force in clashes with police. The critique of nonviolence and advocacy for more martial approaches was first articulated by such nationalist groups as Hong Kong Indigenous and the Hong Kong National Party, whose journal *Comitium* provided the most systematic critique of the tactical "uselessness" of nonviolent civil disobedience in a politically unjust society, as discussed in chapter 2. The 2019 protests marked the first application of this approach on a large scale, in response to the police force's increasingly aggressive suppression tactics. The police came to protests over the summer of 2019 armed with batons, tear gas, bean bag rounds, rubber bullets, and eventually real bullets. Protesters also came in full protest gear with gas masks, goggles, gloves, and hard hats. When police fired tear gas, protestors did not flee; they were ready to either extinguish the canisters or throw them back to police. When police charged, protesters were ready to escape and regroup elsewhere, or even in some cases to fight. The once unthinkable vision of young people dressed in black bloc gear and gas masks engaging in standoffs and clashes with police suddenly became a predictable weekly if not at times daily event in the second half of 2019. This approach, which brought new vitality and force into the protest movement, owed a considerable debt to Hong Kong nationalists' pioneering critique of nonviolent protest and promotion of more martial approaches to resistance.

The independence movement's appeals to international politicians and calls for international alliances also had a major influence on the 2019 protests. Building upon Wan Chin's insight from his first city-state book that China needed Hong Kong just as much as Hong Kong needed China, advocates of self-determination and independence had been appealing to international politicians to change their Hong Kong policy for years. When Chan Ho-tin delivered a letter to the US Consulate in Hong Kong calling for the cancellation of the Hong Kong Policy Act in 2017, as discussed in chapter 2, the move was deeply controversial, as was nearly everything that the boundary-pushing

Hong Kong National Party did. Yet just two years later, on September 7, 2019, I joined a massive rally marching past the US Consulate in Hong Kong with tens of thousands of people calling for the cancellation of the Hong Kong Policy Act. When the United States passed the Hong Kong Human Rights and Democracy Act just a little over two months later, a testament to the success of lobbying for greater pressure on the Hong Kong and Chinese governments, crowds gathered for a Thanksgiving party at Central's Chater Garden, celebrating the bill. The July 2020 announcement of the US revocation of Hong Kong's special trade status and subsequent announcement of sanctions on a number of senior political figures in the Hong Kong government was a direct product of the protest movement's determined lobbying efforts, methods that can be traced back to the independence movement's early advocacy for international sanctions on the Hong Kong and Chinese governments.

The deeper one looks, the deeper the influence of the independence discussion on the 2019 protest movement appears. For example, the movement's slogan, "liberate Hong Kong, revolution of our times (*gwongfuhk Heunggong, sihdoih gaakmihng*)," is a quote from independence activist Edward Leung, currently serving a six-year prison sentence on charges of rioting and assaulting a police officer. Protestors even wrote a national anthem, "Glory to Hong Kong," that could be heard everywhere throughout the city in the autumn of 2019. Its lyrics read:

Break now the dawn, liberate our Hong Kong
In common breath: Revolution of our times
May people reign, proud and free, now and evermore
Glory be to thee, Hong Kong.

Returning to the question of the five demands and independence, although none of the protesters' five demands explicitly relates to independence, there is also no way to deny the fact that these demands could never be realized under Beijing's control. In this sense, as Lewis Loud has argued, the protest movement is an independence movement that dare not speak its own name.[3]

Yet far more than any particular insight or tactic or aspiration derived from the independence discussion, the 2019 protest movement shared with this discussion the will to break apart old orthodoxies and seek out new paths forward. Just as the Hong Kong nationalism discussion has been a conversation trying out new models derived from a collective enlightenment regarding the failed orthodoxies of the past, so the protest movement of 2019 became a living protest laboratory developing new tactics to free Hong Kong from the increasingly powerless protest methods of the past. In both cases, there is an awakening, a refusal to abide by the old once-dominant orthodoxies, and a corresponding will to generate new knowledge, imagining new paths forward for the city.

This dynamism, abandoning old methodologies and seeking out new possibilities, stands in stark contrast to the government's all too predictable hardline response to these developments. The Hong Kong-China tensions that began with the proposal for national security legislation in 2002, producing the largest protest in Hong Kong's history on July 1, 2003, came full circle with the largest protests in Hong Kong's history in 2019, producing a National Security Law forced on the city in June 2020. In violation of established procedure and indeed of any even remotely reasonable interpretation of the Basic Law, the National Security Law was written and legislated not in Hong Kong, as stipulated in Article 23, but rather in Beijing, then forced on the city on June 30, 2020, via a very creative reading of Annex III of the Basic Law.

The National Security Law focuses on four main offenses: separatism, subversion, terrorism, and collusion with foreign forces. The first offense, secession, very clearly targets the Hong Kong nationalist debate and everyone who has been involved therein. The law explicitly states that the charge of secession does not require the use or threat of force, essentially enabling prosecution for speech and thought crimes. What type of speech related to Hong Kong-China relations is now legal or illegal? Is it still possible to have a conversation that imagines a different relationship, or is the simple discussion of such a possibility in and of itself invariably grounds for imprisonment? Will this academic monograph researched in Hong Kong still be considered "legal" in Hong Kong? The answers to these questions remain unclear, but with the passage of time it becomes increasingly clear that one must lean toward caution, as such speech crimes are punishable under the law by a maximum sentence of life in prison.

The jarring contrast between the vagueness of the offenses and the severity of the punishment reveals the National Security Law's underlying truth. Despite the endlessly growing mountain of commentaries on the National Security Law and its implications, there is really no point to be found in dwelling on its details: whether the way in which the law was drafted and implemented is constitutional, whether detainees will have a right to legal representation, or whether the offenses listed in the law conflict with other laws protecting freedom of speech or association. None of this is of any consequence now. The

National Security Law is not required to be constitutional or to make sense. It is simply a blank check that the central government wrote itself to act as it pleases in Hong Kong, a counter-enlightenment drive to suppress discussion and discovery, overriding all legally guaranteed freedoms and rights in the city. As first articulated in Jack Lee's reflections on Tibet and Hong Kong, discussed in chapter 1, was there ever any chance that One Country, Two Systems could produce a different outcome?

Hong Kong independence activists, facing the expansion of the Chinese Communist Party's security state into Hong Kong, have been given three options: fade into silence, flee into exile, or go to prison. Fading into silence seemed a possibility at first, but recent developments indicating that the National Security Law can be enforced retroactively mean that even fading into silence has an element of considerable risk. One activist told me that on account of his past public comments on Hong Kong-China relations, basically anything that he said today could be reinterpreted in such a way as to provide a pretext for sending him to prison under the National Security Law. If, for example, he embraced the central state's ultimate ideal of political correctness and declared that Hong Kong is in fact part of China, his utterance of this assertion would be read as insincere at best, or at worst as a thinly veiled and now seemingly illegal call for international sanctions on both China and Hong Kong. Even his silence on such matters could prove the state's presumption of guilt. Another activist, who subsequently fled abroad, told me before his departure that his family was expecting a knock on the door from the national security forces any day to take him away. Once one becomes the target of political elimination under the National Security Law, almost anything that one does can be read as a violation of this law.

As a result, many independence activists have chosen to flee overseas. Seeking refuge in Taiwan, the United Kingdom, the United States, and Australia, these young people have had to uproot their entire lives on account of the illegal passage in Beijing of a law for nominally autonomous Hong Kong. Some already facing charges from the 2019 protests have skipped bail to seek refuge overseas. Some have left via legal means, and others have smuggled themselves out of the city that they love to start over on the other side of the world simply to be able to live and to think another day. The National Security Law, in its raw exercise of power for the purpose of silencing the Hong Kong nationalist discussion, is at the same time the ultimate testament to the insights of this discussion: that it is a fatal mistake to trust the Chinese Communist Party's legal guarantees, that there is no hope for Hong Kong's freedoms and way of life as part of the People's Republic of China, and that One Country, Two Systems is destined to become One Country, One System.

As advocates of Hong Kong independence flee their homeland to seek refuge in countries around the world, they will find no comfort in knowing that all that they predicted and warned us about has come true. Nevertheless, in this truth, their ideas live on.

CHARACTER GLOSSARY WITH CANTONESE (YALE) AND MANDARIN (PINYIN) ROMANIZATION

BAT PIHNGDANG TIUHFUN/BU PINGDENG TIAOKUAN 不平等條款
BUNTOH MAHNJYU CHIHNSIN/BENTU MINZHU QIANXIAN 本土民主前線
BUNTOH WAHNDUHNG/BENTU YUNDONG 本土運動
BAGGIO LEUNG/LIANG SONGHENG 梁頌恆
CHAN HO TIN/CHEN HAOTIAN 陳浩天
CHENG CHUNG-TAI/ZHENG SONGTAI 鄭松泰
CHIN WAN/CHEN YUN 陳雲
CHINGNIHN SANJING/QINGNIAN XINZHENG 青年新政
DAAIH HEUNGGONG JYUYIH/DA XIANGGANG ZHUYI 大香港主義
DAAIH WAAN KEUI/DAWAN QU 大灣區
DAAIHGA DOU HAIH JUNGGWOKYAHN/DAJIA DOU SHI ZHONGGUOREN 大家都係中國人
DAIYEUK JINGJIH/DIYUE ZHENGZHI 締約政治
DUHK/DU 獨
DUHK/DU 毒
DUHKLAAHP/DULI 獨立
GEIBUNFAAT GOILEUHNG CHOYIH/JIBENFA GAILIANG CHUYI 基本法改良芻議
GEUIMAHN/JUMIN 居民
GINKAW HEUNGGONG MAHNJUHK/JIANGUO XIANGGANG MINZU 建構香港民族
GONGDUHK/GANGDU 港獨
GUNGMAHN/GONGMIN 公民
GUYIH/GU'ER 孤兒
GWONGFUHK HEUNGGONG, SIHDOIH GAAKMIHNG/GUANGFU XIANGGANG, SHIDAI GEMING 光復香港, 時代革命
HAAKGING/HEIJING 黑警
HAAKGING OT, GINGSOU 3P/HEIJING OT, JINGSAO 3P 黑警OT，警嫂3P

HAHM GAA LING/ QUAN JIA SI 冚家伶

HEIMOHNG JINGJIH/XIWANG ZHENGZHI 希望政治

HEUNGGONG/XIANGGANG 香港

HEUNGGONG GINGCHAAT JIFAAT FAANFAAT/XIANGGANG JINGCHA ZHIFA FANFA 香港警察知法犯法

HEUNGGONG KONGJAANG WAHNDUHNG/XIANGGANG KANGZHENG YUN-DONG 香港抗爭運動

HEUNGGONG MAHNJUHK, CHIHNTOUH JIHKYUT/XIANGGANG MINZU, QIANTU ZIJUE 香港民族，前途自決

HEUNGGONG MAHNJUHK, MIHNGWAHN JIHKYUT/XIANGGANG MINZU, MINGYUN ZIJUE 香港民族，命運自決

HEUNGGONG MAHNJUHK DONG/XIANGGANG MINZU DANG 香港民族黨

HEUNGGONG MAHNJUHK LEUHN/XIANGGANG MINZU LUN 香港民族論

HEUNGGONG YAHN/XIANGGANG REN 香港人

HONFUHK/HANFU 漢服

HOHKSAANG DUHKLAAHP LYUHNMAHNG/XUESHENG DULI LIANMENG 學生獨立聯盟

JOUHFAN YAUHLEIH/ZAOFAN YOULI 造反有理

JUHKKWAN/ZUQUN 族群

JUNGGWOK/ZHONGGUO 中國

JUNGGWOK JIHKMAHN BAKYUN/ZHONGGUO ZHIMIN BAQUAN 中國殖民霸權

JUNGGWOK JIHKMAHN JYUYIH/ZHONGGUO ZHIMIN ZHUYI 中國殖民主義

JUNGYIH/ZHONGYI 眾議

JYUKYUHN GAAUYIHK/ZHUQUAN JIAOYI 主權交易

LAM HONG CHING/LIN GUANGZHENG 林匡正

LEUHN GWAIYING: WUIH DOU YINGJIH HEUNGGONG/LUN GUIYING: HUIDAO YINGZHI XIANGGANG 論歸英：回到英治香港

LEUNG KAI-PING/LIANG JIPING 梁繼平

LEUNG TIN-KEIH/LIANG TIANQI 梁天琦

LEWIS LOUD/LUSIDA 盧斯達

LIUHGAAI GEIBUN FAAT/LIAOJIE JIBEN FA 瞭解基本法

MAHNFA GINGWOK/WENHUA JIANGUO 文化建國

MAHNFA JUNGGWOK/WENHUA ZHONGGUO 文化中國

MAHNJYU/MINZHU 民主

MAHNJYU KONG'GUHNG LEUHN/MINZHU KANG'GONG LUN 民主抗共論

MAHNJYU WUIHGWAI LEUHN/MINZHU HUIGUI LUN 民主回歸論

MAHNJUHK/MINZU 民族

SHA TIN/SHATIAN 沙田

SHEUNG SHUI/SHANGSHUI 上水

SIHNGBONG JYUKYUHN/CHENGBANG ZHUQUAN 城邦主權

SIHNGBONG LEUHN/CHENGBANG LUN 城邦論

SIU KIT/XIAO JIE 蕭傑

SYUNGUEI YUH FOGUEI/XUANJU YU KEJU 選舉與科舉

TAI PO/DAPU 大浦

TUEN MUN/DUNMEN 屯門

TSUI SING YAN/XU CHENG'EN 徐承恩

WAH-HAH MAHNFA/HUAXIA WENHUA 華夏文化

WAH-HAH/HUAXIA 華夏

WAIHMAHN LEUHN/YIMIN LUN 遺民論

WOH LEIH FEI/HE LI FEI 合理非

WUIHGWAI/HUIGUI 回歸

YAU WAI-CHING/YOU HUIZHEN 游蕙禎

YUEN LONG/YUANLANG 元朗

YUEN YUEN-LUNG/ 袁源隆

NOTES

INTRODUCTION

1. Many different terms have been used to describe the notable shift in identity formations in Hong Kong since 2011, including localism, nationalism, and as shown in chapter 3, secessionism. This book follows the lead of both Wu Rwei-ren and Eric Tsui in calling this identity formation nationalism. See Wu Rwei-ren, "The Lilliputian Dreams: Preliminary Observations of Nationalism in Okinawa, Taiwan, and Hong," *Nations and Nationalism* 22, no. 4 (2016): 686–705; and Tsui Sing Yan, *Sisok gabong: Junggwok jihkmahn jyuyih kohng chiuh hah dik Heunggong* [Reflections on my homeland: Hong Kong under Chinese colonization] (Taipei: Avanguard Publishing, 2019).

2. United Press International (UPI), "Text of Address by Jiang Zemin," June 30, 1997, www.upi.com/Archives/1997/06/30/Text-of-address-by-Jiang-Zemin /8090867643200/.

3. On the lack of consultation with and consent from the Hong Kong people in negotiating the city's handover to China, see Ian Scott, *Political Change and the Crisis of Legitimacy in Hong Kong* (Honolulu: University of Hawaii Press, 1989).

4. There was a cottage industry in the publishing world in the 1990s predicting a dire fate for Hong Kong under Chinese Communist Party rule. Although dismissed and even mocked in the immediate post-1997 era of relative autonomy as sensationalized and outdated Cold War–style alarmism, the more pessimistic predictions contained in these studies have with the passage of time proven themselves to be too optimistic. Three examples of this genre are George L. Hicks, *Hong Kong Countdown* (Hong Kong: Writers' & Publishers' Cooperative, 1989); Mark Roberti, *The Fall of Hong Kong: China's Triumph and Britain's Betrayal* (New York: John Wiley & Sons, 1996); and Jamie Allen, *Seeing Red: China's Uncompromising Takeover of Hong Kong* (Singapore: Butterworth-Heinemann Asia, 1997).

5. On the risks to legally guaranteed rights in national security legislation for Hong Kong, see Thomas Kellogg, "Legislating Rights: Basic Law Article 23, National Security, and Human Rights in Hong Kong," *Columbia Journal of Asian Law* 17 (2004): 307–369.

6. On the National Education Program and its construction of Chinese nationalism for Hong Kong, see Kevin Carrico, "From Citizens Back to Subjects: Constructing National Belonging in Hong Kong's National Education Center," in *From a British to a Chinese Colony? Hong Kong before and after the 1997 Handover*, ed. Gary Chi-hung Luk (Berkeley: Institute of East Asian Studies China Research Monograph, 2017), 259–284. On the Anti-National Education Movement and its impact on localist politics, see Sebastian Veg, "The Rise of 'Localism' and Civic Identity in Post-Handover Hong Kong," *China Quarterly* 230 (June 2017): 323–347.

7. For a detailed history of the Umbrella Revolution, see Kong Tsung-gan, *Umbrella: A Political Tale from Hong Kong* (Detroit: Pema Press, 2017). The edited volume *Take Back Our Future* also provides a thought-provoking introduction to the events of 2014, their origins, and their legacies. See Ching Kwan Lee and Ming Sing, eds., *Take Back Our Future: An Eventful Sociology of the Hong Kong Umbrella Movement* (Ithaca, NY: Cornell University Press, 2019).

8. Chin Wan, *Heunggong sihngbong leuhn* [On Hong Kong as a city-state] (Hong Kong: Enrich Publishing, 2011).

9. *Undergrad* Editorial Board, ed., "*Heunggong mahnjuhk, mihngwahn jihkyut*" [Hong Kong nationality, self-determination of our own future], *Undergrad* (February 2014); and *Undergrad* Editorial Board, ed., *Heunggong mahnjuhk leuhn* [Hong Kong nationalism] (Hong Kong: Hong Kong University Undergraduate Student Union Publishing, 2015).

10. Amy Qin and Tiffany May, "For Some in Hong Kong, New Bridge Has a Downside: 'That Kind of Tourist,'" *New York Times*, November 23, 2018, www.nytimes .com/2018/11/23/world/asia/china-hong-kong-tung-chung.html.

CHAPTER I. HONG KONG ETHNOGENESIS

1. Public Opinion Programme, "Ethnic Identity-Chinese in Broad Sense (per Poll, by Age Group), August 1997–June 2019," last updated June 2019, www.hkupop.hku .hk/english/popexpress/ethnic/eidentity/chibroad/poll/datatables.html. The full details of ethnic identity and other polling can be read at Public Opinion Programme, the University of Hong Kong, "People's Ethnic Identity," last updated June 2019 www .hkupop.hku.hk/english/popexpress/ethnic/index.html.

2. Gene Lin, "CUHK Survey Finds Nearly 40% of Young Hongkongers Want Independence after 2047," *Hong Kong Free Press*, July 25, 2016, https://hongkongfp .com/2016/07/25/17-hongkongers-support-independence-2047-especially-youth -cuhk-survery/. The full survey results can be read at Centre for Communication and Public Opinion Survey, "Public Opinion and Political Development in Hong Kong: Survey Results," July 2016, http://www.com.cuhk.edu.hk/ccpos/images/news/Task Force_PressRelease_160722c_English.pdf.

3. Zhu Jie and Zhang Xiaoshan, *Critique of Hong Kong Nativism: From a Legal Perspective* (Singapore: Springer, 2019).

4. The Chinese Association of Hong Kong-Macao Studies, "About Us," www .cahkms.org/HKMAC/webView/mc/AboutUs_1.html?0101&%E6%9C%AC%E4 %BC%9A%E7%AE%80%E4%BB%8B.

5. On official Chinese academia's forced integration of Hong Kong's history into preformed Sinocentric narratives, see Wong Wang-Chi, *Lihksi dik chahmchuhng: Chuhng Heunggong hon Junggwok daaihluhk dik Heunggongsi leuhnseuht* [The burden of history: A Hong Kong perspective on the mainland discourse of Hong Kong history] (Hong Kong: Oxford University Press, 2000).

6. Zhu and Zhang, *Critique of Hong Kong Nativism*, 10.

7. Ibid., 4, 10.

8. Steve Tsang, *A Modern History of Hong Kong* (London: I.B. Tauris, 2007): 180–181.

9. Zhu and Zhang, *Critique of Hong Kong Nativism*, 4.

10. Ibid, 31–32.

11. Ibid., 116–117.

12. Ibid., 31.

13. Ibid., 20.

14. Ibid., 16–17, 30–32.

15. Ibid., 20.

16. Ibid., 166–167.

17. Ibid., 8, 87, 118.

18. Ibid., 5.

19. Ibid., 38.

20. Ibid.

21. Ibid., 91.

22. G. William Skinner and Edwin A. Winckler, "Compliance Succession in Rural Communist China: A Cyclical Theory," in *A Sociological Reader on Complex Organizations*, ed. Amitai Etzioni (New York: Holt, Rinehart, and Wilson, 1969), 410–438.

23. Ibid., 410.

24. Ibid., 414–415.

25. Ibid., 416–418

26. Ibid., 418–420.

27. Ibid., 420.

28. Ibid., 424.

29. Ibid., 414–415, 424.

30. Ibid., 424.

31. Ibid., 422.

32. Ibid., 424–425.

33. Ibid., 424–425.

34. What Wu Rwei-ren calls "the built-in centralizing tendency of the Chinese state" and what Stein Ringen calls "controlocracy." See Wu Rwei-ren, "The Lilliputian

Dreams: Preliminary Observations of Nationalism in Okinawa, Taiwan, and Hong," *Nations and Nationalism* 22 no. 4 (2016): 690; and Stein Ringen, *The Perfect Dictatorship: China in the 21st Century* (Hong Kong: Hong Kong University Press, 2016).

35. There are notable parallels in this noncompliance cycle of mutual provocation with the insecurity dilemma within the China-Tibet conflict as outlined by Tsering Topgyal in *China and Tibet: The Perils of Insecurity* (London: Hurst, 2016).

36. James Hsiung, "Introduction: The Paradox Syndrome and Update," in *Hong Kong the Super Paradox: Life after Return to China*, ed. James Hsiung (New York: St. Martin's Press, 2000), 1.

37. James Hsiung, "The Hong Kong SAR: Prisoner of Legacy or History's Bellwether?," in *Hong Kong the Super Paradox: Life after Return to China*, ed. James Hsiung (New York: St. Martin's Press, 2000), 329, 341.

38. Ibid., 331.

39. Thomas Kellogg, "Legislating Rights: Basic Law Article 23, National Security, and Human Rights in Hong Kong," *Columbia Journal of Asian Law* 17 (2004), 312. See also Benny Tai, "The Principle of Minimum Legislation for Implementing Article 23 of the Basic Law," *Hong Kong Law Journal* 32 (2002): 579–612.

40. Kellogg, "Legislating Rights," 317 (treason); 324–325 (sovereignty); 341–344 (subversion and state secrets); and 344–345 ("illegal" organizations); see also Suzanne Pepper, *Keeping Democracy at Bay: Hong Kong and the Challenges of Chinese Political Reform* (Lanham, MD: Rowman & Littlefield, 2008), 356–357; and Carole Petersen, "Hong Kong's Spring of Discontent: The Rise and Fall of the National Security Bill in 2003," in *National Security and Fundamental Freedoms: Hong Kong's Article 23 Under Scrutiny*, ed. Carole Petersen, Fu Hualing, and Simon N. M. Young (Hong Kong: Hong Kong University Press, 2005) 24–28.

41. Carole Petersen, "National Security Offences and Civil Liberties in Hong Kong: A Critique of the Government's 'Consultation' on Article 23 of the Basic Law," *Hong Kong Law Journal* 32 (2002): 457–470.

42. In a fascinating case of the history of the city coming full circle, there was a second meeting of national security legislation and a pandemic in 2020, when Beijing forced the National Security Law on Hong Kong amid the COVID-19 pandemic.

43. Susan Sontag, *Illness as Metaphor and AIDS and Its Metaphors* (London: Picador, 2001).

44. Zhao Jinqiu, "The SARS Epidemic under China's Media Policy," *Media Asia* 30, no. 4 (January 2003): 191–196.

45. Eric Kit-wai Ma and Joseph Man Chan, "Global Connectivity and Local Politics: SARS, Talk Radio, and Public Opinion," in *SARS: Reception and Interpretation in Three Chinese Cities*, ed. Deborah Davis and Helen Siu (London: Routledge, 2007), 30.

46. On explication as a defining feature of modernity, undermining aspects of life that are unthought or taken for granted, see Peter Sloterdijk, *Terror from the Air* (Los Angeles: Semiotext(e), 2009).

47. Ma Ngok, "Civil Society in Self-Defense: The Struggle against National Security Legislation in Hong Kong," *Journal of Contemporary China* 14, no. 44 (2005): 465, 480.

48. For a thought-provoking introduction to the central government's "new Hong Kong policy" and its role in developing a peripheral counternationalism in Hong Kong, see Brian Fong, "One Country, Two Nationalisms: Center-Periphery Relations between Mainland China and Hong Kong, 1997–2016," *Modern China* 43, no. 5 (2017): 523–556. Wu Rwei-ren also proposes a framework of nationalism and counternationalism, although Wu sees this defensive counternationalism as emerging on the foundations of a protonational community formed over the course of the preceding century and a half. See Wu, "The Lilliputian Dreams." Both Fong and Wu trace Chinese state-driven centralization in the political, economic, and ideological/cultural fields since 1997.

49. Manisa Piuchan, Chi Wa Chan, and Jack Kaale, "Economic and Socio-cultural Impacts of Mainland Chinese Tourists on Hong Kong Residents," *Kasetsart Journal of Social Sciences* 39 (2018): 9.

50. Ibid., 14.

51. Wu, "Lilliputian Dreams," 690.

52. As Michael Davis observes in his 2007 study of democratization in Hong Kong, "Pro-Beijing and progovernment leaders in Hong Kong frequently worry that democracy poses a risk to stability. The opposite may be true in Hong Kong. The lack of democracy in Hong Kong's liberal constitutional system may pose the greatest risk to stability, as the government veers from crisis to crisis." See Michael C. Davis, "Interpreting Constitutionalism and Democratization in Hong Kong," in *Interpreting Hong Kong's Basic Law: The Struggle for Coherence*, ed. Hualing Fu, Lison Harris, and Simon N. M. Young (London: Palgrave Macmillan, 2007): 90.

53. Davis, "Interpreting Constitutionalism and Democratization in Hong Kong," 79; Alvin Y. H. Cheung, "Road to Nowhere: Hong Kong's Democratization and China's Obligations under Public International Law," *Brooklyn Journal of International Law* 40, no. 2 (2015): 483–484.

54. Davis, "Interpreting Constitutionalism and Democratization in Hong Kong," 80; Cheung, "Road to Nowhere," 483–484.

55. Cheung, "Road to Nowhere," 484–485.

56. Ibid.

57. Ibid., 503.

58. A personal recounting of the national education experience can be found in Kevin Carrico, "From Citizens Back to Subjects: Constructing National Belonging in Hong Kong's National Education Center," in *From a British to a Chinese Colony? Hong Kong before and after the 1997 Handover*, ed. Gary Chi-hung Luk (Berkeley: University of California Press, 2017): 259–284.

59. Ibid.

60. Ibid. A detailed narration of the rise of Scholarism (which eventually became Demosistō) and its impacts on political activism in Hong Kong can be found in Lam Hong Ching, *Hohkmahn duhkbaahk* [Scholarism monologues] (Hong Kong: Subculture, 2013).

61. The markedly nonautonomous fates of China's various "autonomous regions" meant that naming Hong Kong an "autonomous region" would have been far too

ominous. The name Special Administrative Region was given, suggesting a newfound promise of autonomy. Unfortunately, the fates of special administrative regions under Beijing's control are now similar to the fates of its autonomous regions: namely, nonautonomous.

62. Chin Wan, *Heunggong sihngbong leuhn* [On Hong Kong as a city-state] (Hong Kong: Enrich Publishing, 2011).

63. Ibid., 21–22.

64. Ibid., 22.

65. Ibid.

66. Ibid.

67. Ibid., 26.

68. A recommendation that I have applied in writing this book. See ibid., 26–27, 30.

69. Ibid., 40.

70. Ibid., 22.

71. Ibid.

72. Ibid., 58–59.

73. James Mann, *The China Fantasy: Why Capitalism Will Not Bring Democracy to China* (New York: Penguin, 2008).

74. Chin, *Heunggong sihngbong leuhn*, 11, 37.

75. Ibid., 37.

76. Ibid., 23, 51–52.

77. Ibid.

78. Ibid.

79. Ibid., 18–59.

80. Basic Law of the Hong Kong Special Administrative Region of the People's Republic of China, accessed March 2019, www.basiclaw.gov.hk/en/basiclawtext /images/basiclaw_full_text_en.pdf.

81. Ibid.

82. Ibid.

83. See the discussion of the political controversy surrounding this case in Anne R. Fokstuen, "The 'Right of Abode' Cases: Hong Kong's Constitutional Crisis," *Hastings International and Comparative Law Review* 26 (2003): 265–288. Tensions between the Hong Kong and Chinese legal systems emerging in this and other cases are also introduced in Johannes Chan, "Judicial Independence: Controversies on the Constitutional Jurisdiction of the Court of Final Appeal of the Hong Kong Special Administrative Region," *International Lawyer* 33 (1999): 1015–1040.

84. Tsui Sing Yan, *Heunggong: Watchou dik gabong, buntou gundim dik Heunggong yuhnlauh si* [Hong Kong: A national history, second edition] (Taipei: Rive Gauche Publishing, 2019), 453.

85. Ibid., 453.

86. Fokstuen, "The 'Right of Abode' Cases," 271–272.

87. Tsui, *Heunggong: Watchou dik gabong*, 453.

88. See the discussion of Basic Law interpretations in Siu Kit, *Wohngtin giksaat bong* [Heaven's hit list] (Hong Kong: Passiontimes, 2018), 72–76.

89. See, for example, the call to ensure that "Hong Kong's next generation understands the Basic Law" in Central Government of the People's Republic of China, "*Xianggang tequ 22 ri juban 'jiben fa banbu 16 nian yantao hui'*" [Hong Kong SAR hosts a conference on the 16th anniversary of the Basic Law], www.gov.cn/jrzg/2006-04/22/content_260906_2.htm; the promotion of studying the Basic Law in Xinhua News, "*Xianggang juban jianianhua huodong tuiguang jiben fa*" [Hong Kong hosts a carnival to promote the Basic Law], *Xinhua News*, February 21, 2009, http://news.sohu.com/20090221/n262382186.shtml; and Central Government of the People's Republic of China "*Xianggang juban jiben fa banbu 25 zhounian zhanlan*" [Hong Kong hosts an exhibition to mark the twenty-fifth anniversary of the Basic Law], April 4, 2015, www.gov.cn/xinwen/2015-04/04/content_2842992.htm.

90. Carrico, "From Citizens Back to Subjects."

91. See Louis Althusser, "Ideology and Ideological State Apparatuses," in *Lenin and Philosophy and Other Essays* (New York: Monthly Review Press, 1971), 127–186.

92. André Glucksmann, *The Master Thinkers* (New York: Harper & Row, 1980), 11–20.

93. Ibid., 13.

94. Ibid., 20.

95. Ibid., 13.

96. Lewis Loud, "*Syunguei yuh foguei*" [Elections as an imperial examination], in *Ngoh maihsat joih jeh cheuhng jihkmahn yauhhei* [I am lost in this colonial game] (Hong Kong: Ideate Trails Press, 2018), 26–30.

97. A thoughtful discussion of the controversies surrounding the commemoration of the June 4 massacre and pan-Chinese nationalism in Hong Kong can be found in Sebastian Veg, "The Rise of 'Localism' and Civic Identity in Post-Handover Hong Kong: Questioning the Chinese Nation-state." *China Quarterly* 230 (June 2017): 323–347.

98. Loud, "*Syunguei yuh foguei*," 28.

99. Ibid., 27.

100. See Malte Philipp Kaeding, "The Rise of 'Localism' in Hong Kong," *Journal of Democracy* 28, no. 1 (January 2017): 158.

101. Loud, "*Syunguei yuh foguei*," 26.

102. Ibid., 27–29.

103. Ibid., 27.

104. Ibid., 27.

105. Ibid., 27.

106. See Ambrose Yeo-chi King, "Administrative Absorption of Politics in Hong Kong: Emphasis on the Grassroots Level," *Asian Survey* 15, no. 5 (May 1975): 422–439; and Lewis Loud, "*Syunguei yuh foguei*," 27.

107. Loud, "*Syunguei yuh foguei*," 28.

108. Hong Kong Trade and Industry Department, "Mainland and Hong Kong Closer Economic Partnership Agreement," 2003, www.tid.gov.hk/english/cepa/legal text/fulltext.html.

109. Bruno Cabrillac, "A Bilateral Trade Agreement between Hong Kong and China: CEPA," *China Perspectives* 54 (July–August 2004): 1.

110. Kelvin Chan, "Economists Say CEPA Benefits HK and the Mainland," *South China Morning Post*, September 13, 2003, /www.scmp.com/article/427772/economists -say-cepa-benefits-hk-and-mainland.

111. Maurice Godelier, *The Enigma of the Gift* (Chicago: University of Chicago Press, 1999), 101; and Marcel Mauss, *The Gift: Expanded Edition* (Chicago: Hau Books, 2016), 69.

112. Mauss, *Gift*, 72–73.

113. Godelier, *Enigma of the Gift*, 86, 120.

114. Siu Kit, *Heunggong buntoh wahnduhng si I* [A history of the localist movement in Hong Kong, vol. 1] (Hong Kong: Passiontimes, 2019), 38.

115. Siu, *Wohngtin giksaat bong*, 82.

116. Tsui, *Heunggong: Watchou dik gabong*, 477; see also Kiano Yim-mei Luk, "How Does Mainlandization Affect Hong Kong's Tourism Industry," in *Mainlandization of Hong Kong: Pressures and Responses*, ed. Joseph Yu-shek Cheng, Jacky Chau-kiu Cheung, and Beatrice Kit-fun Leung (Hong Kong: City University of Hong Kong Press, 2017), 162.

117. Tsui, *Heunggong: Watchou dik gabong*, 477.

118. Luk, "How Does Mainlandization Affect Hong Kong's Tourism Industry," 151–152; and Piuchan et al., "Economic and Socio-cultural Impacts of Mainland Chinese Tourists," 9.

119. Hong Kong Tourism Board, "Annual Report, 2014/15, Tourism Performance," www.discoverhongkong.com/eng/about-hktb/annual-report/annual-report-20142015 /tourism-performance/.

120. Lam Hong Ching, *Heunggong kongjaang wahnduhng si: Chobaaih dik saamsahp nihn fausik* [A history of Hong Kong's struggle, vol. 1, Dissecting 30 years of failure] (Hong Kong: Subculture, 2014), 101.

121. Siu, *Wohngtin giksaat bong*, 83; and Lam, *Heunggong kongjaang wahnduhng si*, 103.

122. Lam, *Heunggong kongjaang wahnduhng si*, 100–101; and Siu, *Wohngtin giksaat bong*, 83.

123. Siu, *Wohngtin giksaat bong*, 83; and Lam, *Heunggong kongjaang wahnduhng si*, 101–102.

124. Tania Branigan, "Chinese Figures Show Fivefold Rise in Babies Sick from Contaminated Milk," *Guardian*, December 2, 2008, www.theguardian.com/world /2008/dec/02/china.

125. Luk, "How Does Mainlandization Affect Hong Kong's Tourism Industry," 160.

126. Lam, *Heunggong kongjaang wahnduhng si*, 103.

127. Luk, "How Does Mainlandization Affect Hong Kong's Tourism Industry," 160; and Piuchan, Chan, and Kaale, "Economic and Socio-cultural Impacts of Mainland Chinese Tourists," 12.

128. Local Studio, *Hong Kong Is Not China* (Hong Kong: Local Studio, 2015).

129. Ibid.

130. Ibid.

131. Ibid.

132. Ibid.

133. Ibid.

134. See Jean-François Lyotard, *La Guerre des Algériens: Écrits, 1956–1963*, ed. Mohammed Ramdani (Paris: Galilée, 1989). The Algerian differend is given its most powerful articulation in Ramdani's introduction to this volume, Mohammed Ramdani, "L'Algérie: Un différend," in Lyotard, *La Guerre des Algériens: Écrits, 1956–1963*, ed. Mohammed Ramdani (Paris: Galilée, 1989).

135. Jean-François Lyotard, *The Differend: Phrases in Dispute* (Minneapolis: University of Minnesota Press, 1988).

136. Ramdani, "L'Algérie: Un différend," 14–15.

137. See James Williams, "Impasse," in *Lyotard and the Political* (London: Routledge, 2000).

138. Jack Lee (writing under the pseudonym Cheung Si-chai), "*Heunggong sihfau yingyauh mahnjuhk jihkyut dik kyuhnlei*" [Should Hong Kong have the right to self-determination?], in *Undergrad* Editorial Board, ed., "*Heunggong mahnjuhk, mihngwahn jihkyut*" [Hong Kong nationality, self-determination of our own future], *Undergrad* (February 2014): 34–37.

139. Ibid.

140. Tsering Woeser, *Tibet on Fire: Self-Immolations against Chinese Rule* (New York: Verso, 2016).

141. Lam, *Heunggong kongjaang wahnduhng si*, 105.

142. Cheung Yuk-man, "'Liberate Hong Kong, the Revolution of Our Times': The Birth of the First Orient Nation in the Twenty-First Century," in *Research Handbook on Nationalism*, ed. Liah Greenfeld and Zeying Wu (Cheltenham, UK: Edward Elgar, 2020), 313.

143. Kevin Carrico, *The Great Han: Race, Nationalism, and Tradition in China Today* (Oakland: University of California Press, 2017).

144. On the events of August 31, 2019, in Prince Edward Station, see Robyn Dixon and Ryan Ho Kilpatrick, "'I Thought I Was about to Die': Eyewitnesses Describe Brutal Beatings by Hong Kong Police," *Los Angeles Times*, September 2, 2019, www.latimes.com/world-nation/story/2019-09-02/hong-kong-police-violence-protesters-eyewitnesses.

CHAPTER 2. TWO SYSTEMS, TWO COUNTRIES

1. Readers interested in a complementary history of these developments should refer to Tsui Sing Yan, *Heunggong: Watchou dik gabong, buntou gundim dik Heunggong yuhnlauh si* [Hong Kong: A national history, second edition] (Taipei: Rive Gauche Publishing, 2019). Other useful contributions, from various political

perspectives, include Lam Hong Ching, *Heunggong kongjaang wahnduhng si I: Chobaaih dik saamsahp nihn fausik* [A history of Hong Kong's struggle, vol. 1, Dissecting 30 years of failure] (Hong Kong: Subculture, 2014); Lam Hong Ching, *Heunggong kongjaang wahnduhng si II: Jung-gong deuikyit* [A history of Hong Kong's struggle, vol. 2, The Hong Kong-China standoff] (Hong Kong: Subculture, 2015); Siu Kit, *Heunggong buntoh wahnduhng si I* [A history of the localist movement in Hong Kong, vol. 1] (Hong Kong: Passiontimes, 2019); and Siu Kit, *Heunggong buntoh wahnduhng si II* [A history of the localist movement in Hong Kong, vol. 2] (Hong Kong: Passiontimes, 2019).

2. An informative discussion of Chin Wan and his intervention in Hong Kong political culture can be found in Sebastian Veg, "The Rise of 'Localism' and Civic Identity in Post-Handover Hong Kong: Questioning the Chinese Nation-state," *China Quarterly* 230 (June 2017): 323–347.

3. Chin Wan, *Heunggong sihngbong leuhn* [On Hong Kong as a city-state] (Hong Kong: Enrich Publishing, 2011).

4. Ibid., 21.

5. Ibid., 65.

6. Ibid., 62.

7. Ibid., 67.

8. Ibid., 65; 93–94.

9. Ibid., 93. See also Aristotle, *The Politics*, trans. T. A. Sinclair and rev. Trevor J. Saunders (New York: Penguin, 1982).

10. Hong Kong was first ceded to the United Kingdom in 1841, a reality that was subsequently affirmed by the Treaty of Nanking in 1842 and the city's official establishment as a crown colony in 1843.

11. Chin, *Heunggong sihngbong leuhn*, 101–102; and Chin Wan, *Heunggong waihmahn leuhn* [On Hong Kong as a bastion of loyalism] (Hong Kong: Subculture Publishing, 2013), 53.

12. Chin, *Heunggong sihngbong leuhn*, 105.

13. Chin, *Heunggong waihmahn leuhn*, 53.

14. Ibid., 40, 53.

15. Ibid., 53.

16. Chin, *Heunggong sihngbong leuhn*, 85-86.

17. Ibid., 86.

18. Ibid., 86.

19. Ibid., 85–86.

20. Ibid., 56, 118.

21. Ibid., 69–72.

22. Ibid., 134.

23. Ibid., 10–12, 136, 213.

24. Ibid., 213.

25. Ibid., 202.

26. Ibid., 113, 136, 173.

27. Ibid., 133, 147–149.

28. Ibid., 8, 55–59.

29. Ibid., 55, 58–59.

30. Ibid., 210. See also a similar assertion on page 59.

31. Chin, *Heunggong waihmahn leuhn*, 35-36.

32. Ibid., 36–37.

33. On arborescence, territorialization, and deterritorialization, see Gilles Deleuze and Felix Guattari, *A Thousand Plateaus: Capitalism and Schizophrenia*, vol. 2 (Minneapolis: University of Minnesota Press, 1987).

34. Chin, *Heunggong waihmahn leuhn*, 35, 120.

35. Ibid., 37.

36. Ibid., 36.

37. Ibid., 36.

38. Ibid., 41–51.

39. Ibid., 47.

40. See the discussion of "the feudal" in Albert Feuerwerker, "China's Modern Economic History in Communist Chinese Historiography," *China Quarterly* 22 (June 1965): 31–61.

41. Chin, *Heunggong waihmahn leuhn*, 42–43; and Li Feng, *Early China: A Social and Cultural History* (Cambridge: Cambridge University Press, 2013), 128–129. On the definition of feudalism and its use in discussions of Chinese history, see also Li Feng, "'Feudalism' and Western Zhou China: A Criticism," *Harvard Journal of Asiatic Studies* 63, no. 1 (2003): 115–144.

42. Chin, *Heunggong waihmahn leuhn*, 42–43.

43. Wang Fei-ling, *The China Order: Centralia, World Empire, and the Nature of Chinese Power* (Albany: State University of New York Press, 2017).

44. Ibid., 32–35.

45. Ibid., 39–47, 51–55. On "the warring state," see also Kenneth Dean and Brian Massumi, *First and Last Emperors: The Absolute State and the Body of the Despot* (New York: Autonomedia, 1992).

46. Wang, *China Order*, 55–59.

47. Chin, *Heunggong waihmahn leuhn*, 41–44.

48. Ibid., 45–46.

49. Ibid., 43.

50. Ibid., 54–56.

51. Ibid., 55.

52. Ibid., 44, 55–56.

53. Ibid., 47, 55–56.

54. Ibid., 57.

55. Ibid., 56–57.

56. Ibid., 56.

57. Ibid., 56.

58. Ibid., 57.

59. On Han Clothing and identity, see Kevin Carrico, *The Great Han: Race, Nationalism, and Tradition in China Today* (Berkeley: University of California Press, 2017).

60. Tsui, *Heunggong: watchou dik gabong*, 520.

61. Chin Wan, *Sihngbong jyukyuhn leuhn* [On Hong Kong as a sovereign city-state] (Hong Kong: Subculture Publishing, 2015); and Chin Wan, *Heimohng jingjih: Sihngbong jyukyuhn leuhn II* [The politics of hope: On Hong Kong as a sovereign city-state II] (Hong Kong: Subculture Publishing, 2016).

62. Basic Law of the Hong Kong Special Administrative Region of the People's Republic of China, accessed March 2019, www.basiclaw.gov.hk/en/basiclawtext /images/basiclaw_full_text_en.pdf.

63. Chin, *Heimohng jingjih*, 78–79.

64. Ibid., 78, 86, 88.

65. Ibid., 88.

66. Ibid., 88–89.

67. Ibid., 84–88.

68. Ibid., 88–89.

69. Ibid., 88.

70. Chin, *Heimohng jingjih*, 79; and Chin, *Sihngbong jyukyuhn leuhn*, 80-81.

71. Chin, *Heimohng jingjih*, 79.

72. Ching Cheong, "*Chung sahpbaatdaaih hon Heunggong deihah Jungguhng dongyuhn kwaimouh*" [An assessment of the number of underground CCP members in Hong Kong based on insights from the 18th Party Congress], *Mingpao*, November 28, 2012 (no longer on Mingpao site; reprinted at www.hkfront.org/20121201ch.htm).

73. Bernard Yam, "Cross-Border Childbirth between Mainland China and Hong Kong: Social Pressures and Policy Outcomes," *PORTAL: Journal of Multidisciplinary International Studies* 8, no. 2 (2011): 1–13.

74. Margaret Harris Cheng, "Hong Kong Attempts to Reduce Influx of Pregnant Chinese," *Lancet* 369 (2007): 981–982.

75. Cheng Ka Ming, "Medical Tourism: Chinese Maternity Tourism to Hong Kong," *Current Issues in Tourism* 19, no. 14 (2016): 1479–1486.

76. Sharon LaFraniere, "Mainland Chinese Flock to Hong Kong to Give Birth," *New York Times*, February 22, 2012, www.nytimes.com/2012/02/23/world/asia /mainland-chinese-flock-to-hong-kong-to-have-babies.html.

77. Chin, *Sihngbong jyukyuhn leuhn*, 80–81.

78. Ibid., 82, 162.

79. Chin, *Heimohng jingjih*, 80; and Chin, *Sihngbong jyukyuhn leuhn*, 162–167.

80. Kris Cheng, "Lingnan University President Warns Localist Professor to 'Mind Your Words or Suffer the Consequences," *Hong Kong Free Press*, November 12, 2015, https://hongkongfp.com/2015/11/12/lingnanu-president-warns-localist-prof-to-mind -your-words-or-suffer-the-consequences/.

81. Although Chin's bid for the Legislative Council was unsuccessful, nationalist candidates with philosophies inspired by his won almost a fifth (19 percent) of the popular vote in the 2016 election, signaling a massive shift in the city's political culture.

See Malte Philipp Kaeding, "The Rise of 'Localism' in Hong Kong," *Journal of Democracy* 28, no. 1 (January 2017): 167.

82. Cheng Chung-tai and Jonathan Kan, *Geibunfaat goileuhng choyih* [A preliminary discussion of reforms to the Basic Law] (Hong Kong: Passiontimes, 2017).

83. Ibid., 31.

84. Ibid., 63–64.

85. Ibid., 163.

86. Ibid., 132.

87. Ibid., 143.

88. Ibid., 145.

89. *Undergrad* Editorial Board, ed., "*Heunggong mahnjuhk, mihngwahn jihkyut*" [Hong Kong nationality, self-determination of our own future], *Undergrad* (February 2014); and *Undergrad* Editorial Board, ed., *Heunggong mahnjuhk leuhn* [Hong Kong nationalism] (Hong Kong: Hong Kong University Undergraduate Student Union Publishing, 2015).

90. Leung Kai-ping, Introduction to *Undergrad* Editorial Board, ed., "*Heunggong mahnjuhk, mihngwahn jihkyut*" [Hong Kong nationality, self-determination of our own future," *Undergrad* (February 2014): 23. Leung later became the sole protester to reveal his face during the occupation of the city's Legislative Council on July 1, 2019, delivering a moving speech on the rationale for the occupation and the need for protestors to hold their ground.

91. Leung, Introduction, 23. Tsui's quotation comes from Tsui Sing Yan, *Sihngbong gauhsih: Sahpyih bun syu hon Heunggong buntou si* [A history of the city-state: Reading Hong Kong local history through twelve books] (Hong Kong: Red Publishing, 2014), 72.

92. Leung, Introduction, 23.

93. See, for example, Liah Greenfeld, *Nationalism: Five Roads to Modernity* (Cambridge, MA: Harvard University Press, 1993) or Liah Greenfeld, *Nationalism: A Short History* (Washington, DC: Brookings Institution Press, 2019).

94. Leung, Introduction, 23.

95. Jonathan Rée, "Internationality," *Radical Philosophy* 60 (Spring 1992): 3–11.

96. A thoughtful overview of the case and its implications can be found in Karen Kong, "*Kong Yunming v. Director of Social Welfare*: Implications for Law and Policy on Social Welfare," *Hong Kong Law Journal* 44, no. 1 (2014): 67–82.

97. Leung Kai-ping, "*Jungwuhn chithaahn jangyih yuh buntou jingjih guhngtungtai*" [The local political community and the controversy surrounding the removal of welfare eligibility limits], in *Undergrad* Editorial Board, ed., "*Heunggong mahnjuhk, mihngwahn jihkyut*" [Hong Kong nationality, self-determination of our own future], *Undergrad* (February 2014): 24–26.

98. Liberal Party, "Survey on the Removal of Welfare Eligibility Limits," January 6, 2014, www.liberal.org.hk/index.php?option=com_content&view=article&id=900& mid=49&lang=tc&__cf_chl_captcha_tk__=5131a30cdd5bb6d09a69c78261f65c861 beb7fc7-1588591776-0-AWj2ivFFFrsIsT66nC909U205h8vUdNHIIqgdYjJac79jl

TIIxthR59Hı5Q6VFYkwOa9ıVkI6u8RMPVDXXYjAh_YLAipg8kxvWtJOG4
KJMABısz3ppYv-BGerwcuTkaTeJ6lrWCuV5B-ozygdlhZ6jORlcZYduh
UaxljıobudNUSrsp9ıXk6ıpPKMNZIb2fadauNKAzVT5gDNKD9iAUHyolUj
_yN_093hR7QVpdt5OuRmw38qm8_GHuXucEmLx4xOqlcOSuo2_wCluCn
QMWxMbnZkWtAEYcFqzlY_2zIN6-uFblsaTYqagoL5_oT2SpıerE-MHYDg
Iph2iRfZTfiQojHijlxDDdN3-GCfZGJHDoj29WxNsJ-2SVeOZfje-8hD3nDp
VDLxXIXlExmD2mda6itDgNob_5CoO9eQ3ch909QObUfG70CBAV5Ujo
NCQXJfJ46tygv5_HzfNPQbmJjvQknG4qDgSfQYGFcuobo4SxQGoXMhlkAEs
UyGr_Qjoı6VMzpMgZun5PeLJ8P-vNRfkjnIAyEtı6QVıbgLGfovCBSrR4z
_aGwroebiCWt62nOieW_dvKFtqeyImM7aMVz62sN_ffgTLFlzızii-3TxNk9
UdHFbXUQv-ıuYGZYlFpnEQ.

99. Leung, *"Jungwuhn chithaahn jangyih,"* 24.

100. Ibid., 24.

101. Ibid., 25.

102. See Kevin Carrico, "Swarm of the Locusts: The Ethnicization of Hong Kong-China Relations," in *Yellow Perils: China Narratives in the Contemporary World*, ed. Franck Billé and Sören Urbansky (Honolulu: University of Hawaii Press, 2018), 197–220; and Kevin Carrico, "From Citizens Back to Subjects: Constructing National Belonging in Hong Kong's National Education Centre," in *From a British to a Chinese Colony: Hong Kong before and after the 1997 Handover*, ed. Gary Chi-hung Luk (Berkeley: Institute of East Asian Studies China Research Monograph, 2017), 259–284.

103. Niklas Luhmann, *Political Theory in the Welfare State* (Berlin: Walter De Gruyter, 1990), 43.

104. Jonathan Friedman, *PC Worlds: Political Correctness and Rising Elites at the End of Hegemony* (New York: Berghahn Books, 2019).

105. Luhmann, *Political Theory in the Welfare State*, 44.

106. Ibid., 66.

107. Jack Lee, *"Heunggong sihfau yingyauh mahnjuhk jihkyut dik kyunlei"* [Should Hong Kong have the right to self-determination?], in *Undergrad* Editorial Board, ed., *"Heunggong mahnjuhk, mihngwahn jihkyut"* [Hong Kong nationality, self-determination of our own future], *Undergrad* (February 2014): 34–37.

108. Ibid., 35.

109. Ibid., 35.

110. Ibid., 35.

111. Ibid., 35.

112. Ibid., 35.

113. Joseph Lian Yi-zheng appears to have been the first commentator to draw upon Stalin's characterization of a nationality to reimagine Hong Kong identity. See Lian Yi-zheng, *"Taahm wuhjiu gwokjihk: Leuhn gongyahn sihngwaih siusou mahnjuhk* [Of passports and nationalities: On designating the Hong Kong people as a minority nationality," *Hong Kong Economic Journal*, November 6, 2012. wwwı.hkej.com/daily news/article/id/644727/%E8%AB%87%E8%AD%B7%E7%85%A7%E5%9C%8B%E7

%B1%8D%E2%80%94%E2%80%94%E8%AB%96%E6%B8%AF%E4%BA%BA%E6%88
%90%E7%82%BA%E5%B0%91%E6%95%B8%E6%B0%91%E6%97%8F

114. On the concept of a difference that makes a difference, see Gregory Bateson's definition of information in "Form, Substance, and Difference," in *Steps to an Ecology of Mind* (Chicago: University of Chicago Press, 1972), 454–471.

115. Wong Chun Kit, Introduction to *Heunggong mahnjuhk leuhn* [Hong Kong nationalism], ed. *Undergrad* Editorial Board (Hong Kong: Hong Kong University Undergraduate Student Union Publishing, 2015), 13–21.

116. Ibid., 17.

117. Ibid., 17–18.

118. Ibid., 18.

119. Lee, *"Heunggong sihfau yingyauh mahnjuhk jihkyut dik kyunlei,"* 36.

120. International Covenant on Civil and Political Rights, accessed February 20, 2020, www.ohchr.org/en/professionalinterest/pages/ccpr.aspx; and International Covenant on Economic, Social, and Cultural Rights, accessed February 20, 2020, www.ohchr.org/en/professionalinterest/pages/cescr.aspx .

121. United Nations General Assembly, "General Assembly Resolution 1514 of 14 December 1960: Declaration on the Granting of Independence to Colonial Countries and People," www.ohchr.org/EN/ProfessionalInterest/Pages/Independence.aspx.

122. Lee, *"Heunggong sihfau yingyauh mahnjuhk jihkyut dik kyunlei,"* 36.

123. Carole Petersen, "Not an Internal Affair: Hong Kong's Right to Internal Autonomy and Self-Determination under International Law," *Hong Kong Law Journal* 49, no. 3 (2019): 894–895.

124. Lee, *"Heunggong sihfau yingyauh mahnjuhk jihkyut dik kyunlei,"* in *Heunggong mahnjuhk leuhn* [Hong Kong nationalism], ed. *Undergrad* Editorial Board (Hong Kong: Hong Kong University Undergraduate Student Union Publishing, 2015), 75–76. Also quoted in Tsui, *Heunggong, watchou dik gabong*, 525.

125. A thorough overview of the 2016 Legislative Council election, the role of Hong Kong nationalists therein, and their transformation of the city's political landscape can be found in Kaeding, "Rise of 'Localism' in Hong Kong."

126. Stand News, *"Chingnihn sanjing dang luhk joujik jou lyuhnmahng jin laahpwuih, cheung 2021 Heunggong jihkyut gungtauh"* [Youngspiration and five other organizations establish an alliance to win seats in the legislative council, call for a 2021 referendum on self-determination], Stand News, April 10, 2016, www.thestandnews.com/politics /%E9%9D%92%E5%B9%B4%E6%96%B0%E6%94%BF%E7%AD%89%E5%85%AD %E7%B5%84%E7%B9%94-%E7%B5%84%E8%81%AF%E7%9B%9F%E6%88%B0%E7 %AB%8B%E6%9C%83-%E5%80%A12021%E9%A6%99%E6%B8%AF%E8%87%AA %E6%B1%BA%E5%85%AC%E6%8A%95/.

127. Tsui, *Heunggong, watchou dik gabong*, 531.

128. Joshua Wong (with Jason Ng), *Unfree Speech: The Threat to Global Democracy and Why We Must Act Now* (New York: W. H. Allen, 2020), 58.

129. Siu Kit, *Wohngtin giksaat bong* [Heaven's hit list] (Hong Kong: Passiontimes, 2018), 191–192.

130. Petersen, "Not an Internal Affair," 885–886.

131. Ibid., 896–897.

132. On the escalating challenges facing human rights lawyers in China today, see Eva Pils, "The Party's Turn to Public Repression: An Analysis of the '709' Crackdown on Human Rights Lawyers in China," *China Law and Society Review* 3, no. 1 (2018): 1–48.

133. James Griffiths, "Hong Kong Moves to Disqualify More Pro-democracy Lawmakers," CNN, December 2, 2016, https://edition.cnn.com/2016/12/02/asia/hong-kong-lawmakers-oathgate/index.html.

134. Venus Wu and Greg Torode, "Hong Kong Lawmakers Condemn 'Unlawful' Disqualification of Candidate," Reuters, January 29, 2018, www.reuters.com/article/us-hongkong-politics/hong-kong-lawyers-condemn-unlawful-disqualification-of-candidate-idUSKBN1FI0U4.

135. Laignee Barron, "Hong Kong Democracy Activist Joshua Wong Disqualified from Upcoming Election," *Time*, October 29, 2019, https://time.com/5712824/joshua-wong-hong-kong-disqualified-district-elections/.

136. RTHK, "Demosistō Drops 'Self-Determination' Clause," RTHK, January 11, 2020, https://news.rthk.hk/rthk/en/component/k2/1502283-20200111.htm?spTabChangeable=0.

137. *Undergrad* Editorial Board, ed., "*Heunggong, mahnjyu, duhklaahp*" [Hong Kong, democracy, independence], *Undergrad* (September 2014).

138. Yuen Yuen-lung, "*Jeh sihdoih dik naahp-haam*" [An era's call to arms: Xianggang, minzu, duli], in *Undergrad* Editorial Board, ed., "*Heunggong, mahnjyu, duhklaahp*" [Hong Kong, democracy, independence], *Undergrad* (September 2014): 31; the Tien quote is discussed in *Apple Daily*, "*Tihn Bakjeun waaileuhn: jan pousyun yuh gongduhk mouh yih*," *Apple Daily*, July 18, 2014, https://hk.appledaily.com/local/20140718/2S2BOTIY73HAO6PDBCNDD2X2SY/.

139. Yuen, "*Jeh sihdoih dik naahp-haam*," 31.

140. Ibid., 31.

141. The press conference that launched the Hong Kong National Party can be viewed in full on YouTube at SOCrecHK, "28MAR2016 *gindong syunyihn- Heunggong Mahnjuhk dong gindong geihjewuih* (1/3)" [March 28, 2016 announcement of the founding of the party—Hong Kong National Party press conference], https://youtu.be/DVSZakCo9nE.

142. Hong Kong National Party, eds., *Comitium*, nos. 1–3 (2016–2017).

143. The fourth, unpublished issue of *Comitium* was slated to include an article I penned entitled, "The Basic Law Is Basically Garbage." This article was subsequently published by *Local News* on September 24, 2018, the day that the Hong Kong National Party was declared an illegal organization. See Kevin Carrico, "The Basic Law is Basically Garbage," *Local News*, September 24, 2018, www.localpresshk.com/2018/09/basic-garbage/.

144. Kai Keih, "*Chungpo mouhleih yihnsan dik Junggwok jihkmahn bakyun: Shi Shumei 'wahyuh yuhhaih' leihleuhn dik kaisih*" [Disrupting China's ever-expanding colonial

hegemony: Insights from Shih Shu-mei's Sinophone Theory], *Comitium*, no. 1 (July 2016): 13–19.

145. Ibid., 13–14.

146. Shih Shu-mei, "The Concept of the Sinophone," *PMLA* 126, no. 3 (May 2011): 710. A general introduction to Sinophone theory is available at Shih Shu-mei, Tsai Chien-hsin, and Brian Bernards, eds. *Sinophone Studies: A Critical Reader* (New York: Columbia University Press, 2013).

147. Shih, "Concept of the Sinophone," 711–714.

148. Kai, "*Chungpo mouhleih yihnsan dik Junggwok jihkmahn bakyun*," 19.

149. Jason Chow, "*Ginkaw Heunggong mahnjuhk*" [Constructing a Hong Kong nationality], *Comitium*, no. 1 (July 2016): 8–11.

150. Ibid., 9.

151. Ibid., 9.

152. Ibid., 9.

153. Ibid., 9–11.

154. Ibid., 11.

155. Ibid., 11.

156. Ibid., 9–11.

157. Quenthai, "*Jungwah mahnjuhk jyuyih deui Heunggong dik yihchuhng jihkmahn*" [Chinese nationalism's dual colonization of Hong Kong], *InMedia HK*, July 25, 2015. https://www.inmediahk.net/node/1036196

158. Chow, "*Ginkaw Heunggong mahnjuhk*," 11.

159. Quenthai, "*Chuhng faanjihk gokdouh hon 'Heunggong mahnjuhk leuhn' dik batjuk*" [A critique of *Hong Kong Nationalism* from an anti-colonial perspective], *Comitium*, no. 2 (January 2017): 44–51.

160. Ibid., 45.

161. See Chow, "*Ginkaw Heunggong mahnjuhk*," 11.

162. Rogers Brubaker, *Citizenship and Nationhood in France and Germany* (Cambridge, MA: Harvard University Press, 1992).

163. I too have been guilty of the rush to affirm civic nationalism to the idealistic exclusion of other possibilities. See, for example, Carrico, "Swarm of the Locusts."

164. Quenthai, "*Chuhng faanjihk gokdouh hon 'Heunggong mahnjuhk leuhn' dik batjuk*," 47–48.

165. Benedict Anderson, *Imagined Communities: On the Origins and Spread of Nationalism* (London: Verso, 1983), 7; and Martin Heidegger, "The Age of the World Picture," in *The Question Concerning Technology and Other Essays* (New York: Garland Publishing, 1977), 142.

166. Quenthai, "*Chuhng faanjihk gokdouh hon 'Heunggong mahnjuhk leuhn' dik batjuk*," 47–48.

167. Ibid., 47–48.

168. Ibid., 48–49.

169. Ibid., 49.

170. Ibid., 49.

171. Ibid., 48–49.

172. Ibid., 49–51.

173. Ibid., 49–51.

174. Fredrik Barth, introduction to *Ethnic Groups and Boundaries: The Social Organization of Culture Difference*, ed. Fredrik Barth (Long Grove: Waveland Press, 1998), 9–38 (relationally across a boundary); and Quenthai, "*Chuhng faanjihk gokdouh hon 'Heunggong mahnjuhk leuhn' dik batjuk,*" 49–51.

175. Ibid., 50–51.

176. Ibid., 50–51.

177. Kai, "*Chungpo mouhleih yihnsan dik Junggwok jihkmahn bakyun.*"

178. Chow, "*Ginkow Heunggong mahnjuhk.*"

179. Quenthai, "*Chuhng faanjihk gokdouh hon 'Heunggong mahnjuhk leuhn' dik batjuk.*"

180. Translation of this phrase is based on the translation of a section of this comment included in Xi Jinping's essay "Foster and Practice Core Socialist Values from Childhood," in *The Governance of China* (Beijing: Foreign Languages Press, 2014), 201.

181. Hong Kong National Party Facebook page, "*Heunggong mahnjuhk dong hungjohk jingjih kaimuhng gaiwaahk sanmahn gou*" [Press release on Hong Kong National Party middle school political enlightenment scheme], September 19, 2016, www.facebook.com/hknationalparty/posts/541142572751368/.

182. Mingpao, "*Mahnjuhk dong: 80 junghohk yahp 'kaimuhng gaiwaahk,' haauhjeung chik 'heung sailou maaihsau bat douhdak'*" [[National Party: 80 middle schools involved in "enlightenment scheme," school principal declares "targeting kids is immoral"], *Mingpao*, September 20, 2016, https://news.mingpao.com/pns/%E6%B8%AF%E8%81%9E/article/20160920/s00002/1474308150162/%E6%B0%91%E6%97%8F%E9%BB%A8-80%E4%B8%AD%E5%AD%B8%E5%85%A5%E3%80%8C%E5%95%9F%E8%92%99%E8%A8%88%E5%8A%83%E3%80%8D-%E6%A0%A1%E9%95%B7%E6%96%A5%E3%80%8C%E5%90%91%E7%B4%B0%E8%B7%AF%E5%9F%8B%E6%89%8B%E4%B8%8D%E9%81%93%E5%BE%B7%E3%80%8D

183. Hong Kong National Party Facebook page, "*Heunggong mahnjuhk dong yu Toihwaan cheutjihk ajau yahnkyuhn baakhoih yuh jikyut gwokhai geije wuih sanmahn gou*" [Press release on Hong Kong National Party's attendance at the "Human rights, persecution, and self-determination" international press conference held in Taiwan], December 9, 2016, www.facebook.com/hknationalparty/posts/578527842346174/.

184. The website of the Free Indo-Pacific Alliance can be found at http://fipa.asia/en/. The PRC state-owned newspaper *Ta Kung Pao*, directly under the control of the central government's liaison office in Hong Kong, reported on Chan Ho-tin's interactions with Mongolian independence activists in Japan in 2016 in the article "'*Heunggong mahnjuhk dong' Chan Ho-tin gungyihn ngaugit 'Muhngduhk'*" [Hong Kong National Party's Andy Chan openly colludes with "Mongolian independence"], *Ta Kung Pao*, November 12, 2016, http://news.takungpao.com.hk/hkol/topnews/2016-11/3390941.html.

185. Hong Kong National Party Facebook page, "*Mahnjuhk dong heung Meihgwok jyugong lihngsihgun gaau chingyuhnseun, yiukauh cheuixiao Heunggong gwaanhaih faat*"

[National Party delivers petition to United States' Consulate in Hong Kong, requesting that the US abolish the Hong Kong Policy Act], August 24, 2017, www.facebook.com /hknationalparty/posts/698259103706380/.

186. Lam Jeunhim, *"Chan Ho-tin chuk Dahklohngpou tuhngsih jaichoih Jung Gong, Gongfu gap wuihying Heunggong sih daanduhk gwaanseui kuei"* [Andy Chan calls on Trump to sanction both China and Hong Kong, the Hong Kong government urgently responds "Hong Kong is a separate customs territory"], *Apple Daily*, August 20, 2018, https://hk.news.appledaily.com/local/daily/article/20180820/20480322.

187. SOCrecHK, "28MAR2016 *gindong syunyihn*."

188. Jilaahn Yuhngyihp, *"Mouhyuhng ji yuhng: Gungmahn bat hahpjok wahnduhng"* [The use of the useless: on civil disobedience], *Comitium*, no. 2 (January 2017): 36–43.

189. Ibid., 38–39.

190. Ibid., 38–39.

191. Ibid., 38–39.

192. Ibid., 40–41.

193. Ibid., 40–41.

194. Ibid., 41.

195. *Apple Daily*, *"Hohksaang duhklaahp lyuhnmahng: Gongduhk haih bitseui jau dik louh"* [Students' Independence Union: Hong Kong independence is the only path forward], *Apple Daily*, September 28, 2018, https://hk.news.appledaily.com/local /realtime/article/20180928/58736008.

196. Mouhyihn, *"Heunggong doyuhn mahnfa buiging* [Hong Kong's multicultural background]," in *Leuhn gwaiying: wuih dou yingjih Heunggong* [On returning to the UK: recapturing a British-ruled Hong Kong], 81.

197. Mouhyihn, *"Wuihdou yingjih jingfu gwoheui dik doihyuh"* [Recapturing the UK's Hong Kong governance model], in *Leuhn gwaiying: Wuih dou yingjih Heunggong* [On returning to the UK: Recapturing a British-ruled Hong Kong], 32-33; Mouhyihn, *"Heunggong doyuhn mahnfa buiging"* [Hong Kong's multicultural background], in *Leuhn gwaiying: Wuih dou yingjih Heunggong* [On returning to the UK: Recapturing a British-ruled Hong Kong] (Hong Kong: Passiontimes, 2015), 80–81; and Lady Kylie, *"Sowaih 'gwaiying' sih sahnmo yat wuihsih"* [What is this "returning to the UK" idea?]," in *Leuhn gwaiying: Wuih dou yingjih Heunggong* [On returning to the UK: Recapturing a British-ruled Hong Kong] (Hong Kong: Passiontimes, 2015), 26.

198. Bruce Gilley, "The Case for Colonialism" (withdrawn from *Third World Quarterly* after publication), accessed at www.nas.org/academic-questions/31/2/the_case _for_colonialism.

199. Gilley, "Case for Colonialism," 3.

200. Peter Sloterdijk, "What Happened in the Twentieth Century? A Critique of Extremist Reason," in *What Happened in the Twentieth Century?* (London: Polity, 2018), 55–81.

201. The failure to implement full and genuine democracy under colonial rule is of course a significant contributor to the current dire state of affairs. The story of this failure is, however, vastly more complex than generally assumed. For more details on

the role of the People's Republic of China in suppressing political reforms before 1997, see Gwynn Guilford, "The Secret History of Hong Kong's Stillborn Democracy," *Quartz*, October 11, 2014, https://qz.com/279013/the-secret-history-of-hong-kongs-stillborn-democracy/.

202. Mouhyihn, "*Wuihdou yingjih jingfu gwoheui dik doihyuh*," 32; and Nihngsi, "*Gwaiying bat sih waihliuh geinihm yingjih sihkeih*" [Returning to the UK is not just for nostalgia]," in *Leuhn gwaiying: Wuih dou yingjih Heunggong* [On returning to the UK: Recapturing a British-ruled Hong Kong] (Hong Kong: Passiontimes, 2015), 94.

203. Lady Kylie, "*Wuihgwai wuih neih louh juhk* [Return? Return to your mom!], in *Leuhn gwaiying: wuih dou yingjih Heunggong* [On returning to the UK: Recapturing a British-ruled Hong Kong] (Hong Kong: Passiontimes, 2015), 70; and Jiwaih, "*Heunggong, jauhsih Heunggong yahn dik Heunggong*" [Hong Kong is the Hong Kong people's Hong Kong], in *Leuhn gwaiying: Wuih dou yingjih Heunggong* [On returning to the UK: Recapturing a British-ruled Hong Kong] (Hong Kong: Passiontimes, 2015), 92.

204. Mouhyihn, "*Wuihdou yingjih jingfu gwoheui dik doihyuh*," 33; Mouh Loihyauh, "*Yingsuhk jihjih sihngbong yuh waihdoleiha sik wohngga jihkmahndeih* [A UK-held self-ruling city-state and a Victorian-style royal colony]," in *Leuhn gwaiying: Wuih dou yingjih Heunggong* [On returning to the UK: Recapturing a British-ruled Hong Kong] (Hong Kong: Passiontimes, 2015), 124–125; and Lady Kylie, "*Sowaih 'gwaiying' sih sahnmo yat wuihsih*," 26.

205. Lady Kylie, "*Sowaih 'gwaiying' sih sahnmo yat wuihsih*," 26–27.

206. Joint Declaration of the Government of the United Kingdom of Great Britain and Northern Ireland and the Government of the People's Republic of China on the Question of Hong Kong, www.cmab.gov.hk/en/issues/jd2.htm.

207. Ibid.

208. Petersen, "Not an Internal Affair," 896–897.

209. Lady Kylie, "*Sowaih 'gwaiying' sih sahnmo yat wuihsih*," 22.

210. Ibid., 22; Mouh Loihyauh, "*Yingsuhk jihjih sihngbong yuh waihdoleiha sik wohngga jihkmahndeih*," 124.

211. Lady Kylie, "*Gongduhk waahk gwaiying batsih naahnyih dik mahntaih sih muhtfaat batjouh dik mahntaih*" [Hong Kong independence or returnism: Not a question of what is easier or harder, but rather a question of necessity], in *Leuhn gwaiying: Wuih dou yingjih Heunggong* [On returning to the UK: Recapturing a British-ruled Hong Kong] (Hong Kong: Passiontimes, 2015), 141.

212. See the analysis and critique of these various proposals for Hong Kong's future in Lady Kylie, "*Sowaih 'gwaiying' sih sahnmo yat wuihsih*," 24.

213. Lady Kylie, "*Sowaih 'gwaiying' sih sahnmo yat wuihsih*," 22; and Lady Kylie, "*Gongduhk waahk gwaiying batsih naahnyih dik mahntaih sih muhtfaat batjouh dik mahntaih*," 141.

214. Lady Kylie, "*Sowaih 'gwaiying' sih sahnmo yat wuihsih*," 22.

215. Nihngsi, "*Jihkboulohtaap yuh Heunggong* [Gibraltar and Hong Kong]," in *Leuhn gwaiying: Wuih dou yingjih Heunggong* [On returning to the UK: Recapturing a British-ruled Hong Kong] (Hong Kong: Passiontimes, 2015), 137–139.

216. Ibid., 137–138.

217. David Lambert, "'As Solid as the Rock'? Place, Belonging and the Local Appropriation of Imperial Discourse in Gibraltar," *Transactions of the Institute of British Geographers* New Series 30 (2005): 206–220.

218. Ibid.

219. Mouh Loihyauh, "*Saibaanngah mahnjyufa hauh maauhteuhn* [Tensions after Spain's democratization]," in *Leuhn gwaiying: Wuih dou yingjih Heunggong* [On returning to the UK: Recapturing a British-ruled Hong Kong] (Hong Kong: Passiontimes, 2015), 138.

220. Lady Kylie, "*Sowaih 'gwaiying' sih sahnmo yat wuihsih*," 22; and Nihngsi, "*Jihkboulohtaap yuh Heunggong*," 137–138.

221. Lady Kylie, "*Sowaih 'gwaiying' sih sahnmo yat wuihsih*," 22; and Nihngsi, "*Jihkboulohtaap yuh Heunggong*," 137–138.

222. Ibid.; and Lady Kylie, "*Sowaih 'gwaiying' sih sahnmo yat wuihsih*," 22.

223. Peter Sloterdijk, *Critique of Cynical Reason* (Minneapolis: University of Minnesota Press, 1987): 13.

224. Ibid., 11.

225. Ibid., 14.

CHAPTER 3. SEEING (EXACTLY) LIKE A STATE: KNOWLEDGE/POWER IN THE HONG KONG-CHINA RELATIONSHIP

1. Chen Hao, "*Yu shi ju jin yingdui 'gangdu' 'ruan baoli'*" [Keeping up with the times in responding to abuse by "Hong Kong independence forces"], *Journal of the Fujian Institute of Socialism* 104, no. 5 (2014): 104.

2. Chen, "*Yu shi ju jin*," 104.

3. Ibid.

4. Ibid.

5. Ibid., 105–106.

6. Ibid., 106.

7. Edward Said, *Orientalism* (New York: Penguin, 2003), 41, 6.

8. Said, *Orientalism*, 42.

9. Ibid., 5.

10. Ibid., 39, 43.

11. Ibid., 3.

12. Sadik Jalal al-'Azm. "Orientalism and Oriental-ism in Reverse," *Khamsin*, no. 8 (1981): 5–26.

13. Gerd Baumann, "Grammars of Identity/Alterity: A Structural Approach." In *Grammars of Identity/Alterity: A Structural Approach*, ed. Gerd Baummann and Andre Gingrich (New York: Berghahn Books, 2004), 19.

14. Ibid., 19–20.

15. Ibid., 20.

16. Ibid., 21–24.

17. Ibid., 25.

18. Ibid., 26.

19. See Magnus Fiskesjö, "'The Legacy of the Chinese Empires Beyond 'the West and the Rest,'" *Education about Asia* 22, no. 1 (2017): 6–10; and Dru Gladney, "Representing Nationality in China: Refiguring Majority/Minority Identities." *Journal of Asian Studies* 53, no. 1 (1994): 92–123.

20. Sean Roberts, "The Biopolitics of China's 'War on Terror' and the Exclusion of the Uyghurs," *Critical Asian Studies* 50, no. 2 (2018): 232–258.

21. Stevan Harrell, "Introduction: Civilizing Projects and the Reaction to Them," in *Cultural Encounters on China's Ethnic Frontiers*, ed. Steven Harrell (Seattle: University of Washington Press, 1995), 3–36.

22. Louis Althusser, "Ideology and Ideological State Apparatuses," in *Lenin and Philosophy and Other Essays* (New York: Monthly Review Press, 1971), 175.

23. On this notion of the human ability to step outside of "the they," see Hubert L. Dreyfus, *Being-in-the-World: A Commentary on Heidegger's "Being and Time"* (Cambridge, MA: MIT Press, 1991).

24. Such conditions of production, one would think, should be a point of consideration for a Marxist academic, but seem instead to be a blind spot.

25. See Said, *Orientalism*, 7.

26. Xi Jinping, speech at Hong Kong civil servants' oath ceremony, July 1, 2017, https://orientaldaily.on.cc/cnt/news/20170702/00176_014.html, quoted in Li Qin, "'Xiaoyuan gangdu' sichao de fazhan mailuo, xingcheng yuanyin ji zhili qishi" [The pro-independence movement on Hong Kong's campus: Its evolution, causes, and implications], *Hong Kong-Macao Studies* 2 (2019): 60.

27. Gene Lin, "CUHK Survey Finds That Nearly 40% of Young Hongkongers Want Independence after 2047," *Hong Kong Free Press*, July 25, 2016, https://hongkongfp.com/2016/07/25/17-hongkongers-support-independence-2047-especially-youth-cuhk-survery/.

28. Susan Blum, *Portraits of "Primitives": Ordering Human Kinds in the Chinese Nation* (Lanham, MD: Rowman & Littlefield, 2001).

29. Tian Feilong, "Dawan qu jianshe shiye xia de Xianggang bentu zhili xin silu" [New directions in the administration of Hong Kong from the perspective of developing the Greater Bay Area], *Journal of Guangzhou Institute of Socialism* 2, no. 65 (2019): 5–20.

30. Ibid., 9–10.

31. William Callahan, *Contingent States: Greater China and Transnational Relations* (Minneapolis: University of Minnesota Press, 2004), 158.

32. Sang Pu, *Junggwok dik guyih: Heunggong yahn* [China's orphan: The Hong Kong people] (Hong Kong: Subculture, 2017).

33. Tian, "Dawan qu," 5.

34. Huang Chenpu, "'Qingnianhua' Gangdu sixiang de chengyin ji benzhi" [The causes and essence of young people's 'Hong Kong independence' thought], *Journal of Guangdong Youth Vocational College* 31, no. 1 (February 2017): 17. This argument is also articulated in Wei Nanji, "Xianggang qingnian bentupai de zhengzhi jueqi yu zouxiang" [The

political rise and future direction of Hong Kong's young localists], *China Youth Research* (May 2018): 12–18.

35. Huang, 17.

36. Ibid., 17–18.

37. Feng Qingxiang and Xu Haibo, "*Xianggang 'gangdu' xianxiang shuyuan yu xiaojie*" [Origins of the "Hong Kong independence" phenomenon and its elimination], *Theoretical Research* 340, no. 2 (April 2017): 49. For other examples of this narrative, see Chen Yi, "*Xiangdui boduogan yu Xianggang qingnian de zhengzhi xinren*" [Relative deprivation and political trust among youth in Hong Kong], *Hong Kong-Macao Studies* 3 (2019): 35–44; Li Weishun, "'*Gangdu' wenti de weihai, yuanyou ji duice*" [The origins and dangers of "Hong Kong independence," as well as countermeasures], *Practice and Theory of SEZs*, no. 6 (2017): 60; and Wang Junjun "*Shilun 'gangdu' de xingcheng yuanyin, jiben tedian ji celue xuanze*" [A preliminary examination of the causes and basic characteristics of Hong Kong independence, as well as options for responding to this phenomenon], *Journal of Guangdong Institute of Socialism* 69, no. 4 (October 2017): 55.

38. Chen, "*Yu shi ju jin*," 104.

39. Tian, "*Dawan qu*," 7–8.

40. Wang, "*Shilun 'gangdu'*," 55.

41. Tian, "*Dawan qu*," 9–10.

42. See James Pomfret and Venus Wu, "China Pressures Hong Kong to Squash Independence Calls Ahead of Polls: Sources," Reuters, September 6, 2016, www.reuters .com/article/us-hongkong-election-china/china-pressures-hong-kong-to-squash -independence-calls-ahead-of-poll-sources-idUSKCN1175AO.

43. Basic Law of the Hong Kong Special Administrative Region of the People's Republic of China, accessed March 2019, www.basiclaw.gov.hk/en/basiclawtext/.

44. Government of Hong Kong Special Administrative Region Press Releases, "EAC's Request to Sign Confirmation Form Has Legal Basis," July 19, 2016, www.info .gov.hk/gia/general/201607/19/P2016071900950.htm.

45. Hong Kong Watch, "Political Screening in Hong Kong: The Disqualification of Candidates and Lawmakers Ahead of the March By-Elections," March 8, 2018, www .hongkongwatch.org/all-posts/2018/3/7/political-screening-in-hong-kong-a-report -on-the-disqualification-of-candidates-and-lawmakers.

46. "Hong Kong Independence Activist Banned from Elections," DW, July 30, 2016, www.dw.com/en/hong-kong-independence-activist-banned-from-elections/a -19438981.

47. Karen Cheung, "Civic Passion Candidate Says Will Not Advocate Independence through Run; HKNP Convenor Refuses to Answer," *Hong Kong Free Press*, July 27, 2016, https://hongkongfp.com/2016/07/27/civic-passion-candidate-says-will -not-advocate-independence-run-hknp-convenor-refuses-answer/; and Kris Cheng, "Another Pro-independence Candidate Barred from Running in Legco Election," *Hong Kong Free Press*, August 2, 2016, https://hongkongfp.com/2016/08/02/another -pro-independence-candidate-barred-running-legco-election/.

48. Kris Cheng, "Edward Leung of Hong Kong Indigenous Barred from Legco Election," *Hong Kong Free Press*, August 2, 2016, https://hongkongfp.com/2016/08/02/breaking-edward-leung-hong-kong-indigenous-barred-legco-election/.

49. Ellie Ng, "Video: Democratic Lawmakers Stage Protests and Alter Oaths as New Term Kicks Off at Hong Kong Legislature," *Hong Kong Free Press*, October 6, 2016, https://hongkongfp.com/2016/10/12/breaking-democratic-lawmakers-stage-protests-alter-oaths-new-term-kicks-off-hong-kong-legislature/.

50. Zheping Huang and Echo Huang, "A Brief History: Beijing's Interpretations of Hong Kong's Basic Law, from 1999 to the Present Day," *Quartz*, November 7, 2016, https://qz.com/828713/a-brief-history-beijings-interpretations-of-hong-kongs-basic-law-from-1999-to-the-present-day/.

51. See, for example, Devin Lin, Valentin Günther, and Mathias Honer, "Interpreting Article 104: The Way, the How, the Timing," *Hong Kong Law Journal* 47 (2017): 475; and Lo Pui-yin, "Enforcing an Unfortunate, Unnecessary and 'Unquestionably Binding' NPCSC interpretation: The Hong Kong Judiciary's Deconstruction of its Construction of the Basic Law," *Hong Kong Law Journal* 48 (2018): 399.

52. *Ta Kung Pao*, "*Diuhchah: Leung Yau duhklouh kitbei; Gaauyuhk yihmjuhng satbaaih, seui faansi*" [Investigation: Revealing Yau and Leung's path to "independence," a failure in education that requires reflection], *Ta Kung Pao*, November 28, 2016, http://news.takungpao.com.hk/hkol/topnews/2016-11/3396789.html.

53. *Ta Kung Pao*, "*Diuhchah*."

54. Ibid.

55. Han Shanshan, "*Cong shanchuang zhu Gang junying kan 'Gangdu shi' jijin yundong: Tezheng, yuanyin ji weihai*" [Thoughts on the radical Hong Kong independence movement based on the intrusion into the PLA barracks: Characteristics, causes, and risks], *Hong Kong and Macao Studies* 1 (2014): 78.

56. Zhu Jie and Zhang Xiaoshan, "'*Xianggang bentu yishi' de lishixing shuli yu huanyuan*" [A historical narration and restoration of "Hong Kong's sense of nativeness," with a review of the formation and evolution of "Hong Kong independence" thought], *Hong Kong and Macao Studies* 1 (2016): 12–22.

57. Zhu Jie and Zhang Xiaoshan, "*Xianggang jijin bentu zhuyi zhi shehui xinli toushi*" [A psycho-social perspective on radical localism in Hong Kong], *Hong Kong and Macao Studies* 1 (2017): 3–12.

58. This narrative is also deployed (but never cited, indicating the presence of the not-so-hidden script discussed at the end of this chapter) in Zhu Hanqi, "*Gangdu sichao de fenxi yiji yingdui suoshi*" [An analysis of the "Hong Kong independence" trend and countermeasures], *Modern Business Trade Industry* 25 (2018): 134–135; Li Youkun, "*Xianggang chongjian Zhongguo rentong Zhong de zhimin qingjie tanxi*" [An exploration of Hong Kong's colonial complex in the process of reconstructing Chinese identity in the city], *Journal of the Party School of Xinjiang Production and Construction Corps of the Chinese Communist Party* 169, no. 6 (2017): 100–105; Liu Qiang, "*Xianggang qingnian zhengzhi canyu de 'bentuhua' dongxiang ji qi yingdui—dui 'gangdu yiyuan chenguo shijian' de sikao*" [The trend of "localism" in the political participation of Hong Kong youth

and countermeasures—reflections on "Hong Kong independence legislators insulting the nation"], *Chinese Youth Social Science*, no. 2 (2017): 45–46; Feng and Xu, "*Xianggang 'gangdu' xianxiang*"; and Li, "'*Gangdu' wenti*."

59. Zhu and Zhang, "*Xianggang bentu yishi*," 13.

60. Ibid., 14.

61. Zhu and Zhang, "*Xianggang jijin bentu zhuyi*," 5.

62. Zhu and Zhang, "*Xianggang bentu yishi*," 15.

63. Zhu and Zhang, "*Xianggang jijin bentu zhuyi*," 6.

64. Ibid.

65. Ibid., "*Xianggang jijin bentu zhuyi*," 6.

66. See Benedict Anderson, *The Specter of Comparisons: Nationalism, Southeast Asia and the World* (New York: Verso, 1998).

67. Zhu and Zhang, "*Xianggang jijin bentu zhuyi*," 6.

68. Zhu and Zhang, "*Xianggang bentu yishi*," 18.

69. Zhu and Zhang, "*Xianggang jijin bentu zhuyi*," 6.

70. Wang Wanli, "'*Gangdu' sichao de yanhua qushi yu fali yingdui*" [The evolutionary trend and legal response to the thought of "Hong Kong independence"], *Hong Kong-Macao Studies* 1 (2017): 19.

71. Said, *Orientalism*, 41, 6.

72. Chen Guanghan and Li Xiaoying. "*Yi fazhan jingji he gaishan minsheng wei zhongxin ningju Xianggang gongshi*" [Consolidate a Hong Kong consensus via economic development and livelihood improvement], *Hong Kong-Macao Studies* 3 (2015): 3–9.

73. Chen and Li, "*Yi fazhan jingji he gaishan minsheng*," 4–5.

74. Ibid., 7–9.

75. Emily Yeh, *Taming Tibet: Landscape Transformation and the Gift of Chinese Development* (Ithaca, NY: Cornell University Press, 2013) (Tibet). See Xinhua News, "Vocational Training and Education in Xinjiang," Xinhua News, August 16, 2019, www.xinhuanet.com/english/2019-08/16/c_138313359.htm.

76. See, for example, Tian, "*Dawan qu*."

77. Feng and Xu, "*Xianggang 'gangdu' xianxiang shuyuan yu xiaojie*," 47.

78. Basic Law of the Hong Kong Special Administrative Region of the People's Republic of China.

79. Ibid.

80. Li Yiyi, "'*Gangdu' yanxing de shibie jiqi falü guizhi—yi 'Xianggang jibenfa' di ershisan tiao lifa wei shijiao*" [Detection and legal regulation of "Hong Kong Independence" speech: A perspective from Article 23 of the Hong Kong Basic Law], *Hong Kong-Macao Studies* 2 (2018): 50.

81. Wang Fuchun, "*Lun Xianggang tequ fan fenlie guojia lifa*" [On establishing an anti-secession law for the HKSAR], *Local Legislation Journal* 3, no. 3 (May 15, 2018): 78–85.

82. Luo Weijian, "'*Gangdu' yanxing de weifaxing fenxi jiqi falü guizhi—Aomen fayuan anli de qishi* [Analysis of illegality about statements and actions of "Hong Kong independence" and the legal regulations: Enlightenments from the case of Macao courts]," *Hong Kong-Macao Studies* 4 (2016): 22–29.

83. Ibid., 24.

84. Ibid.

85. Ibid.

86. Wang, "*Lun Xianggang tequ fan fenlie guojia lifa,*" 80–81.

87. Han, "*Cong shanchuang zhu Gang junying,*" 79–80.

88. Chen Yijian and Huang Tong, "*Ezhi 'gangdu' zhi lifa gouxiang*" [Legislative design of regulating the so-called Hong Kong separatist activities], *Local Legislation Journal* 2, no. 6 (November 15, 2017): 32.

89. Zhu Jie and Zhang Xiaoshan, "*Zhuquan, guojia anquan yu zhengzhi gaige: 'Gangdu' de 'jiben fa' fangkong jizhi*" [Sovereignty, national security, and political reform: Prevention mechanism against "Hong Kong independence" under the Hong Kong Basic Law], *Journal of Jianghan University* (Social Science Edition) 33, no. 4 (August 2016): 15; and Li Yiyi, "'*Gangdu' yanxing,*" 40.

90. Li Yiyi, "'*Gangdu' yanxing,*" 51; similar ideas can be found in Luo, "'*Gangdu' yanxing,*" 25.

91. Luo, "'*Gangdu' yanxing,*" 23.

92. Elson Tong, "Pro-independence Hong Kong National Party Appeals against Companies Registry's Denial of Registration," *Hong Kong Free Press*, April 11, 2017, https://hongkongfp.com/2017/04/11/pro-independence-hong-kong-national-party-appeals-companies-registrys-denial-registration/.

93. Austin Ramzy, "Hong Kong Bars Pro-independence Candidate from Election," *New York Times*, July 30, 2016, www.nytimes.com/2016/07/31/world/asia/hong-kong-bars-pro-independence-candidate-from-election.html.

94. Kris Cheng, "Explainer: How Hong Kong Is Seeking to Ban a Pro-independence Party Using Existing National Security Laws," *Hong Kong Free Press*, July 19, 2018, https://hongkongfp.com/2018/07/19/explainer-hong-kong-seeking-ban-pro-independence-party-using-existing-national-security-laws/.

95. Carole Petersen, "Prohibiting the Hong Kong National Party: Has Hong Kong Violated the International Covenant on Civil and Political Rights?," *Hong Kong Law Journal* 48 (2018): 789–805.

96. Ibid., 797.

97. Ibid., 801–802.

98. Ibid., 803–804.

99. Ibid., 793–794.

100. Ibid.

101. Ibid.

102. Ibid.

103. Ibid., 796–797.

104. Arthur Shek, "*Chan Ho-tin mh haih yahn*" [Andy Chan is not a human being], *Hong Kong Economic Times*, August 17, 2018, https://invest.hket.com/article/2139897/%E9%99%B3%E6%B5%A9%E5%A4%A9%E5%94%94%E4%BF%82%E4%BA%BA.

105. Zhu and Zhang, "*Zhuquan, guojia anquan yu zhengzhi gaige,*" 12.

106. Li, "'Xiaoyuan gangdu'," 52.

107. On this topic, see Yinghong Cheng, Discourses of Race and Rising China (London: Palgrave Macmillan, 2019).

108. See Kevin Carrico, "Eliminating Spiritual Pollution: A Genealogy of Closed Political Thought in China's Era of Opening," China Journal, no. 78 (July 2017): 100–119.

109. Ibid.

110. On the biopolitical implications of such degenerative distance from the norm, see Roberto Esposito, Bios: Biopolitics and Philosophy (Minneapolis: University of Minnesota Press, 2008), 119.

111. Margaret Wong, "China Raps Hong Kong over Criticism: Further Erosion Seen in Autonomy," Associated Press, May 9, 2004. http://archive.boston.com/news/world/articles/2004/05/09/china_raps_hong_kong_over_criticism/.

112. Ibid.

113. Li, "Xianggang chongjian Zhongguo rentong," 100–105.

114. Ibid., 103

115. Shek, "Chan Ho-tin."

116. Ibid.

117. Ibid.

118. Ibid.

119. Esposito, Bios, 126.

120. Li, "Xianggang chongjian Zhongguo rentong," 104.

121. Ibid.

122. See Esposito's discussion of degeneration in Bios, 121.

123. See Esposito, Bios, 121.

124. Li, "Xianggang chongjian Zhongguo rentong," 102. A similar argument is pursued in Liu Xiulun and Ye Xinlu, "'Gangdu' fenli zhuyi dui qingnian guojia rentong de yingxiang yu yingdui celüe" [Influence of "Hong Kong independence movement" separatism on the youth's national identity and its countermeasures], Contemporary Youth Research 357, no. 6 (2018): 126.

125. Li, "Xianggang chongjian Zhongguo rentong," 104.

126. Gilles Deleuze and Felix Guattari, Anti-Oedipus: Capitalism and Schizophrenia (Minneapolis: University of Minnesota Press, 1977), 168; see also the discussion of the Oedipus complex as the blackmail of desire in Rob Weatherill, The Anti-Oedipus Complex: Lacan, Critical Theory and Postmodernism (London: Routledge, 2017), 23.

127. Niklas Luhmann, Social Systems (Stanford, CA: Stanford University Press, 1995), 373–374.

128. Hui Lei, "Genchu 'zhengzhi bingdu,' Xianggang you luan zhuangzhi fan zhenggui" [Eliminate political viruses, so that Hong Kong can recover to normal], Wen Wei Po, July 3, 2020, http://paper.wenweipo.com/2020/07/03/PL2007030004.htm.

129. Luhmann, Social Systems, 370.

130. See Esposito, Bios, 116.

131. The notion of a hegemonic counter-enlightenment is based in Peter Sloterdijk's reinterpretation of enlightenment via dialogue and nondialogue in *Critique of Cynical Reason* (Minneapolis: University of Minnesota Press, 1987).

132. Wang, *"Lun Xianggang tequ fan fenlie guojia lifa,"* , 81.

133. See Jiang Shigong, *Zhongguo Xianggang: Wenhua yu Zhengzhi de Shiye* [China's Hong Kong: A political and cultural perspective] (Hong Kong: Oxford University Press, 2008).

134. The idea that people in Hong Kong do not understand China or even Hong Kong is a common theme throughout these official academic studies, seen in Peng Ai, *"Xianggang qingshaonian guojia rentong kunjing ji duice fenxi"* [Analysis of the challenges of national identification among Hong Kong youth identification and possible policy responses], *Course Education Research* 32 (2018): 20–21; Li Peng, *" 'Gangdu' sichao de xingqi, zhuzhang jiqi weihai lunxi"* [An analysis of the origins, main proposals, and harms of the "Hong Kong independence" trend], *Social Sciences in Heilongjiang*, no. 4 (2017): 19–24; Wang, *"Shilun 'gangdu'"*; and Han, *"Cong shanchuang zhu Gang junying."*

135. Said, *Orientalism*, 3.

136. Ibid.

137. Tsui Sing Yan, *Sihngbong gauhsih: Sahpyih bun syu hong Heunggong buntou si* [A history of the city-state: Reading Hong Kong local history through twelve books] (Hong Kong: Red Publishing, 2014), 72.

CONCLUSION

1. Cheung Yuk-man, *"'Liberate Hong Kong, the Revolution of Our Times': The Birth of the First Orient Nation in the Twenty-First Century,"* in *Research Handbook on Nationalism*, ed. Liah Greenfeld and Zeying Wu (Cheltenham, UK: Edward Elgar, 20200, 328.

2. Lewis Loud, "Hong Kong's Protestors Are Resisting China with Anarchy and Principle," *New York Times*, June 28, 2019, www.nytimes.com/2019/06/28/opinion /hong-kong-protests-extradition-china.html.

3. Lewis Loud, "Hong Kong and the Independence Movement That Doesn't Know Itself," *New York Times*, September 27, 2019, www.nytimes.com/2019/09/27/opinion /hong-kong-umbrella.html.

BIBLIOGRAPHY

Al-Azm, Sadik Jalal. "Orientalism and Orientalism in Reverse." *Khamsin*, no. 8 (1981): 5–26.

Allen, Jamie. *Seeing Red: China's Uncompromising Takeover of Hong Kong*. Singapore: Butterworth-Heinemann Asia, 1997.

Althusser, Louis. "Ideology and Ideological State Apparatuses." In *Lenin and Philosophy and Other Essays*, 127–186. New York: Monthly Review Press, 1971.

Anderson, Benedict. *Imagined Communities: Reflections on the Origins and Spread of Nationalism*. New York: Verso, 1983.

———. *The Specter of Comparisons: Nationalism, Southeast Asia and the World*. New York: Verso, 1998.

Apple Daily. "Hohksaang duhklaahp lyuhnmahng: Gongduhk haih bitseui jau dik louh" [Students' Independence Union: Hong Kong independence is the only path forward]. September 28, 2018. Accessed April 1, 2020. https://hk.news.appledaily.com/local/realtime/article/20180928/58736008.

———. "Tihn Bakjeun waaileuhn: jan pousyun yuh gongduhk mouh yih" [James Tian's crazy comment: Genuine universal suffrage no different from Hong Kong independence]. July 18, 2014. Accessed July 2020. https://hk.appledaily.com/local/2014 0718/2S2BOTIY73HAO6PDBCNDD2X2SY/.

Aristotle. *The Politics*. Translated by T. A. Sinclair. Revised by Trevor J. Sauders. New York: Penguin, 1982.

Barron, Laignee. "Hong Kong Democracy Activist Joshua Wong Disqualified from Upcoming Election." *Time*, October 29, 2019. Accessed February 10, 2020. https://time.com/5712824/joshua-wong-hong-kong-disqualified-district-elections/.

Barth, Fredrik. Introduction to *Ethnic Groups and Boundaries: The Social Organization of Culture Difference*, edited by Fredrik Barth, 9–38. Long Grove, IL: Waveland Press, 1998.

Basic Law of the Hong Kong Special Administrative Region of the People's Republic of China. Accessed March 2019. www.basiclaw.gov.hk/en/basiclawtext/images /basiclaw_full_text_en.pdf.

Bateson, Gregory. "Form, Substance, and Difference." In *Steps to an Ecology of Mind*, 454–471. Chicago: University of Chicago Press, 1972.

Baumann, Gerd. "Grammars of Identity/Alterity: A Structural Approach." In *Grammars of Identity/Alterity: A Structural Approach*, edited by Gerd Baummann and Andre Gingrich, 18–50. New York: Berghahn Books, 2004.

Blum, Susan. *Portraits of "Primitives": Ordering Human Kinds in the Chinese Nation.* Lanham, MD: Rowman & Littlefield, 2001.

Branigan, Tania. "Chinese Figures Show Fivefold Rise in Babies Sick from Contaminated Milk." *Guardian*, December 2, 2008. Accessed March 2021. www.theguardian .com/world/2008/dec/02/china.

Brubaker, Rogers. *Citizenship and Nationhood in France and Germany.* Cambridge, MA: Harvard University Press, 1992.

Cabrillac, Bruno. "A Bilateral Trade Agreement between Hong Kong and China: CEPA." *China Perspectives* 54 (July–August 2004): 1–13.

Callahan, William. *Contingent States: Greater China and Transnational Relations.* Minneapolis: University of Minnesota Press, 2004.

Carrico, Kevin. "The Basic Law Is Basically Garbage." *Local News.* September 24, 2018. Accessed March 2021. https://www.localpresshk.com/2018/09/basic-garbage/.

———. "Eliminating Spiritual Pollution: A Genealogy of Closed Political Thought in China's Era of Opening." *China Journal*, no. 78 (July 2017): 100–119.

———. "From Citizens Back to Subjects: Constructing National Belonging in Hong Kong's National Education Center." In *From a British to a Chinese Colony? Hong Kong before and after the 1997 Handover*, edited by Gary Chi-hung Luk, 259–284. Berkeley: Institute of East Asian Studies China Research Monograph, 2017.

———. *The Great Han: Race, Nationalism, and Tradition in China Today.* Oakland: University of California Press, 2017.

———. "Swarm of the Locusts: The Ethnicization of Hong Kong-China relations." In *Yellow Perils: China Narratives in the Contemporary World*, edited by Franck Billé and Sören Urbansky, 197–220. Honolulu: University of Hawaii Press, 2018.

Central Government of the People's Republic of China. "*Xianggang juban jiben fa banbu 25 zhounian zhanlan*" [Hong Kong hosts an exhibition to mark the twenty-fifth anniversary of the Basic Law]. April 4, 2015. Accessed May 2019. www.gov.cn /xinwen/2015–04/04/content_2842992.htm.

———. "*Xianggang tequ 22 ri juban 'jiben fa banbu shiliu nian yantao hui'*" [Hong Kong SAR hosts a conference on the 16th anniversary of the Basic Law]. Accessed May 2019. www.gov.cn/jrzg/2006–04/22/content_260906_2.htm.

Centre for Communication and Public Opinion Survey. "The Identity and National Identification of Hong Kong People: Survey Results." July 2016. Accessed May 2019. www.com.cuhk.edu.hk/ccpos/en/research/Identity_Survey%20Results_2016 _ENG.pdf.

Chan, Johannes. "Judicial Independence: Controversies on the Constitutional Jurisdiction of the Court of Final Appeal of the Hong Kong Special Administrative Region." *International Lawyer* 33 (1999): 1015–1040.

Chan, Kelvin. "Economists Say CEPA Benefits HK and the Mainland." *South China Morning Post*, September 13, 2003. Accessed August 2019. www.scmp.com/article /427772/economists-say-cepa-benefits-hk-and-mainland.

Chen Guanghan and Li Xiaoying. "*Yi fazhan jingji he gaishan minsheng wei zhongxin ningju Xianggang gongshi*" [Consolidate a Hong Kong consensus via economic development and livelihood improvement]. *Hong Kong-Macao Studies* 3 (2015): 3–9.

Chen Hao. "*Yu shi ju jin yingdui 'gangdu' 'ruan baoli'*" [Responding to the domestic violence of HK independence in step with the times]. *Journal of the Fujian Institute of Socialism* 104, no. 5 (2015): 104–106.

Chen Yi. "*Xiangdui boduogan yu Xianggang qingnian de zhengzhi xinren*" [Relative deprivation and political trust among youth in Hong Kong]. *Hong Kong-Macao Studies* 3(2019): 35–44.

Chen Yijian and Huang Tong. "*Ezhi 'gangdu' zhi lifa gouxiang*" [Legislative design of regulating the so-called Hong Kong separatist activities]. *Local Legislation Journal* 2, no. 6 (November 15, 2017): 28–38.

Cheng Chung-tai and Jonathan Kan. *Geibunfaat goileuhng choyih* [A preliminary discussion of reforms to the Basic Law]. Hong Kong: Passiontimes, 2017.

Cheng Ka Ming. "Medical Tourism: Chinese Maternity Tourism to Hong Kong." *Current Issues in Tourism* 19, no. 14 (2016): 1479–1486.

Cheng, Kris. "Another Pro-independence Candidate Barred from Running in Legco Election." *Hong Kong Free Press*, August 2, 2016. Accessed August 2020. https:// hongkongfp.com/2016/08/02/another-pro-independence-candidate-barred -running-legco-election/.

———. "Edward Leung of Hong Kong Indigenous Barred from Legco Election." *Hong Kong Free Press*, August 2, 2016. Accessed August 2020. https://hongkongfp.com /2016/08/02/breaking-edward-leung-hong-kong-indigenous-barred-legco -election/.

———. "Explainer: How Hong Kong Is Seeking to Ban a Pro-independence Party Using Existing National Security Laws." *Hong Kong Free Press*, July 19, 2018. Accessed August 2020. https://hongkongfp.com/2018/07/19/explainer-hong-kong -seeking-ban-pro-independence-party-using-existing-national-security-laws/.

———. "Lingnan University President Warns Localist Professor to 'Mind Your Words or Suffer the Consequences.'" *Hong Kong Free Press*, November 12, 2015. Accessed March 2021. https://hongkongfp.com/2015/11/12/lingnanu-president-warns-localist -prof-to-mind-your-words-or-suffer-the-consequences/.

Cheng, Margaret Harris. "Hong Kong Attempts to Reduce Influx of Pregnant Chinese." *Lancet* 369 (2007): 981–982.

Cheng Yinghong. *Discourses of Race and Rising China*. London: Palgrave Macmillan, 2019.

Cheung, Alvin Y. H. "Road to Nowhere: Hong Kong's Democratization and China's Obligations under Public International Law." *Brooklyn Journal of International Law* 40, no. 2 (2015): 465–545.

Cheung, Karen. "Civic Passion Candidate Says Will Not Advocate Independence through Run; HKNP Convenor Refuses to Answer." *Hong Kong Free Press*, July 27, 2016. https://hongkongfp.com/2016/07/27/civic-passion-candidate-says-will-not-advocate-independence-run-hknp-convenor-refuses-answer/.

Cheung Yuk-man. "'Liberate Hong Kong, the Revolution of Our Times': The Birth of the First Orient Nation in the Twenty-First Century." In *Research Handbook on Nationalism*, edited by Liah Greenfeld and Zeying Wu, 312–333. Cheltenham, UK: Edward Elgar, 2020.

Chin Wan. *Heimohng jingjih: Sihngbong jyukyuhn leuhn II* [The politics of hope: On Hong Kong as a sovereign city-state II]. Hong Kong: Subculture Publishing, 2016.

———. *Heunggong sihngbong leuhn* [On Hong Kong as a city-state]. Hong Kong: Enrich Publishing, 2011.

———. *Heunggong waihmahn leuhn* [On Hong Kong as a bastion of loyalism]. Hong Kong: Subculture Publishing, 2013.

———. *Sihngbong jyukyuhn leuhn* [On Hong Kong as a sovereign city-state]. Hong Kong: Subculture Publishing, 2015.

Chinese Association of Hong Kong-Macao Studies. "About Us." Accessed September 2019. www.cahkms.org/HKMAC/webView/mc/AboutUs_1.html?0101&%E6%9C%AC%E4%BC%9A%E7%AE%80%E4%BB%8B.

Ching Cheong. "*Chung sahpbaatdaaih hon Heunggong deihah jungguhng dongyuhn kwaimouh*" [An assessment of the number of underground CCP members in Hong Kong based on insights from the 18th Party Congress]. *Mingpao*, November 28, 2012. Accessed April 10, 2020. www.hkfront.org/20121201ch.htm.

Chow, Jason. "*Ginkaw Heunggong mahnjuhk*" [Constructing a Hong Kong nationality]. *Comitium*, no. 1 (July 2016): 8–11.

Davis, Michael C. "Interpreting Constitutionalism and Democratization in Hong Kong." In *Interpreting Hong Kong's Basic Law: The Struggle for Coherence*, edited by Hualing Fu, Lison Harris, and Simon N. M. Young, 77–95. London: Palgrave Macmillan, 2007.

Dean, Kenneth, and Brian Massumi. *First and Last Emperors: The Absolute State and the Body of the Despot*. New York: Autonomedia, 1992.

Deleuze, Gilles, and Felix Guattari. *Anti-Oedipus: Capitalism and Schizophrenia*. Minneapolis: University of Minnesota Press, 1977.

———. *A Thousand Plateaus: Capitalism and Schizophrenia*. Vol. 2. Minneapolis: University of Minnesota Press, 1987.

Dixon, Robyn, and Ryan Ho Kilpatrick. "'I Thought I Was about to Die': Eyewitnesses Describe Brutal Beatings by Hong Kong Police." *Los Angeles Times*, September 2, 2019. Accessed March 2020. www.latimes.com/world-nation/story/2019-09-02/hong-kong-police-violence-protesters-eyewitnesses.

Dreyfus, Hubert. *Being-in-the-World: A Commentary on Heidegger's "Being and Time"*. Cambridge, MA: MIT Press, 1990.

Esposito, Roberto. *Bios: Biopolitics and Philosophy*. Minneapolis: University of Minnesota Press, 2008.

Feng Qingxiang and Xu Haibo. *"Xianggang 'gangdu' xianxiang shuyuan yu xiaojie"* [Origins of the "Hong Kong independence" phenomenon and its elimination]. *Theoretical Research* 340, no. 2 (April 2017): 47–52.

Feuerwerker, Albert. "China's Modern Economic History in Communist Chinese Historiography." *China Quarterly* 22 (June 1965): 31–61.

Fiskesjö, Magnus. "The Legacy of the Chinese Empires Beyond 'the West and the Rest.'" *Education about Asia* 22, no. 1 (2017): 6–10.

Fokstuen, Anne R. "The 'Right of Abode' Cases: Hong Kong's Constitutional Crisis." *Hastings International and Comparative Law Review* 26 (2003): 265–288.

Fong, Brian. "One Country, Two Nationalisms: Center-Periphery Relations between Mainland China and Hong Kong, 1997–2016." *Modern China* 43, no. 5 (2017): 523–556.

Friedman, Jonathan. *PC Worlds: Political Correctness and Rising Elites at the End of Hegemony*. New York: Berghahn Books, 2019.

Gilley, Bruce. "The Case for Colonialism." Withdrawn from *Third World Quarterly* after publication. Accessed April 2020. www.nas.org/academic-questions/31/2/the _case_for_colonialism.

Gladney, Dru. "Representing Nationality in China: Refiguring Majority/Minority Identities." *Journal of Asian Studies* 53, no. 1 (1994): 92–123.

Glucksmann, André. *The Master Thinkers*. New York: Harper & Row, 1980.

Godelier, Maurice. *The Enigma of the Gift*. Chicago: University of Chicago Press, 1999.

Government of Hong Kong Special Administrative Region Press Releases. "EAC's Request to Sign Confirmation Form Has Legal Basis." July 19, 2016. Accessed August 2020. www.info.gov.hk/gia/general/201607/19/P2016071900950.htm.

Greenfeld, Liah. *Nationalism: A Short History*. Washington, DC: Brookings Institution Press, 2019.

———. *Nationalism: Five Roads to Modernity*. Cambridge, MA: Harvard University Press, 1993.

Griffiths, James. "Hong Kong Moves to Disqualify More Pro-democracy Lawmakers." CNN, December 2, 2016. Accessed February 15, 2020. https://edition.cnn.com /2016/12/02/asia/hong-kong-lawmakers-oathgate/index.html.

Guildford, Gwynn. "The Secret History of Hong Kong's Stillborn Democracy." *Quartz*, October 11, 2014. Accessed March 12, 2021. https://qz.com/279013/the -secret-history-of-hong-kongs-stillborn-democracy/.

Han Shanshan. *"Cong shanchuang zhu Gang junying kan 'Gangdu shi' jijin yundong: tezheng, yuanyin ji weihai"* [Thoughts on the Radical Hong Kong Independence Movement Based on the Intrusion into the PLA Barracks: Characteristics, Causes, and Risks]. *Hong Kong and Macau Journal* 1 (2014): 73–82.

Harrell, Stevan. "Introduction: Civilizing Projects and the Reaction to Them." In *Cultural Encounters on China's Ethnic Frontiers*, edited by Stevan Harrell, 3–36. Seattle: University of Washington Press, 1995.

Heidegger, Martin. "The Age of the World Picture." In *The Question Concerning Technology and Other Essays*, 115–154. New York: Garland Publishing, 1977.

Hicks, George. *Hong Kong Countdown*. Hong Kong: Writers' & Publishers' Cooperative, 1989.

"Hong Kong Independence Activist Banned from Elections." DW. July 30, 2016, www.dw.com/en/hong-kong-independence-activist-banned-from-elections/a -19438981.

Hong Kong National Party, eds. *Comitium*, nos. 1–3 (2016–2017).

Hong Kong National Party Facebook page. "*Heunggong mahnjuhk dong junghohk jingjih kaimuhng gaiwaahk sanmahn gou*" [Press release on Hong Kong National Party middle school political enlightenment scheme]. September 19, 2016. Accessed May 12, 2020. www.facebook.com/hknationalparty/posts/541142572751368/.

———. "*Heunggong mahnjuhk dong yu Toihwaan cheutjihk ajau yahnkyuhn baakhoih yuh jikyut gwokjai geije wuih sanmahn gou*" [Press release on Hong Kong National Party's attendance at the "Human rights, persecution, and self-determination" international press conference held in Taiwan]. December 9, 2016. Accessed May 12, 2020. .www.facebook.com/hknationalparty/posts/578527842346174/.

———. "*Mahnjuhk dong heung Meihgwok jyugong lihngsihgun gaau chingyuhnseun, yiu-kauh cheuixiao Heunggong gwaanhaih faat*" [National Party delivers petition to United States' Consulate in Hong Kong, requesting that the US abolish the Hong Kong Policy Act]. August 24, 2017. Accessed May 12, 2020. www.facebook.com /hknationalparty/posts/698259103706380/

Hong Kong Tourism Board. "Annual Report, 2014/15, Tourism Performance." 2015. Accessed March 2019. www.discoverhongkong.com/eng/about-hktb/annual -report/annual-report-20142015/tourism-performance/.

Hong Kong Trade and Industry Department. "Mainland and Hong Kong Closer Economic Partnership Agreement." 2003. Accessed August 2020. www.tid.gov.hk /english/cepa/legaltext/fulltext.html.

Hong Kong Watch. "Political Screening in Hong Kong: The Disqualification of Candidates and Lawmakers Ahead of the March By-Elections," March 8, 2018. Accessed August 2020. www.hongkongwatch.org/all-posts/2018/3/7/political -screening-in-hong-kong-a-report-on-the-disqualification-of-candidates-and -lawmakers.

Hsiung, James. "The Hong Kong SAR: Prisoner of Legacy or History's Bellwether?" In *Hong Kong the Super Paradox: Life after Return to China*, edited by James Hsiung, 307–348. New York: St. Martin's Press, 2000.

———. "Introduction: The Paradox Syndrome and Update." In *Hong Kong the Super Paradox: Life after Return to China*, edited by James Hsiung, 1–31. New York: St. Martin's Press, 2000.

Huang Chenpu. "*'Qingnianhua' Gangdu sixiang de chengyin ji benzhi*" [The causes and essence of young people's "Hong Kong independence" thought]. *Journal of Guangdong Youth Vocational College* 31, no. 1 (February 2017): 15–19.

Huang Zheping and Echo Huang. "A Brief History: Beijing's Interpretations of Hong Kong's Basic Law, from 1999 to the Present Day." *Quartz*, November 7, 2016. Accessed August 2020. https://qz.com/828713/a-brief-history-beijings-interpretations-of-hong-kongs-basic-law-from-1999–to-the-present-day/.

Hui Lei. "*Genchu 'zhengzhi bingdu,' Xianggang you luan zhuangzhi fan zhenggui*" [Eliminate political viruses, so that Hong Kong can recover to normal]. *Wen Wei Po*, July 3, 2020. Accessed August 2020. http://paper.wenweipo.com/2020/07/03/PL2007030004.htm.

International Covenant on Civil and Political Rights. Accessed February 20, 2020. www.ohchr.org/en/professionalinterest/pages/ccpr.aspx.

International Covenant on Economic, Social, and Cultural Rights. Accessed February 20, 2020. www.ohchr.org/en/professionalinterest/pages/cescr.aspx.

Jiang Shigong. *Zhongguo Xianggang: Wenhua yu zhengzhi de shiye* [China's Hong Kong: A political and cultural perspective]. Hong Kong: Oxford University Press, 2008.

Jilaahn Yuhngyihp. "*Mouhyuhng ji yuhng: gungmahn bat hahpjok wahnduhng*" [The use of the useless: on civil disobedience]. *Comitium* 2 (January 2017): 36–43.

Jiwaih. "*Heunggong, jauhsih Heunggong yahn dik Heunggong*" [Hong Kong is the Hong Kong people's Hong Kong]. In *Leuhn gwaiying: wuih dou yingjih Heunggong* [On returning to the UK: Recapturing a British-ruled Hong Kong], 92–94. Hong Kong: Passiontimes, 2015.

Joint Declaration of the Government of the United Kingdom of Great Britain and Northern Ireland and the Government of the People's Republic of China on the Question of Hong Kong. Accessed February 20, 2020. www.cmab.gov.hk/en/issues/jd2.htm.

Kaeding, Malte Philipp. "The Rise of 'Localism' in Hong Kong." *Journal of Democracy* 28, no. 1 (January 2017): 157–171.

Kai Keih. "*Chungpo mouhleih yihnsan dik junggwok jihkmahn bakyun: Shi Shu-mei 'wahyuh' yuhhaih leihleuhn dik kaisih*" [Disrupting China's ever-expanding colonial hegemony: Insights from Shih Shu-mei's Sinophone Theory]. *Comitium*, no. 1 (July 2016): 13–19.

Kellogg, Thomas. "Legislating Rights: Basic Law Article 23, National Security, and Human Rights in Hong Kong." *Columbia Journal of Asian Law* 17 (2004): 307–369.

King, Ambrose Yeo-chi. "Administrative Absorption of Politics in Hong Kong: Emphasis on the Grassroots Level." *Asian Survey* 15, no. 5 (May 1975): 422–439.

Kong, Karen. "*Kong Yunming v. Director of Social Welfare*: Implications for Law and Policy on Social Welfare." *Hong Kong Law Journal* 44, no. 1 (2014): 67–82.

Kong Tsung-gan. *Umbrella: A Political Tale from Hong Kong*. Detroit: Pema Press, 2017.

Lady Kylie. "*Gongduhk waahk gwaiying batsih naahnyih dik mahntaih sih muhtfaat bat-jouh dik mahntaih*" [Hong Kong independence or return-ism: not a question of what is easier or harder, but rather a question of necessity]. In *Leuhn gwaiying: Wuih dou yingjih Heunggong* [On returning to the UK: Recapturing a British-ruled Hong Kong], 140–146. Hong Kong: Passiontimes, 2015.

———. "*Sowaih gwaiying sih sahmmo yat wuihsih*" [What is this "returning to the UK" idea?]. In *Leuhn gwaiying: Wuih dou yingjih Heunggong* [On returning to the UK: Recapturing a British-ruled Hong Kong], 22–30. Hong Kong: Passiontimes, 2015.

———. "*Wuihgwai wuih neih louh juhk*" [Return? Return to your mom!]. In *Leuhn gwaiying: wuih dou yingjih Heunggong* [On returning to the UK: Recapturing a British-ruled Hong Kong], 67–77. Hong Kong: Passiontimes, 2015.

LaFraniere, Sharon. "Mainland Chinese Flock to Hong Kong to Give Birth." *New York Times*, February 22, 2012. Accessed February 19, 2020. www.nytimes.com/2012/02/23/world/asia/mainland-chinese-flock-to-hong-kong-to-have-babies.html.

Lam Hong Ching. *Heunggong kongjaang wahnduhng si I: Chobaaih dik saam sahp nihn fausik* [A history of Hong Kong's struggle, vol. 1, Dissecting 30 years of failure]. Hong Kong: Subculture, 2014.

———. *Heunggong kongjaang wahnduhng si II: Jung-gong deuikyut* [A history of Hong Kong's struggle, vol. 2, The Hong Kong-China standoff]. Hong Kong: Subculture, 2015.

———. *Hohkmahn duhkbaahk* [Scholarism monologues]. Hong Kong: Subculture, 2013.

Lam Jeunhim. "*Chan Ho-tin chuk Dahklohngpou tuhngsih jaichoih Jung Gong, Gongfu gap wuihying Heunggong sih daanduhk gwaanseui kuei*'" [Andy Chan calls on Trump to sanction both China and Hong Kong, the Hong Kong government urgently responds "Hong Kong is a separate customs territory"]. *Apple Daily*, August 20, 2018. Accessed May 1, 2020. https://hk.news.appledaily.com/local/daily/article/20180820/20480322.

Lambert, David. "'As Solid as the Rock'? Place, Belonging and the Local Appropriation of Imperial Discourse in Gibraltar." *Transactions of the Institute of British Geographers New Series* 30 (2005): 206–220.

Lee, Ching Kwan, and Ming Sing, eds. *Take Back Our Future: An Eventful Sociology of the Hong Kong Umbrella Movement*. Ithaca, NY: Cornell University Press, 2019.

Lee, Jack. "*Heunggong sihfau yingyauh mahnjuhk jihkyut dik kyuhnlei?*" [Should Hong Kong have the right to self-determination?]. In *Undergrad Editorial Board*, ed., "*Heunggong mahnjuhk, mihngwahn jihkyut*" [Hong Kong nationality, self-determination of our own future]. *Undergrad* (February 2014): 34–37.

Leung Kai-ping. Introduction to *Undergrad Editorial Board*, ed., "*Heunggong mahnjuhk, mihngwahn jihkyut*" [Hong Kong nationality, self-determination of our own future]. *Undergrad* (February 2014): 22–23.

———. "*Jungwuhn chithaahn jangyih yuh buntou jingjih guhngtuhngtai*" [The local political community and the controversy surrounding the removal of welfare eligibility limits]. In *Undergrad Editorial Board*, ed., "*Heunggong mahnjuhk, mihngwahn jihkyut"* [Hong Kong nationality, self-determination of our own future]. *Undergrad* (February 2014): 24–26.

Li Feng. *Early China: A Social and Cultural History.* Cambridge: Cambridge University Press, 2013.

———. "'Feudalism' and Western Zhou China: A Criticism." *Harvard Journal of Asiatic Studies* 63, no. 1 (2003): 115–144.

Li Peng. "'Gangdu' sichao de xingqi, zhuzhang jiqi weihai lunxi" [An analysis of the origins, main proposals, and harms of the "Hong Kong independence" trend]. *Social Sciences in Heilongjiang*, no. 4 (2017): 19–24.

Li Qin. "'Xiaoyuan gangdu' sichao de fazhan mailuo, xingcheng yuanyin ji zhili qishi" [The pro-independence movement on Hong Kong's campus: Its evolution, causes, and implications]. *Hong Kong-Macao Studies* 2 (2019): 52–61.

Li Weishun. "'Gangdu' wenti de weihai, yuanyou ji duice" [The origins and dangers of "Hong Kong independence," as well as countermeasures]. *Practice and Theory of SEZs*, no. 6 (2017): 59–67.

Li Yiyi. "'Gangdu' yanxing de shibie jiqi falü guizhi- yi 'Xianggang jibenfa' di ershisan tiao lifa wei shijiao" [Detection and legal regulation of "Hong Kong Independence" speech: A perspective from Article 23 of the Hong Kong Basic Law]. *Hong Kong-Macao Studies* 2 (2018): 40–53.

Li Youkun. "Xianggang chongjian Zhongguo rentong Zhong de zhimin qingjie tanxi" [An exploration of Hong Kong's colonial complex in the process of reconstructing Chinese identity in the city]. *Journal of the Party School of Xinjiang Production and Construction Corps of the Chinese Communist Party* 169, no. 6 (2017): 100–105.

Lian Yi-zheng. "Taahm wuhjiu gwokjihk: leuhn gongyahn sihngwaih siusou mahnjuhk" [Of passports and nationalities: On designating the Hong Kong people as a minority nationality]. *Hong Kong Economic Journal*, November 6, 2012. www1.hkej.com /dailynews/article/id/644727/%E8%AB%87%E8%AD%B7%E7%85%A7%E5%9C %8B%E7%B1%8D%E2%80%94%E2%80%94%E8%AB%96%E6%B8%AF%E4%BA %BA%E6%88%90%E7%82%BA%E5%B0%91%E6%95%B8%E6%B0%91%E6 %97%8F.

Liberal Party. "Survey on the Removal of Welfare Eligibility Limits." January 6, 2014. www.liberal.org.hk/index.php?option=com_content&view=article&id=900& mid=49&lang=tc&__cf_chl_captcha_tk__=5131a30cdd5bb6d09a69c78261 f65c861beb7fc7–1588591776–0–AWj2ivFFFrsIsT66nC909U205h8vUdNHIIqgd YjJac79jlTIIxthR59H15Q6VFYkwOa91VkI6u8RMPVDXXYjAh_YLAipg8kxv WtJOG4KJMAB1sz3ppYv-BGerwcuTkaTeJ6lrWCuV5B-ozygdlhZ6jORlc ZYduhUaxlj1obudNUSrsp91Xk61pPKMNZIb2fadauNKAzVT5gDNKD 9iAUHyolUj_yN_093hR7QVpdt5OuRmw38qm8_GHuXucEmLx4xOqlc OSuo2_wCluCnQMWxMbnZkWtAEYcFqzlY_2zIN6–uFblsaTYqagoL5_oT2 Sp1erE-MHYDgIph2iRfZTfiQojHijlxDDdN3–GCfZGJHDoj29WxNs J-2SVeOZfje-8hD3nDpVDLxXIXlExmD2mda6itDgNob_5CoO9eQ3ch909Q ObUfG70CBAV5UjoNCQXJfJ46tygv5_HzfNPQbmJjvQknG4qDgSfQYGF cuobo4SxQGoXMhlkAEsUyGr_Qjo16VMzpMgZun5PeLJ8P-vNRfkjnIAyEt

16QVıbgLGfovCBSrR4z_aGwroebiCWt62nOieW_dvKFtqeyImM7a
MVz62sN_ffgTLFlzızii-3TxNk9UdHFbXUQv-ıuYGZYlFpnEQ.

Lin, Devin, Valentin Günther, and Mathias Honer. "Interpreting Article 104: The Way, the How, the Timing." *Hong Kong Law Journal* 47 (2017): 475.

Lin, Gene. "CUHK Survey Finds Nearly 40% of Young Hongkongers Want Independence after 2047." *Hong Kong Free Press*, July 25, 2016. Accessed February 2020. https://hongkongfp.com/2016/07/25/17–hongkongers-support-independence -2047–especially-youth-cuhk-survery/.

Liu Qiang. "*Xianggang qingnian zhengzhi canyu de 'bentuhua' dongxiang ji qi yingdui- dui 'gangdu yiyuan chenguo shijian' de sikao*" [The trend of "localism" in the political participation of Hong Kong youth and countermeasures—reflections on "Hong Kong independence legislators insulting the nation"]. *Chinese Youth Social Science*, no. 2 (2017): 43–49.

Liu Xiulun and Ye Xinlu. "'*Gangdu' fenli zhuyi dui qingnian guojia rentong de yingxiang yu yingdui celüe*" [Influence of "Hong Kong independence movement" separatism on the youth's national identity and its countermeasures]. *Contemporary Youth Research* 357, no. 6 (2018): 123–128.

Lo Pui-yin. "Enforcing an Unfortunate, Unnecessary and 'Unquestionably Binding' NPCSC Interpretation: The Hong Kong Judiciary's Deconstruction of Its Construction of the Basic Law." *Hong Kong Law Journal* 48 (2018): 38.

Local Studio. *Hong Kong Is Not China*. Hong Kong: Local Studio, 2015.

Loud, Lewis. "*Syunguei yuh foguei*" [Elections as an imperial examination]. In *Ngoh maihsat joih jeh cheuhng jihkmahn yauhhei* [I am lost in this colonial game], 26–30. Hong Kong: Ideate Trails Press, 2018.

———. "Hong Kong and the Independence Movement That Doesn't Know Itself." *New York Times*, September 27, 2019. Accessed August 2020. nytimes.com/2019 /09/27/opinion/hong-kong-umbrella.html.

———. "Hong Kong's Protestors Are Resisting China with Anarchy and Principle." *New York Times*, June 28, 2019. Accessed August 2020. nytimes.com/2019/06/28 /opinion/hong-kong-protests-extradition-china.html.

Luhmann, Niklas. *Political Theory in the Welfare State*. Berlin: Walter De Gruyter, 1990.

———. *Social Systems*. Stanford, CA: Stanford University Press, 1995.

Luk, Kiano. "How Does Mainlandization Affect Hong Kong's Tourism Industry." In *Mainlandization of Hong Kong: Pressures and Responses*, edited by Joseph Yu-shek Cheng, Jacky Chau-kiu Cheung, and Beatrice Kit-fun Leung, 151–188. Hong Kong: City University of Hong Kong Press, 2017.

Luo Weijian. "'*Gangdu' yanxing de weifaxing fenxi jiqi falü guizhi—Aomen fayuan anli de qishi*" [Analysis of illegality about statements and actions of "Hong Kong independence" and the legal regulations: Enlightenments from the case of Macao courts]. *Hong Kong-Macao Studies* 4 (2016): 22–29.

Lyotard, Jean-François. *The Differend: Phrases in Dispute*. Minneapolis: University of Minnesota Press, 1988.

————. *La Guerre des Algériens: Écrits, 1956–1963*. Edited by Mohammed Ramdani. Paris: Galilée, 1989.

Ma, Eric Kit-wai, and Joseph Man Chan. "Global Connectivity and Local Politics: SARS, Talk Radio, and Public Opinion." In *SARS: Reception and Interpretation in Three Chinese Cities*, edited by Deborah Davis and Helen Siu, 19–44. London: Routledge, 2007.

Ma Ngok. "Civil Society in Self-Defense: The Struggle against National Security Legislation in Hong Kong." *Journal of Contemporary China* 14, no. 44 (2005): 465–482.

Mann, James. *The China Fantasy: Why Capitalism Will Not Bring Democracy to China*. New York: Penguin, 2008.

Mauss, Marcel. *The Gift: Expanded Edition*. Chicago: Hau Books, 2016.

Mingpao. "*Mahnjuhk dong: 80 junghohk yahp 'kaimuhng gaiwaahk,' haauhjeung chik 'heung sailou maaihsau bat douhdak*" [National Party: 80 middle schools involved in "enlightenment scheme," school principal declares "targeting kids is immoral"]. *Mingpao*, September 20, 2016. Accessed May 1, 2020. https://news.mingpao.com /pns/%E6%B8%AF%E8%81%9E/article/20160920/s00002/1474308150162/%E6 %B0%91%E6%97%8F%E9%BB%A8-80%E4%B8%AD%E5%AD%B8%E5%85%A5 %E3%80%8C%E5%95%9F%E8%92%99%E8%A8%88%E5%8A%83%E3%80%8D -%E6%A0%A1%E9%95%B7%E6%96%A5%E3%80%8C%E5%90%91%E7%B4%B0 %E8%B7%AF%E5%9F%8B%E6%89%8B%E4%B8%8D%E9%81%93%E5%BE%B7 %E3%80%8D.

Mouh Loihyauh. "*Saibaanngah mahnjyufa hauh maauhteuhn*" [Tensions after Spain's democratization]. In *Leuhn gwaiying: wuih dou yingjih Heunggong* [On returning to the UK: Recapturing a British-ruled Hong Kong], 134–139. Hong Kong: Passiontimes, 2015.

————. "*Yingsuhk jihjih sihngbong yuh waihdoleiha sik wohngga jihkmahndeih*" [A UK-held self-ruling city-state and a Victorian-style royal colony]. In *Leuhn gwaiying: Wuih dou yingjih Heunggong* [On returning to the UK: Recapturing a British-ruled Hong Kong], 124–127. Hong Kong: Passiontimes, 2015.

Mouhyihn. "*Heunggong doyuhn mahnfa buiging*" [Hong Kong's multicultural background]. In *Leuhn gwaiying: Wuih dou yingjih Heunggong* [On returning to the UK: Recapturing a British-ruled Hong Kong], 80–82. Hong Kong: Passiontimes, 2015.

————. "*Wuihdou yingjih jingfu gwoheui dik doihyuh*" [Recapturing the UK's Hong Kong governance model]." In *Leuhn gwaiying: Wuih dou yingjih Heunggong* [On returning to the UK: Recapturing a British-ruled Hong Kong], 31–34. Hong Kong: Passiontimes, 2015.

Ng, Ellie. "Video: Democratic Lawmakers Stage Protests and Alter Oaths as New Term Kicks Off at Hong Kong Legislature." *Hong Kong Free Press*, October 6, 2016. Accessed August 2020. https://hongkongfp.com/2016/10/12/breaking-democratic -lawmakers-stage-protests-alter-oaths-new-term-kicks-off-hong-kong-legislature/.

Nihngsi. "*Gwaiying bat sih waihliuh geinihm yingjih sihkeih*" [Returning to the UK is not just for nostalgia]. In *Leuhn gwaiying: Wuih dou yingjih Heunggong* [On returning to the UK: Recapturing a British-ruled Hong Kong], 94–97. Hong Kong: Passiontimes, 2015.

———."Jihkboulohtaap yuh Heunggong" [Gibraltar and Hong Kong]. In *Leuhn gwaiying: Wuih dou yingjih Heunggong* [On returning to the UK: Recapturing a British-ruled Hong Kong], 137–139. Hong Kong: Passiontimes, 2015.

Peng Ai."Xianggang qingshaonian guojia rentong kunjing ji duice fenxi" [Analysis of the challenges of national identification among Hong Kong youth and possible policy responses]. *Course Education Research* 32 (2018): 20–21.

Pepper, Suzanne. *Keeping Democracy at Bay: Hong Kong and the Challenges of Chinese Political Reform.* Lanham, MD: Rowman & Littlefield, 2008.

Petersen, Carole. "Hong Kong's Spring of Discontent: The Rise and Fall of the National Security Bill in 2003." In *National Security and Fundamental Freedoms: Hong Kong's Article 23 under Scrutiny*, edited by Carole Petersen, Fu Hualing, and Simon N. M. Young, 13–62. Hong Kong: Hong Kong University Press, 2005.

———. "National Security Offences and Civil Liberties in Hong Kong: A Critique of the Government's 'Consultation' on Article 23 of the Basic Law." *Hong Kong Law Journal* 32 (2002): 457–470.

———. "Not an Internal Affair: Hong Kong's Right to Internal Autonomy and Self-Determination under International Law." *Hong Kong Law Journal* 49, no. 3 (2019): 883–904.

———. "Prohibiting the Hong Kong National Party: Has Hong Kong Violated the International Covenant on Civil and Political Rights?" *Hong Kong Law Journal* 48 (2018): 789–805.

Pils, Eva. "The Party's Turn to Public Repression: An Analysis of the '709' Crackdown on Human Rights Lawyers in China." *China Law and Society Review* 3, no. 1 (2018): 1–48.

Piuchan, Manisa, Chi Wa Chan, and Jack Kaale. "Economic and Socio-cultural Impacts of Mainland Chinese Tourists on Hong Kong Residents." *Kasetsart Journal of Social Sciences* 39 (2018): 9–14.

Pomfret, James, and Venus Wu."China Pressures Hong Kong to Squash Independence Calls ahead of Polls: Sources." Reuters, September 6, 2016. Accessed August 2020. www.reuters.com/article/us-hongkong-election-china/china-pressures-hong-kong-to-squash-independence-calls-ahead-of-poll-sources-idUSKCN1175AO.

Powers, John. *The Buddha Party: How the People's Republic of China Works to Define and Control Tibetan Buddhism.* Oxford: Oxford University Press, 2017.

Public Opinion Programme. "Ethnic Identity-Chinese in Broad Sense (per Poll, by Age Group), August 1997–June 2019." Last updated June 2019. Accessed January 2020. www.hkupop.hku.hk/english/popexpress/ethnic/eidentity/chibroad/poll/datatables.html.

———. "People's Ethnic Identity." Last updated June 2019. Accessed January 2020. www.hkupop.hku.hk/english/popexpress/ethnic/index.html.

Qin, Amy, and Tiffany May."For Some in Hong Kong, New Bridge Has a Downside: 'That Kind of Tourist,.'" *New York Times*, November 23, 2018. Accessed

May 2020. www.nytimes.com/2018/11/23/world/asia/china-hong-kong-tung-chung.html.

Quenthai. "*Chuhng faanjihk gokdouh hon 'Heunggong mahnjuhk leuhn' dik batjuk*" [A critique of *Hong Kong Nationalism* from an anti-colonial perspective]. *Comitium*, no. 2 (January 2017): 44–51.

———. "*Jungwah mahnjuhk jyuyih deui Heunggong dik yihchuhng jihkmahn*" [Chinese nationalism's dual colonization of Hong Kong]. InMedia HK, July 25, 2015. Accessed April 18, 2020. www.inmediahk.net/node/1036196.

Ramdani, Mohammed. "L'Algérie: Un différend." In *La Guerre des Algériens: Écrits, 1956–1963*, edited by Mohammed Ramdani, 9–31. Paris: Galilée, 1989.

Ramzy, Austin. "Hong Kong Bars Pro-independence Candidate from Election." *New York Times*, July 30, 2016. Accessed March 2021. www.nytimes.com/2016/07/31/world/asia/hong-kong-bars-pro-independence-candidate-from-election.html.

Rée, Jonathan. "Internationality." *Radical Philosophy* 60 (Spring 1992): 3–11.

Ringen, Stein. *The Perfect Dictatorship: China in the 21st Century*. Hong Kong: Hong Kong University Press, 2016.

Roberti, Mark. *The Fall of Hong Kong: China's Triumph and Britain's Betrayal*. New York: John Wiley & Sons, 1996.

Roberts, Sean. "'The Biopolitics of China's 'War on Terror' and the Exclusion of the Uyghurs." *Critical Asian Studies* 50, no. 2 (2018): 232–258.

RTHK. "Demosistō Drops 'Self-Determination' Clause." RTHK, January 11, 2020. Accessed January 15, 2020. https://news.rthk.hk/rthk/en/component/k2/1502283-20200111.htm?spTabChangeable=0.

Said, Edward. *Orientalism*. New York: Penguin, 2003.

Sang Pu. *Junggwok dik guyih: Heunggong yahn* [China's orphan: The Hong Kong people]. Hong Kong: Subculture, 2017.

Scott, Ian. *Political Change and the Crisis of Legitimacy in Hong Kong*. Honolulu: University of Hawaii Press, 1989.

Shek, Arthur. "*Chan Ho-tin mh haih yahn*" [Andy Chan is not a human being]. *Hong Kong Economic Times*, August 17, 2018. Accessed August 2020. https://invest.hket.com/article/2139897/%E9%99%B3%E6%B5%A9%E5%A4%A9%E5%94%94%E4%BF%82%E4%BA%BA.

Shih Shu-mei. "The Concept of the Sinophone." *PMLA* 126, no. 3 (May 2011): 709–718.

Shih Shu-mei, Tsai Chien-hsin, and Brian Bernards, eds. *Sinophone Studies: A Critical Reader*. New York: Columbia University Press, 2013.

Siu Kit. *Heunggong buntoh wahnduhng si I* [A history of the localist movement in Hong Kong, vol. 1]. Hong Kong: Passiontimes, 2019.

———. *Heunggong buntoh wahnduhng si II* [A history of the localist movement in Hong Kong, vol. 2]. Hong Kong: Passiontimes, 2019.

———. *Wohngtin giksaat bong* [Heaven's hit list]. Hong Kong: Passiontimes, 2018.

Skinner, G. William, and Edwin A. Winckler. "Compliance Succession in Rural Communist China: A Cyclical Theory." In *A Sociological Reader on Complex*

Organizations, edited by Amitai Etzioni, 410–438. New York: Holt, Rinehart, and Wilson, 1969.

Sloterdijk, Peter. *Critique of Cynical Reason*. Minneapolis: University of Minnesota Press, 1987.

——. *Terror from the Air*. Los Angeles: Semiotext(e), 2009.

——. "What Happened in the Twentieth Century? A Critique of Extremist Reason." In *What Happened in the Twentieth Century?*, 55–81. London: Polity, 2018.

SOCrecHK. "*28MAR2016 gindong syunyihn—Heunggong Mahnjuhk dong gindong geihjewuih (1/3)*" [March 28, 2016 announcement of the founding of the party—Hong Kong National Party press conference]. Accessed May 1, 2020. https://youtu.be /DVSZakCo9nE .

Sontag, Susan. *Illness as Metaphor and AIDS and Its Metaphors*. London: Picador, 2001.

Stand News. "*Chingnihn sanjing dang luhk joujik jou lyuhnmahng jin laahp wuih, cheung 2021 Heunggong jihkyut gungtauh*" [Youngspiration and five other organizations establish an alliance to win seats in the legislative council, call for a 2021 referendum on self-determination]. Stand News, April 10, 2016. Accessed April 15, 2016. www .thestandnews.com/politics/%E9%9D%92%E5%B9%B4%E6%96%B0%E6%94 %BF%E7%AD%89%E5%85%AD%E7%B5%84%E7%B9%94–%E7%B5%84%E8%8 1%AF%E7%9B%9F%E6%88%B0%E7%AB%8B%E6%9C%83–%E5%80%A12021% E9%A6%99%E6%B8%AF%E8%87%AA%E6%B1%BA%E5%85%AC%E6 %8A%95/.

Ta Kung Pao. "*Diuhchah: Leung Yau duhklouh kitbei; Gaauyuhk yihmjuhng satbaaih, seui faansi*" [Investigation: Revealing Yau and Leung's path to "independence"; a failure in education that requires reflection]. *Ta Kung Pao*, November 28, 2016. Accessed July 2020. http://news.takungpao.com.hk/hkol/topnews/2016–11 /3396789.html.

——. "'*Heunggong mahnjuhk dong*' *Chan Ho-tin gungyihn ngaugit 'Muhngduhk*'" [Hong Kong National Party's Andy Chan openly colludes with "Mongolian independence"]. *Ta Kung Pao*, November 12, 2016. Accessed March 26, 2020. http:// news.takungpao.com.hk/hkol/topnews/2016–11/3390941.html.

Tai, Benny. "The Principle of Minimum Legislation for Implementing Article 23 of the Basic Law." *Hong Kong Law Journal* 32 (2002): 579–612.

Tian Feilong. "*Dawan qu jianshe shiye xia de Xianggang bentu zhili xin silu*" [New directions in the administration of Hong Kong from the perspective of developing the Greater Bay Area]. *Journal of Guangzhou Institute of Socialism* 65, no. 2 (2019): 5–20.

Tong, Elson. "Pro-independence Hong Kong National Party Appeals against Companies Registry's Denial of Registration." *Hong Kong Free Press*, April 11, 2017. Accessed March 2021. https://hongkongfp.com/2017/04/11/pro-independence -hong-kong-national-party-appeals-companies-registrys-denial-registration/.

Tsang, Steve. *A Modern History of Hong Kong*. London: I. B. Tauris, 2007.

Tsering Topgyal. *China and Tibet: The Perils of Insecurity*. London: Hurst, 2016.

Tsering Woeser. *Tibet on Fire: Self-Immolations against Chinese Rule*. New York: Verso, 2016.

Tsui Sing Yan. *Heunggong: Watchou dik gabong, buntou gundim dik Heunggong yuhn-lauh si* [Hong Kong: A national history, second edition]. Taipei: Rive Gauche Publishing, 2019.

———. *Sihngbong gauhsih: Sahpyih bun syu hon Heunggong buntou si* [A history of the city-state: Reading Hong Kong local history through twelve books]. Hong Kong: Red Publishing, 2014.

———. *Sisok gabong: Junggwok jihkmahn jyuyih kohng chiuh hah dik Heunggong* [Reflections on my homeland: Hong Kong under Chinese colonization]. Taipei: Avanguard Publishing, 2019.

Undergrad Editorial Board, ed. *Heunggong mahnjuhk leuhn* [Hong Kong nationalism]. Hong Kong: Hong Kong University Undergraduate Student Union Publishing, 2015.

———. "*Heunggong mahnjuhk, mihngwahn jihkyut*" [Hong Kong nationality, self-determination of our own future]. *Undergrad* (February 2014).

———. "*Heunggong, mahnjyu, duhklaahp*" [Hong Kong, democracy, independence]. *Undergrad* (September 2014).

United Nations General Assembly. "General Assembly Resolution 1514 of 14 December 1960: Declaration on the Granting of Independence to Colonial Countries and People." December 14, 1960. https://www.ohchr.org/EN/Professional Interest/Pages/Independence.aspx.

United Press International (UPI). "Text of Address by Jiang Zemin." June 30, 1997. www.upi.com/Archives/1997/06/30/Text-of-address-by-Jiang-Zemin/80908 67643200/.

Veg, Sebastian. "The Rise of 'Localism' and Civic Identity in Post-Handover Hong Kong." *China Quarterly* 230 (June 2017): 323–347.

Wang Fei-ling. *The China Order: Centralia, World Empire, and the Nature of Chinese Power*. Albany: State University of New York Press, 2017.

Wang Fuchun. "*Lun Xianggang tequ fan fenlie guojia lifa*" [On establishing an anti-secession law for the HKSAR]. *Local Legislation Journal* 3, no. 3 (May 15, 2018): 78–85.

Wang Junjun. "*Shilun 'gangdu' de xingcheng yuanyin, jiben tedian ji celue xuanze*" [A preliminary examination of the causes and basic characteristics of Hong Kong independence, as well as options for responding to this phenomenon]. *Journal of Guangdong Institute of Socialism* 69, no. 4 (October 2017): 55–57.

Wang Wanli. "'*Gangdu' sichao de yanhua qushi yu fali yingdui*" [The evolutionary trend and legal response to the thought of "Hong Kong independence"]. *Hong Kong-Macao Studies* 1 (2017): 13–25.

Weatherill, Rob. *The Anti-Oedipus Complex: Lacan, Critical Theory and Postmodernism*. London: Routledge, 2017.

Wei Nanji. "*Xianggang qingnian bentupai de zhengzhi jueqi yu zouxiang*" [The political rise and future direction of Hong Kong's young localists]. *China Youth Research* (May 2018): 12–18.

Williams, James. *Lyotard and the Political*. London: Routledge, 2000.

Wong Chun Kit. Introduction to *Heunggong mahnjuhk leuhn* [Hong Kong national-ism], edited by *Undergrad* Editorial Board, 13–21. Hong Kong: Hong Kong University Undergraduate Student Union Publishing, 2015.

Wong, Joshua (with Jason Ng). *Unfree Speech: The Threat to Global Democracy and Why We Must Act Now.* New York: W. H. Allen, 2020.

Wong, Margaret. "China Raps Hong Kong over Criticism: Further Erosion Seen in Autonomy." Associated Press, May 9, 2004. Accessed August 2020. http://archive.boston.com/news/world/articles/2004/05/09/china_raps_hong_kong_over_criticism/.

Wong Wang-chi. *Lihksi dik chahmchuhng: Chuhng Heunggong hon Junggwok daaihluhk dik Heunggongsi leuhnseuht* [The burden of history: A Hong Kong perspective on the mainland discourse of Hong Kong history]. Oxford: Oxford University Press, 2000.

Wu, Venus, and Greg Torode. "Hong Kong Lawmakers Condemn 'Unlawful' Disqualification of Candidate." Reuters, January 29, 2018. Accessed March 30, 2020. www.reuters.com/article/us-hongkong-politics/hong-kong-lawyers-condemn-unlawful-disqualification-of-candidate-idUSKBN1FIoU4.

Wu Rwei-ren. "The Lilliputian Dreams: Preliminary Observations of Nationalism in Okinawa, Taiwan and Hong Kong." *Nations and Nationalism* 22, no. 4 (2016): 686–705.

Xi Jinping. "Foster and Practice Core Socialist Values from Childhood." In *The Governance of China*, 200–205. Beijing: Foreign Languages Press, 2014.

Xinhua News. "Vocational Training and Education in Xinjiang." *Xinhua News,* August 16, 2019. www.xinhuanet.com/english/2019-08/16/c_138313359.htm.

———. "*Xianggang juban jianianhua huodong tuiguang jiben fa*" [Hong Kong hosts a carnival to promote the Basic Law]. *Xinhua News,* February 21, 2009. Accessed July 2020. http://news.sohu.com/20090221/n262382186.shtml.

Yam, Bernard. "Cross-Border Childbirth between Mainland China and Hong Kong: Social Pressures and Policy Outcomes." *PORTAL: Journal of Multidisciplinary International Studies* 8, no. 2 (2011): 1–13.

Yeh, Emily. *Taming Tibet: Landscape Transformation and the Gift of Chinese Development.* Ithaca, NY: Cornell University Press, 2013.

Yuen Yuen-lung. "*Jeh sihdoih dik naahp-haam: Heunggong, mahnjyu, duhklaahp*" [An era's call to arms: Hong Kong, democracy, independence]. In *Undergrad* Editorial Board, ed., "*Heunggong, mahnjyu, duhklaahp*" [Hong Kong, democracy, independence]. *Undergrad* (September 2014): 30–32.

Zhao Jinqiu. "The SARS Epidemic under China's Media Policy." *Media Asia* 30, no. 4 (January 2003): 191–196.

Zhu Hanqi. "*Gangdu sichao de fenxi yiji yingdui suoshi*" [An analysis of the "Hong Kong independence" trend and countermeasures]. *Modern Business Trade Industry* 25 (2018): 134–135.

Zhu Jie and Zhang Xiaoshan. *Critique of Hong Kong Nativism: From a Legal Perspective.* Singapore: Springer, 2019.

———. "'Xianggang bentu yishi' de lishixing shuli yu huanyuan" [A historical narration and restoration of "Hong Kong's sense of nativeness," with a review of the formation and evolution of "Hong Kong independence" thought]. *Hong Kong and Macao Studies* 1 (2016): 12–22.

———. "Xianggang jijin bentu zhuyi zhi shehui xinli toushi [A Psycho–social Perspective on Radical Localism in Hong Kong]." *Hong Kong and Macao Studies* 1 (2017): 3–12.

———. "Zhuquan, guojia anquan yu zhengzhi gaige: 'gangdu' de 'jiben fa' fangkong jizhi" [Sovereignty, national security, and political reform: Prevention mechanism against "Hong Kong Independence" under the Hong Kong Basic Law]. *Journal of Jianghan University (Social Science Edition)* 33, no. 4 (August 2016): 12–19.

INDEX

Founded in 1893,
UNIVERSITY OF CALIFORNIA PRESS
publishes bold, progressive books and journals
on topics in the arts, humanities, social sciences,
and natural sciences—with a focus on social
justice issues—that inspire thought and action
among readers worldwide.

The UC PRESS FOUNDATION
raises funds to uphold the press's vital role
as an independent, nonprofit publisher, and
receives philanthropic support from a wide
range of individuals and institutions—and from
committed readers like you. To learn more, visit
ucpress.edu/supportus.